W9-BTH-107

Engaging Minds

Engaging Minds: Cultures of Education and Practices of Teaching explores the diverse beliefs and practices that define the current landscape of formal education. The third edition of this introduction to current interdisciplinary studies of teaching and teacher education is restructured around four prominent "moments" in formal education:

- Standardized Education – began to unfold in the 1600s, when public education was invented as a response to the cultural convulsions of industrialization, urbanization, and imperialism.
- Authentic Education – rose to prominence over the last century as researchers began to untangle the complexity of human cognition.
- Democratic Citizenship Education – fuelled by civil rights movements of the 1960s, with the realization that schools often contribute to (or at least help to perpetuate) inequities and injustices.
- Systemic Sustainability Education – an emerging trend, as schools and other cultural institutions find themselves out of step with the transition from a mechanization-focused industrialized society to an ecologically minded and information-based society.

These moments serve as the foci of the four sections of the book, each with three chapters dealing respectively with history, epistemology, and pedagogy within the moment. This structure makes it possible to read the book in two ways – either "horizontally" through the four in-depth treatments of the moments or "vertically" through coherent threads of history, epistemology, and pedagogy. Pedagogical features include suggestions for delving deeper to get at subtleties that can't be simply stated or appreciated through reading alone, several strategies to highlight and distinguish important vocabulary in the text, and more than 150 key theorists and researchers included among the search terms and in the Influences section rather than a formal reference list.

Brent Davis is Professor and Distinguished Research Chair in Mathematics Education in the Werklund School of Education, University of Calgary, Canada.

Dennis Sumara is Dean of the Werklund School of Education, University of Calgary, Canada.

Rebecca Luce-Kapler is Associate Dean of Graduate Studies and Research in the Faculty of Education, Queen's University, Canada.

Engaging Minds

Cultures of Education and Practices of Teaching • THIRD EDITION

Brent Davis, Dennis Sumara, and Rebecca Luce-Kapler

Routledge
Taylor & Francis Group

NEW YORK AND LONDON

First published 2015
by Routledge
711 Third Avenue, New York, NY 10017

and by Routledge
2 Park Square, Milton Park, Abingdon, Oxon, OX14 4RN

Routledge is an imprint of the Taylor & Francis Group, an informa business

First edition published by Lawrence Erlbaum Associates, Inc., 2000
Second edition published by Routledge, 2008.

Library of Congress Cataloging-in-Publication Data
Davis, Brent.
    Engaging minds : cultures of education and practices of teaching / by Brent Davis, Dennis Sumara, Rebecca Luce-Kapler.
    pages cm
    Includes bibliographical references and index.
    1. Learning. 2. Teaching. I. Sumara, Dennis J., 1958- II. Luce-Kapler, Rebecca. III. Title.
    LB1060.D38 2015
    370.15'23--dc23
    2014049244

ISBN: 978-1-138-90540-5 (hbk)
ISBN: 978-1-138-90541-2 (pbk)
ISBN: 978-1-315-69589-1 (ebk)

Typeset in Palatino and Myriad Pro
by Brent Davis.

Publisher's Note:
This book has been prepared from camera-ready copy provided by the authors.

Contents

Acknowledgments

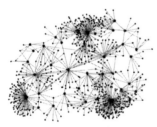

We would like to recognize those teachers, researchers, and scholars who have labored to interrupt the assumptions and norms that frame popular understandings of education and teaching. Only a handful of these persons could be mentioned in the pages that follow, but we acknowledge our work is only made possible by theirs.

More locally, we are indebted to undergraduate and graduate students, colleagues, reviewers, and family members whose careful readings and focused responses of the first and second editions of *Engaging Minds* have contributed in many and substantial ways to this version. As well, we note the critical assistance of several people who responded to drafts of this edition, including Dave Carlgren, Avis Beek, Roy Norris, Janice Beler, Cully Robinson, Garette Tebay, Natalie Prytuluk, Crystal MacArthur, David Ikenouve, Anne Daniel, Kathleen Kellock, Bernita Leahy, Ugur Parlar, Violet Baron, Moshe Renert, and Veronika Bohaç Clarke. Special gratitude is extended to Mick Elliott whose patient accommodations helped immensely in keeping the project on track.

Most of the new images for this edition were drawn by Wayne Eng, with some contributions from Kathleen Ralph and Jenny Arntzen.

We acknowledge the contributions of our editor, Naomi Silverman, whose gentle provocations and skillful interventions helped to bring this work to form.

Prologue

What's teaching?

Or, more precisely, how might we describe a teaching that fits with the time and place we find ourselves?

On the surface, these questions might sound like simple ones. But they're not, as evidenced by an incredible array of synonyms and metaphors for *teach* in the English language. Here are the first 100 that popped up when we entered the word in a few online thesauruses.

ADMONISH	DIRECT ATTENTION TO	GIVE AN IDEA OF	INFILTRATE	PROFESS
ADVISE	DISCIPLINE	GIVE NEW IDEAS	INFIX	PRIME
BEAT INTO	DISSEMINATE	GIVE THE FACTS	INFORM	PUT UP TO
BRAINWASH	DRAW IN	GRAFT	INFUSE	PUT IN THE WAY OF
BREAK	DRAW OUT	GROUND	INGRAFT	QUALIFY
BREAK IN	DRILL	GUIDE	INITIATE	READ A LESSON
BREED	EDIFY	HABITUATE	INOCULATE	REAR
BRIEF	EDUCATE	HOLD FORTH	INSTILL	SCHOOL
BRING FORWARD	ENLARGE THE MIND	ILLUSTRATE	INSTRUCT	SERMONIZE
BRING UP	ENLIGHTEN	IMBUE	INTERPRET	SET RIGHT
BRING UP TO	EXERCISE	IMPART	INURE	SHAPE
CATECHIZE	EXPLAIN	IMPLANT	LECTURE	SHARPEN
COACH	EXPOUND	IMPREGNATE	MORALIZE	SHARPEN THE WITS
COMMUNICATE	FAMILIARIZE WITH	IMPRESS UPON THE MIND	NURTURE	SHOW
CONVERT	FORM	IMPRESS UPON MEMORY	OPEN EYES	SHOW THE ROPES
CONVINCE	GIVE A DISCOURSE	IMPROVE	POLISH UP	SOW THE SEEDS OF
CRAM	GIVE INSTRUCTION	IMPROVE MIND	POUND INTO	TAKE IN HAND
DEMONSTRATE	GIVE A LECTURE	INCEPT	PRACTICE	TAME
DEVELOP	GIVE A LESSON	INCULCATE	PREACH	TRAIN
DIRECT	GIVE A SERMON	INDOCTRINATE	PREPARE	TUTOR

Clearly there's a wide range of interpretation.

Having taught for several decades – and having had to negotiate meanings and understandings with students, colleagues, parents, and others – we knew to expect some variety before we went to the thesauruses. Even so, we were taken aback at the mixture of sensibilities that seems to be present in this list. In particular,

- There is a surprising number of words that we have never used to refer to teaching ourselves (and, in fact, quite a few words we've never used to refer to anything).
- The list is missing many currently popular synonyms (e.g., FACILITATE, CHALLENGE, DESIGN, ENGAGE, EMPOWER, GIVE VOICE, …).
- There seem to be some strong and unexpected themes in the list (e.g., many terms cluster around somewhat forceful and violent notions, including BEAT INTO, BREAK, CRAM, DISCIPLINE, DRILL, INCULCATE, PUT IN THE WAY OF, SHOW THE ROPES, and TAME).
- Considered all together, there are some massively different and not-easily-reconciled beliefs about teaching presented (e.g., BRAINWASH *vs.* NURTURE, or DRAW OUT *vs.* DRAW IN).

The word *teaching* traces back to the Proto-Indo-European word *deik-*, meaning "to point out." Its most ancient meanings, then, are about orienting attentions and alerting consciousness. In fact, the index finger was once known as "the teaching finger," or simply "the teacher."

Of course, as an insightful group of teacher candidates argued when presented with a similar list, it comes from outside the field of education. One might justly expect popular opinion to be all over the map. Surely a different picture would emerge if the list were assembled from the vocabulary teachers actually use to describe their work.

Unfortunately that's not the case – and, in fact, that's the realization that drives this book. The same vast range of perspectives found in popular opinion (and in online thesauruses) is present among professional educators. But, there's one important difference. Among the vocabularies for teaching used by teachers, the distinctions tend to be subtler and harder to notice.

These varied vocabularies and fine-grained distinctions reveal the tangled webs of belief and practice that currently exist in education – and that's why they serve as a particular emphasis in this book. But to be clear, the project here isn't to nitpick about words. Rather, synonyms and metaphors serve as entry points to our real interest: the very practical question of how to teach.

More specifically, our intention with this book is to invite you into the challenge of describing a conception of teaching that fits the current era. An important starting place in this project is to notice that every entry in the list on page 1 was first used as both a *description of* and a *prescription for* teaching, and so it makes sense to try to figure out what an educator in the 1600s might have been pointing to when choosing to characterize the work of teaching in terms of EDIFYING, IMPREGNATING, or INSTRUCTING. Something specific was being flagged, some deep beliefs about learning and knowledge were being asserted, and a particular set of actions was being recommended.

The book's structure

We use that point – that is, that distinctive vocabularies of teaching have both theoretical and practical implications – to structure this book. As it turns out, these distinctive vocabularies are also related to specific eras, cultural trends, and social movements. New terms pop into the language in clusters, and these small explosions of vocabulary always occur alongside shifts in collective sensibility. For that reason, we look at four historical moments in particular, each associated with a distinctive set of teaching practices:

- STANDARDIZED EDUCATION: The first of these moments began in the 1600s and 1700s, when public education was invented as a response to the cultural convulsions of industrialization, urbanization, and imperialism. Teaching came to be modeled after working on a factory line.
- AUTHENTIC EDUCATION: The second moment occurred over the last century as researchers began to untangle the complexity of human cognition and educators realized the inadequacies of commonsense beliefs about learning. Teaching became less directive and more attentive to individuals.
- DEMOCRATIC CITIZENSHIP EDUCATION: The third moment was fueled by civil rights movements of the

The word *education* derives from Latin *educare*, which in turn derives from *ex-* + *ducere*, "to lead/draw out." The first uses in English date back to the mid-1400s.

1960s, with the realization that schools often contribute to (or at least help to perpetuate) inequities and injustices. Teaching came to be seen in terms of an ethical endeavor contributing to social justice.

- SYSTEMIC SUSTAINABILITY EDUCATION: The fourth moment is the current one, as schools and other cultural institutions find themselves out of step with the transition from a mechanization-focused, industrialized society to an ecologically minded, information-based society. Teaching is coming to be seen in terms of helping to develop awareness of self, others, humanity, and the more-than-human world.

Importantly, we don't mean to suggest that these are the only four moments that merit consideration. Indeed, these aren't even adequate for making sense of the full scope of sensibilities presented in the list on page 1.

Of course, a reason our range is narrower is that formal education extends much further into the past than the 1600s. The decision to start the discussion with events that unfolded a mere 400 years ago means that we might gloss over some important shaping moments for teaching. Most obvious, perhaps, we run the risk of ignoring when and how some vital terms entered the language, such as *educate* from ancient Greek and *teach* from Old English.

There are many, many synonyms for *teaching* that reflect senses of NURTURANCE and CULTIVATION, including some that have faded into obscurity. For instance, MANURING was once a popular term for the work of the teacher, related to "working the earth" and, more anciently, to "work of the hand." No doubt its more recent association with "spreading dung" contributed to its disuse.

We don't disregard this issue, but we address it by backfilling as we go along rather than making it a primary focus. The simple fact is that no matter where we elected to start the discussion, it would be in the middle of something. That said, the decision to begin with the creation of the modern public school isn't at all arbitrary. Many of the entries in our list of synonyms for teaching on page 1 entered the language at that particular moment, and a significant portion of the remainder entered since. And so the invention of public schooling is much more than a convenient historical marker. It was a defining moment for teaching, and its descriptions of teaching continue to echo through all levels of education.

Why the focus on language?

There are many ways to frame a discussion of contemporary teaching, and many sources that can be used to provide evidence for the different mindsets, goals and practices that have given shape to schooling. These sources include historical texts, works of art, policy papers, curriculum documents, and teachers' memoirs.

While we use these and other artifacts to make sense of different perspectives on teaching, we focus most of the discussion through the lens of vocabulary because language preserves a memory of earlier insights while it frames current possibilities. As such, vocabularies do more than guide practice. They can signal where ideas came from, they can point toward particular theoretical commitments, and – perhaps most importantly – they can give insight into why certain practices and beliefs are so resistant to change. Language holds a key for understanding why, for example, today's classrooms tend to look very much like classrooms from a century ago – whereas the structures outside the classroom are so, so different. And that key can be used to unlock new possibilities.

Through all of this, it's important to emphasize that we're not looking to propose or impose a new vocabulary – that is, to define an up-to-date, universalized, all-encompassing, ideal perspective on teaching. Quite the contrary, we believe such a goal to be nonsense. For two reasons.

One reason is that human culture is a complex phenomenon, and its complexity makes it impossible to replace one perspective with another. Humanity carries its history of thinking along in its customs, its languages, and its artifacts – and so despite the distaste one might feel toward, for example, a ram-it-in-cram-it-in mode of teaching, that conception is knitted into the culture of education. It may be suppressed, but it will always be present in one form or another. Our focus on language helps us to foreground this point. It's useful to be aware of the residues from earlier thinking that are carried in common vocabularies. If habits of speaking are ignored, they hold power over the speakers.

The word *literate* derives from the Latin *litteraturs*, meaning both "acquainted with the letters of the alphabet" and "learned."

That is, knowing the letters was what once separated the learned from the unlearned. While the meaning of literate has broadened to refer to other competencies (e.g., scientific literacy), those references are always to bodies of knowledge that rely on formal symbol systems.

Another reason to be wary of a one-size-fits-all description of teaching is that conceptions must be appropriate to situations, and situations can vary dramatically in today's world. A pre-industrialized setting where citizens are grappling with poverty, have unreliable access to electricity, and are debating such issues as "Should girls be permitted to attend school?" will need a very different model of teaching to one in which the pressing educational issues include a declining enrolment in engineering and the sciences, bullying, and spotty performances on international achievement tests. A focus on vocabulary helps us to be mindful of the wheres and whens.

That returns us to the question driving this work: how might we describe a teaching that fits with the time and place we find ourselves? In light of the above points, one of the most important words in this question is *fits*. We're not after something perfect or ideal. We want an education that makes sense where it is enacted.

The trouble with vocabulary

One of the major obstacles to overcome for a newcomer to any profession is its vocabulary. Every established profession has one, and maintaining a mastery over it is often cited as one of the most challenging obstacles for its members. This is as true of teaching as any other domain.

The apple is by far the most common image associated with teaching. But why was this chosen as an icon of the profession?

The answer to this question reveals some deep-seated assumptions about not just the role of the teacher, but the processes of learning and the nature of knowledge.

Some critics choose to view professional vocabularies as deliberate strategies to exclude non-professionals. From an insider's perspective, however, this is nonsense. Words are chosen and invented to focus attentions on specific aspects of the work. Teachers (and lawyers, and physicians, and nurses, and pharmacists …) must be aware of and attentive to subtle distinctions that won't matter to most, and specialized vocabularies make it easier to flag and catalogue these distinctions.

In other words, we acknowledge upfront that we might be amplifying an already difficult issue by inviting readers not only to learn new vocabularies, but to interrogate those vocabularies. To ease this issue, we use the margins of this text to highlight important terms and to point to additional resources for those who wish to delve more deeply into particular words, notions, and topics.

Again, vocabulary isn't our focus; it's our way in. That is, we're not aiming to ensure readers become more fluent speakers of teacherese or to master a jargon, but to offer a means to organize and relate relevant terms. Our main strategy in this regard is to anchor vocabularies to sensibilities. In the hope to support readers' efforts to this end, we have made use of the following features:

- Each moment starts with a title page, offering abstracts of the entire section and of each of its three chapters. It also includes some suggestions for locating illustrative clips on YouTube. We strongly recommend lingering on these pages and, especially, checking out some of the videos.
- That title page is followed by a chart that includes a sampling of the vocabulary tied to key events, theoretical developments, and educational trends associated with the moment. We hope these charts are useful as both previews and reviews. (The complete chart is included in the Epilogue.)
- Each of the four moments follows the same structure, opening with a chapter on history and context, followed by a chapter on associated beliefs on knowledge and learning, and closing with a chapter on conceptions of teaching.
- We use several strategies for highlighting and distinguishing important vocabulary in the text. *Italics* are used often, to flag major nodes in the network of educational vocabulary. SMALL CAPS are used to draw attention to vital metaphors for knowledge, learning, or teaching. **Boldface** is used to identify inquiry and search terms that we found particularly useful.

Our hope is that these devices will offer occasions for you to engage with (rather than merely "receive") issues and content.

We must also mention a feature that is common to almost every academic text that we've omitted. You

Margin notes are used for a few different purposes, but mainly to underscore and emphasize core vocabulary through rephrased definitions and/or visual metaphors.

won't find a formal reference list, although there is a graphic (pp. 244–245) in which we've collected and organized the names of thinkers and researchers who have been particularly influential within different moments in education. A rationale for this move is provided on pages 125–126, embedded in a discussion of evolving sensibilities around participation, authority, and authorship.

We close this Prologue with a few questions that we've used in many of our courses with pre-service and practicing teachers. In fact, each chapter ends with similar "suggestions for delving deeper." These activities are designed to get at nuances and subtleties that can't be simply stated. As well, and as every experienced educator knows, engaging in such activities can support much richer understandings and appreciations than reading alone. To that end, and in keeping with currently prominent pedagogical advice, we recommend a mix of personal reflection, small-group discussion, and large-group comparison – the reasons for which will unfold through Moments 2, 3, and 4.

We used many sources to develop definitions, identify synonyms, and trace etymologies of key terms. The following free sites were particularly useful:
- dictionaryofeducation.co.uk
- etymonline.com
- visualthesaurus.com
- visuwords.com
- wikipedia.com

Suggestions for delving deeper

1. Look back at the list of synonyms of teaching of page 1. Which have you used to describe teaching. Which align with your current understanding of the word? Which do you find distasteful or offensive? (We recommend that you start lists in response to these sorts of questions so that they can be revisited in later sections.)

2. Many, many currently popular metaphors for and descriptions of teaching are absent from the list on page 1. What other terms would you include? What sorts of orienting sensibilities or common themes are there in the terms that resonate with you? To what extent are those themes present in the prepared list?

3. Revisit the words you've identified in the preceding exercises. Bearing in mind that they are both *descriptions* and *prescriptions*, what advice might they communicate to educators? How do they frame relationships with students? What do they foreground for the role of the teacher?

1600   1700   1800   1900   2000

MYSTICIST, RELIGIOUS, AND OTHER EDUCATIONAL SENSIBILITIES

STANDARDIZED EDUCATION

AUTHENTIC EDUCATION

DEMOCRATIC CITIZENSHIP EDUCATION

SYSTEMIC SUSTAINABILITY EDUCATION

MOMENT 1 •
standardized education

In brief ...

The term "Standardized Education" refers to those approaches to schooling that emphasize common programs of study, age-based grade levels, and uniform performance outcomes. The movement drew much of its inspiration and content from ancient traditions
and religion, but its main influences have been industry and the physical sciences.

1.1 • The context ...

The phenomenon of Standardized Education began to emerge in the 1700s and 1800s.
Triggered by a cluster of entangled events – including the rise of modern science, industrialization, urbanization, and European expansionism – the need arose for a school system
that could keep youth occupied and prepare them for the workforce.

1.2 • On knowledge and learning ...

With the principal influences coming from the industry and the physical sciences, knowledge came to be viewed mainly in terms of COMMODITIES and OBJECTS. Learning, correspondingly, was framed as ACQUISITION and INTERNALIZATION.

1.3 • On teaching ...

Teaching came to be understood in terms of DELIVERY and INSTRUCTION. Industry-influenced
concerns with standards – with regard to quality control, efficiency, and so on – were
imposed on both the expectations of students and the work of teachers.

Take a glimpse ...

Suggested YouTube searches: [traditional schooling] [direct instruction] [classroom man-
agement] [back-to-basics education]

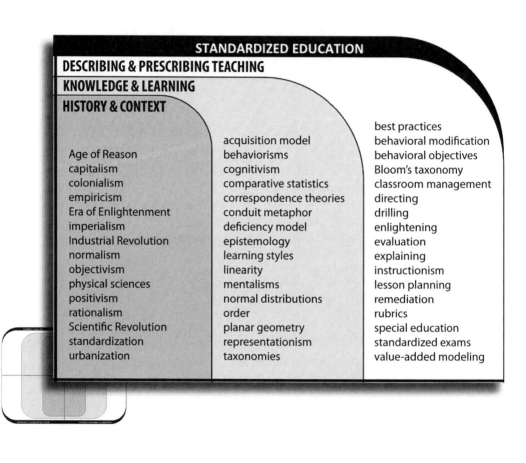

STANDARDIZED EDUCATION

DESCRIBING & PRESCRIBING TEACHING

KNOWLEDGE & LEARNING

HISTORY & CONTEXT

		best practices
	acquisition model	behavioral modification
Age of Reason	behaviorisms	behavioral objectives
capitalism	cognitivism	Bloom's taxonomy
colonialism	comparative statistics	classroom management
empiricism	correspondence theories	directing
Era of Enlightenment	conduit metaphor	drilling
imperialism	deficiency model	enlightening
Industrial Revolution	epistemology	evaluation
normalism	learning styles	explaining
objectivism	linearity	instructionism
physical sciences	mentalisms	lesson planning
positivism	normal distributions	remediation
rationalism	order	rubrics
Scientific Revolution	planar geometry	special education
standardization	representationism	standardized exams
urbanization	taxonomies	value-added modeling

iconic visual metaphor:

UNIDIRECTIONAL ARROW

1.1 The Emergence of Standardized Education

We've just asserted that the notions of "teacher" and "teaching" are hotly contested.

Despite the great range of beliefs on these matters, however, some perspectives are encountered much more frequently than others. One in particular seems to prevail in the popular mindset, and it's easily illustrated through an image search of the word *teacher*. We've just done exactly that, and the images below are reflective of the first five pictures that came up today:

Of course, image searches aren't exactly scientifically rigorous research exercises, but we believe this sort of result gives a few clues into popular assumptions on what teaching is all about – that is, in this case, that teaching typically involves standing in front of people with a view toward DEMONSTRATING, HIGHLIGHTING, TELLING, or otherwise DISSEMINATING knowledge. (Many other issues are presented in these images, but we'll leave those for later chapters.)

As it turns out, that meaning has been particularly stable in English for many centuries. Indeed, it traces back at least to the origins of the word *teach*, which is derived from the Proto-Indo-European word *deik-*, "to show, point out." It is also related to the Old English *tacn*, meaning "sign" or "mark," and the root of the modern word *token*. The notion of teaching, that is, originally had to do with GESTURING TOWARD RELEVANT

This compiled image on this page is highly reflective of but not identical to the result of our Google Image search of **teacher**. To avoid copyright issues, the graphic was assembled from images provided courtesy of Thinkstock.com.

SIGNS, of ORIENTING ATTENTIONS TOWARD SIGNIFICANT FEATURES, of POINTING.

Given this history, it's perhaps not surprising that the act of pointing is so prominent across the images above. Nor is it surprising that teaching has long been synonymous with DIRECTING, LEADING, and related notions. All of these terms share senses of orienting toward a common goal.

But the conception of teaching that is most commonsensical today involves much more than POINTING and DIRECTING. The task of the professional educator is framed by responsibilities for planning, measuring, and reporting in an outcomes-driven, evaluation-heavy, and accountability-laden culture of COMMAND-and-CONTROL teaching. A more complete sense of what's being portrayed in images collected above is captured by such synonyms as DEMONSTRATE, INSTRUCT, TRAIN, ASSIGN, PRESCRIBE, PERSUADE, INFORM, EDIFY, SUPERVISE, INDOCTRINATE, and DISCIPLINE. These and other words were part of a convulsion of new terminology for teaching that occurred roughly 400 years ago. More broadly, this new vocabulary was part of an emergent conception of education as *standardizable*.

The story of how the word *standardized* came to be so tightly coupled to *education* is an interesting and instructive one. Knowing a bit about it is useful for understanding some of the structures of contemporary schooling and some of the nuances of popular interpretations of teaching. Indeed, in many ways, the notion of *standardizing* is thoroughly represented in many of the images on the previous page.

Before going there, however, we invite you to think about the sorts of images and associations that you have for "standardized education." What comes to mind?

Different people will answer in different ways, but our experience has been that some recollections are particularly popular. These include thoughts of standardized examinations, standardized ("common" or "core") curricula, standardized lesson plans, and standardized classroom formats. More subtly, the idea shows up in standards of student behavior, professional standards for teachers, and the many, many

If we were pressed to choose an icon for Standardized Education, it would be the arrow. The image is implicit in some of the movement's defining principles. Instances include ...

... the belief that *teaching causes learning*, which is tied to a linear, cause⇨effect sensibility ...

... the conception of *progress through schooling*, which is framed as incremental movement along a linear trajectory ...

... notions of *orders* and *hierarchies*, which pervade disciplines, achievement levels, administrative structures ....

documents bearing the word *Standards* put out by teachers' organizations, ministries of education, and groups of concerned citizens.

These elements certainly resonate with us. For our own part, however, the most salient details summoned by the phrase "standardized education" are the aspects of formal education that are typically represented using points, lines, and rectangles – of, for example, bulleted lists of learning objectives, linear trajectories through lessons, or the rectangular schedule pasted on the corner of a rectangular desk organized in a rectangular array with other desks in a rectangular room along a rectangular hall in a rectangular school on a rectangular city block in a rectangulated city.

There is an implicit geometry here. We delve into some of its qualities in Chapter 1.2, insofar as it relates to the structures associated with modern schools and theories and metaphors used to describe knowledge and learning. For now, though, the goal is to offer a partial answer to the questions of how, when, and where the prevailing model of education as a standardized endeavor arose.

Ancient forerunners of the modern school

In a sense, it's ridiculous to talk about the beginnings of education. Humanity is a teaching species; the practice of deliberately passing accumulated knowledge from one generation to the next extends much further back than any historical account.

However, it's a different story with the matter of **formal education** – that is, with those social institutions designed to gather and disseminate insights through enrolling and teaching a body of students. There are some reasonably clear records on when these practices began to appear. In particular, across cultures, one of the major precursors of formal educational systems was the development of some form of writing – a technology that made it possible for groups of people to record and store their knowledge in a new and powerful way. In a sense, the invention of systems of writing compelled the invention of formal education – for two reasons. Firstly, mastering the skill of writing is cogni-

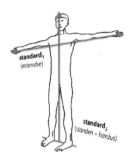

The word *standard* has many definitions, but they cluster around notions of authority, commonality, normality, and acceptability.

Its roots are contested, with two major theories. One traces standard to the Old French *estendre*, "to stretch out" (linked to the English extend), which is likely the sense that came to be associated with standardized measures. A second etymology links standard to the Gothic *standan + hardus*, "to stand hard," suggesting senses of vertical uprightness and rallying point (as in a military standard).

tively demanding, requiring consistent instruction and persistent practice that can only be ensured through a formal setting. Secondly, as writing advanced and texts of knowledge accumulated, needs arose for strategies to preserve and disseminate that knowledge – means that were more consistent, accessible, and reliable than those that relied on families, clans, gilds, or religious orders. Those needs, in turn, spurred the education of small armies of scribes and record keepers.

It is thus that the first formal educational institutions appeared in ancient Egypt in the 3rd millennium BCE, and in China, the Indian Subcontinent, the Middle East, northern Africa, and southern Europe in the 2nd millennium BCE. For the most part, these ancient institutions likely bore little resemblance to modern schools. Nevertheless, their influence is still discernible. As detailed below, there are similarities in curriculum content and organizational structures. But the most significant influence seems to be on conceptions of teaching. Some of the most widely used synonyms for *teacher*, including EDUCATOR and PEDAGOGUE, derive from this era – and, along with these words, some of the most enduring attitudes among educators toward NURTURING, FOSTERING, and CULTIVATING the learner.

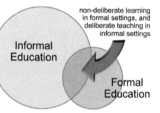

non-deliberate learning in formal settings, and deliberate teaching in informal settings

Informal Education

Formal Education

When the modifier *formal* is used in describe to *education*, it refers to deliberately structured, institution-based activities. (In contrast, *informal education* refers to settings that have less structured curriculum and teaching but are still learning-focused, such as museums, playgrounds, and zoos.)

Among the many differences between the first institutions for formal education and today's schools, two are particularly notable. The first had to do with who was served by formal education. In the ancient world, this opportunity was reserved for elites – principally, males from privileged financial, religious, military, and/or political backgrounds. Given this detail, as might be expected, foci varied greatly according to what different groups deemed educationally important. What was taught depended on who opened the school, who funded it, and who could afford it. However, despite the many geographical, cultural, temporal, and class differences, two subjects tended to feature prominently: literacy and mathematics.

At first glance, this detail might be taken to suggest that things haven't changed all that much over the last few thousand years. Compared to today, however, the topics of reading, writing, and arithmetic were treated in wildly different ways. A sense of this difference might be gleaned by researching the histories of such words as *grammar, spell,* and *mathematics*. All of these terms were at one time associated with deep spiritual knowledge (and even occult and magical lore in some settings) – whereas, within a modern frame of Standardized Education, these and other topics are seen mainly as skills or well-defined competencies.

Conflicting sensibilities on the focus of schooling

This detail – that is, the varied and conflicting conceptions of knowledge that are at play in different models of education – may be the most important one addressed in this book, as the issue is far from settled. In fact, over the past half-century, it has resurfaced with a vengeance and is now at the core of many, if not most, debates about schooling.

The word *school* is derived from Greek *skhole*, "spare time, leisure, ease; learned discussion," as exemplified in Raphael's masterpiece *The School of Athens*. The current meaning of "a building for instruction" was first recorded in the 1590s. This usage is associated with a shift in conceptions of knowledge, as *episteme* (practical know-how) eclipsed *gnosis* (deep, spiritual knowledge).

It's a matter that is at least touched on in every chapter. For now, the interesting point is that the institutions for formal education in the ancient world were centrally concerned with a very different type of knowledge than most of today's schools. Unfortunately, this point is a little difficult to make. English lacks a precise vocabulary to signal this difference between the type of knowledge that was the focus of ancient institutions and the type of knowledge that is the focus today. For that reason, we turn to other languages.

Except for modern English, in almost every European language (in fact, in every language for which we have been able to query a native speaker), there is a pairing of words used to signal two distinct subcategories for *knowledge*. These dyads include the Greek *gnosis* and *episteme*, the Latin *mythos* and *logos*, the French *connaissance* and *savoir*, and the German, *kennen* and *wissen*. If you were to enter any of these terms into most online translators, the English correlate is likely to come out as some cognate of the word *know*. Yet each word pairing points to a vital distinction that isn't directly named in English.

One category of knowledge that is being signaled – and the subject of *gnosis, mythos, connaissance,* and *kennen* – has to do with deep knowledge of animate forms, spiritual insight, wise judgments, and ethical action. *Gnosis*-knowledge is oriented to the meanings of existence, and it tends to be represented through more artistic genres such as poetry, parable, fable, myth, and allegory. Such devices are invoked to communicate understandings that can't be expressed directly and explicitly. They provide a means into important ethical, psychological, social, civic, and cultural insights of a society.

The other category – and the object of *episteme*, *logos*, *savoir*, and *wissen* – has more to do with facts, skills, and, readily stated truths. *Episteme*-knowledge encompasses understandings of cause–effect events, logical implications, procedural knowledge, everyday know-how, and practiced skills. Whereas the category of knowledge discussed in the previous paragraph looks to the mysteries and complexities of existence, this one focuses on the immediate and pragmatic needs of life. Its sources are trial and error, rational inference, experimentation, and empirical evidence.

In ancient times, it was assumed that this latter category of *episteme*-knowledge would take care of itself, and as such it was not addressed through formal education (or, at least, it was only incidentally addressed, as a means to deeper truths). Rather, formal education was devised to help learners develop *gnosis*-knowledge. Where people needed teaching assistance, it was assumed, was around making sense of the profound truths of the universe.

Within this project, a common belief across all western mystical and religious traditions is that humans were once part of a grand-unified whole, but have somehow become separated from that unity. Hence, the core issue in matters of learning and teaching is a restoration of that unity. For the most part, the means of that restoration was believed to reside deeply within the individual knower. The goal was to free it, and teaching techniques such as the **Socratic method** were developed to help people release this knowledge.

Indeed, the word *education* originally referred to precisely this process. To educate was to "draw out," by whatever means, that which was assumed to be woven in one's being. The sentiment that is implicit in

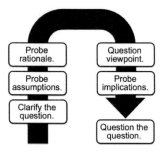

The *Socratic method,* named after the ancient Greek philosopher, is a style of teacher questioning that is intended to alert students to the assumptions, inconsistencies, and gaps in thinking. The intention is to *educe* ("draw out") more defensible, purer insights – which are presumed to already dwell deep inside the learner.

Socrates typically applied this method to such topics as ethics, morality, piety, wisdom, temperance, courage, and justice – that is, matters of *gnosis*-knowledge.

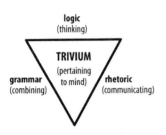

The forerunners of the modern school were mainly concerned with the *liberal arts*, which means "arts that are freeing." The arts served as both curriculum content and pedagogical approach. It was assumed that *gnosis*-knowledge was so elusive and so complex that simplistic, direct instruction was inadequate to support deep, meaningful learning.

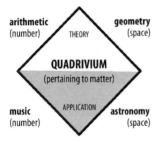

teaching as EDUCATING can also be found in a cluster of terms that includes NURTURING, FOSTERING, and TUTORING, rooted in imagery of suckling, feeding, and protecting.

This attitude toward teaching was associated with a curriculum of **liberal arts** – that is, literally, "arts that are freeing." Disciplines were included on the basis of their soul-nurturing value. In other words, the arts were not seen as disciplines unto themselves, but as means toward the development of one's being and recovery of a lost perfection.

Religion-based forerunners of the modern school

The emphasis on deep, spiritual, wisdom-oriented knowledge prevailed through most of the history of formal schooling, It continued to be the dominant emphasis through the Middle Ages (roughly speaking, about a thousand years ago), by which time control of European formal education for children had been assumed almost entirely by the Church. There were other, more secular options for those with political status or financial means, but for the vast majority of children – actually, for the most part, of young boys – the only option was situated in a local church building.

Education in the early Middle Ages was far from universally accessible. However, in the 1100s, the Church mandated that a MASTER was to be made available in every cathedral to all boys whose families were too poor to pay the fees demanded by the schools. In smaller communities, free schools were also established through parishes and monasteries, with priests and monks serving as teachers.

The purpose of these free schools was unambiguous. They were operated in the service of the Church and were intended mainly to identify and provide early training for children who would become clerics – that is, members of the clergy. That meant that ranking and sorting was a major task of these institutions, and it also meant that they had the spin-off benefit of contributing to a more literate society. For the most part, the curriculum was a combination of religious teachings and elements inherited mainly from ancient Greek and Latin traditions, including particular emphasis on the liberal arts, which included the **quadrivium** of arithmetic, geometry, astronomy, music, and the **trivium** of grammar, rhetoric, and logic.

In part because they dominated the formal educational scene of the era, and in part because they were the first European model for mass education, these institutions have had an immense shaping influence on the modern school. Conceptually, their major contribution has come through the emphasis on *order*, as was articulated most through such innovations as well-structured programs of study and the imperative to rank students.

The commitment to order was no doubt rooted in deep-seated beliefs about the nature of the universe and well-entrenched structures within the Church. By the Middle Ages, the Church was organized into different religious orders, each steeped in protocols and rituals. These orders, ostensibly, were reflective of the rankings and hierarchies among higher beings – that is, an assumed **great chain of being** in the universe. These sensibilities were extended into, imposed upon, and manifest through all aspects of existence, including architecture, social class, and politics.

Much of early formal education was organized around an assumption of the *great chain of being* (Latin *scala naturae*, "ladder of nature"), a concept derived from the ancient Greeks. Assumed to be ordained by the universe, the great chain of being is a strict hierarchical ordering of all matter and life. It starts at God and moves downward to angels, demons, stars, moon, kings, princes, nobles, men, wild animals, domesticated animals, trees, other plants, precious stones, precious metals, and other minerals.

They were also imposed on teaching, which was described and prescribed at the time in terms of INDOCTRINATING, INDUCTING, CONVERTING, TRAINING, DISCIPLINING and otherwise suppressing the base, carnal drives of the innately evil human while enabling individuals to find their proper role in service to the Church. Other titles given to teachers included DOCTOR (related to *doctrine*) and PROFESSOR (as in "profess one's faith"). Embodying the commitment to order, the teacher's task was interpreted in terms of PROFESSING a greater truth with the intention of INDOCTRINATING and INDUCTING (literally, "pull in") flawed, incomplete learners.

Industrialization and standardization

While religion-based institutions of education emphasized order and discipline, they didn't much resemble the modern school. They prepared the ground for an education that involved grades and grading, formally structured curricula, and management of behavior, but exactly what each school did varied massively from one location to the next – indeed, from one master to the next.

The word *inducting* is derived from the same root as *educating*, originally meaning "to pull/draw in." Whereas the focus on TEACHING AS EDUCATING was drawing out a student's inner self, the metaphor of TEACHING AS INDUCTING shifted attentions to pulling a student into a grander order (usually the Church).

In Europe, that changed dramatically in the 1600s and 1700s (and about a century later in North America). The pair of images below illustrates this shift. The image on the left, entitled "The School Master" (by Dutch master Adriaen van Ostade) dates to the mid-1600s and shows the teacher positioned amongst learners of all ages who are engaged in a range of activities. There is order, but this room scarcely resembles a classroom of today.

The image on the right portrays a schoolroom in England in the mid-1700s (artist unknown). Many differences are notable. The teacher is at the side of the room rather than the middle, where he can observe all under his charge and direct the activity. The students are all about the same age, they are organized in straight rows, they are all facing the same direction, they all have their own textbooks, and they're all doing the same thing at the same time.

More concisely, the image on the right depicts not just an *ordered* education, but a *standardized* one.

What happened?

In a nutshell, the Enlightenment.

Generally seen to have begun in the late 1600s, the **Age of Enlightenment** or **Age of Reason** was nothing

short of a cultural convulsion as England and continental Europe transformed in several ways. These included emphases on reason and individualism rather than religion and tradition. Historically, this period is associated with such intertwined developments as the emergence of mass communication through print media, the rise of capitalism, the **Industrial Revolution**, the **Scientific Revolution**, democratization, and European colonialism.

As for what the Enlightenment meant in the lives of individual citizens, the most significant shifts were connected to the emergence of factories. Prior to the Industrial Revolution, the population of Europe was principally rural and work was either close to or in the home. Factories created the need for concentrated labor forces, drawing workers into cities – and this shift toward urbanization fractured the extended family. At the same time it created a need to house children while their parents labored in factories. It also introduced a need for a literate and numerate workforce, as the abilities to read and calculate came to be seen as universal and minimal competencies for the worker.

The industrial factory served as more than a metaphor for the school of the Age of Enlightenment. Buidlings for the standardized school were actually modeled after the factory – as is evident in this image. It's not immediately clear whether the building depicted is a school or a factory.

These combined needs were massive and required a society-level response, which came in the form of the modern school. As mentioned above, the designers of schools in the late 1700s drew some inspiration from earlier instantiations of formal education, including curriculum topics (literacy and mathematics continued at the core) and emphases on order. However, in terms of structure, a new and significant influence was the modern factory with its efficient assembly lines, its standardized outputs, and its capacity for mass production.

These features were consciously and deliberately incorporated into the new model of the public school. Curricula were re-organized to emulate the one-step-at-a-time processes of the **assembly line**. Quality controls, mainly in the form of written tests, were implemented to ensure that outputs were adequate. Large buildings were constructed to accommodate the masses of students, who were separated by grade and subject area. All of these transformations were aspects of standardization – of what was taught, how it was taught, why it was taught, where it was taught, and when it was taught. (Indeed, "who" was taught was also re-interpreted in a standardized, normalized manner, as discussed in the next chapter.)

But the most significant shift associated with the rise of Standardized Education was something far more pervasive and far subtler. It was a change in what schools taught as the emphasis shifted from deep insight to practical know-how – that is, from *gnosis*-knowledge to *episteme*-knowledge. Whereas the main reason children were taught to read, to write, and to do arithmetic prior to the Enlightenment was to afford them access to the deeper truths of the universe, the reason these were taught in the modern school was to ensure they had the minimum basic skills along with an appropriate work ethic for a world of clear-cut roles. Schooling came to be defined not in terms of readiness for life, but of preparation for the job market.

The assembly line, with its parsed and sequenced subtasks, was the major inspiration for a modern curriculum design. As discussed in Chapter 1.2, one of the reasons the model was so powerful was that it meshed with emergent metaphors of knowledge (as an OBJECT) and learning (as ACQUISITION).

The rise of the middle class – education for all

Of course, the situation wasn't nearly as simple as this brief account might suggest. It's also important to mention that schooling through the first century of the Enlightenment had something of a split personality, one that parallels today's distinction between secondary and post-secondary education.

The public school of the early Enlightenment was intended only to provide a basic education, roughly the equivalent of today's upper elementary level. After that, children either went to work or, for an elite (usually according to wealth and class, but ability and other factors sometimes figured in as well), further "secondary" education. Those who aspired to a secondary education encountered a curriculum that was very much like the ones in pre-Enlightenment schooling, with heavy emphases on the liberal arts.

But, of course, things change. By the late-1800s, a large middle class had emerged in the western world. Controlling significant amounts of wealth, members of this class began to demand the same educational opportunities for their children as the nobility and the rich. The result was an education-for-all movement.

In essence, this movement entailed a redefinition of a basic education, as secondary schooling became not only accessible to every child but, by the mid-1900s, mandatory.

This movement also created a problem, however, as it forced a union of two very different models of education. As mentioned, primary schools at the time were focused entirely on the workplace practicality of *episteme*-knowledge, whereas secondary schools still retained some emphasis on deeper meanings associated with *gnosis*-knowledge. There was no easy flow from one to the other. They were seen as largely distinct, self-contained enterprises with very little overlap – not entirely unlike the current separation of secondary and tertiary education. They had different purposes, addressed different content, were geared to different audiences, and had very different outcomes in mind. Primary school was designed to prepare workers; secondary education was intended to prepare society's leaders.

Even though a century has passed since the first efforts to consolidate primary and secondary education, there is still considerable residue from their histories. By way of progress, primary curriculum has come to be more concerned with nurturing understanding, and the secondary curriculum now places much more emphasis on practical knowledge associated with job-preparation. However, the breaks between the levels continue to be apparent in teacher education programs that separate elementary from secondary streams and, more commonly, in cocktail party confessions that "I was good at school until Grade 6" and the dreaded "Why are we doing this?" that's triggered by so many topics in high school. In fact, between elementary and secondary school, there are still major disconnects between notions of what it means to be literate, numerate, and competent across all school disciplines.

That said, the device that was used to pull them together was, plain and simply, standardization. By extending the use of such tools of uniform curricula, formal testing, and rectangulated buildings from the primary level, secondary schooling was made to at least appear like a complement to primary schooling.

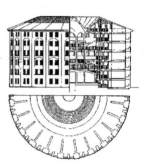

The factory wasn't the only influence on the design of the modern school building.

In the 1700s, an innovative prison design called the *panopticon* (from the Greek *pan-* + *optikon*, "all + for sight") was developed so guards could observe every inmate from a single vantage point. The idea was soon adopted and adapted by many of society's institutions, including hospitals, asylums, ... and schools.

The roles of the *sciences* in defining and shaping teaching is a recurrent theme in this book.

It's important to note at the outset that conceptions of science have evolved dramatically since the Scientific Revolution. Some very diverse perspectives are now represented among its branches (see the margin notes on pages 184–185).

With regard to Standardized Education, images and concepts from the *physical sciences* have had the greatest impact on teaching.

Indeed, a review of the documents and policies written over the last century about secondary schooling will reveal a core emphasis on standards and standardization – an emphasis that had previously been imposed only on the elementary-level schooling.

And there you have it …

It's impossible to understand the complexity of the profession of teaching without having some sense of how the modern school emerged … and how it is evolving. As you've no doubt noticed, it's not easy to present a neutral account of this evolution. We're well aware that we haven't succeeded – but we did confess up front that this history would be partial. There are a few details we'd like to underscore, however, lest we be read as *too* partial.

Firstly, in offering the distinction between two categories of knowledge (*gnosis*-knowledge and *episteme*-knowledge), we don't mean to suggest any sort of ranking. On the contrary, they're both vital to existence, and one would be impoverished without the other. The point is simply that, at some point in its history, the focus of formal education shifted – and shift in focus was so dramatic and complete that many citizens of the modern world are utterly unaware that precursors to public schools were originally invented to serve a very different purpose. Fundamentally, the meaning of *education* changed.

Secondly, in highlighting the contribution of the industrial factory to the structure of the modern school, we do not mean to cast aspersions. Rather, the more benign point is that a society's institutions tend to be influenced by whatever happens to be cutting edge. On that count, schools weren't alone. Government offices, hospitals, prisons, and other cultural institutions were also structured after the model of the industrial factory.

Finally, our intention in flagging some of the incoherent and inconsistent influences on modern schooling is not with the hope that a more coherent and consistent model might somehow emerge. Rather, the point is that, like every complex and evolving entity, the school embodies its entire history. Our aim, then, is to be mindful of the influences that enable and constrain the work of teachers. Once again, awareness opens possibility.

Suggestions for delving deeper

1. Standardized practices continue to dominate the schooling scene. Which aspects of your own educational experience are reflective of the assembly-line approach to schooling? Which aspects are not?

2. Revisit the terms for teaching that you identified as compelling (and/or those your found repulsive) from the Prologue. What are the etymological origins of those words? When might they have come into popular use? Do online searches for images that are currently associated with the terms. Are any of the associations informative? Surprising? Misleading?

3. As mentioned in the Prologue, each synonym for teaching is both a *description* and a *prescription*. That is, it points to both a theory (i.e., literally, a "way of seeing") and a practice. The previous exercise focuses mainly on the former. What sorts of prescriptions for practice are inherent in the terms that you find compelling? That is, what sort of emphases and actions go along with these terms?

1.2 Knowledge and Learning in Standardized Education

It's fair to assume that almost everyone knows what *learning* is. And yet, it may be the most contested notion among educators and educational researchers. We provide overviews of the current theories and opinions in the second chapter of each moment (i.e., Chapters 1.2, 2.2, 3.2, and 4.2). Across the range, there seems to be only one point of convergence, that learning is a process of transforming knowing.

Implicit in every teaching practice are theories of what education is for, what knowledge is, and how learning happens. But you'd be hard pressed to come to that conclusion by looking at the "how to teach" literature.

Every year the **American Educational Research Association** (AERA) hosts a conference that attracts between 10,000 and 20,000 people from around the world. With that sort of attendance, all of the major publishers in the field make sure they're represented in the book display. And so we have a yearly opportunity to scan the latest and greatest tomes on what teaching is all about.

There are always dozens of manuals for pre-service and practicing teachers, and most are little-changed "new" editions of well-established texts. These books are typically 300+ pages long with large glossy layouts, and most of them run between $100 and $200. Without exception, in our experience, they are mainly concerned with teaching practices within a frame of Standardized Education.

We've already flagged that we don't assume that teaching is settled – or even that there can or should be broad agreements on meanings. Rather, we write from the conviction that, for teaching to be relevant, the teacher must have a sense of the theories that enable and constrain practice. On that count, it doesn't make much sense to start out by talking about what teachers should do. Perspectives on that matter are stunningly varied, with only one point of agreement that we can discern – namely that teaching has something to do with triggering *learning*.

That assertion, of course, actually says very little. The range of views on what learning is and how it happens is at least as diverse as the range of thinking on teaching. Also like the notion of teaching, there seems to be just one point of agreement among definitions and theories of learning: they all have something to do with affecting what is known. And that takes us to the question of what it means to *know*.

In the academic world, matters of knowing and learning fall into the domain of **epistemology**, which is concerned with questions of what is known, how knowledge is generated, and how it is learned. It's perhaps the most contested branch of philosophy – as might be expected. Every English speaker has unique understandings of *knowing* and *learning* that are personally compelling. One of the truisms of education is that these sorts of understandings, built up over a lifetime, can be highly resilient because the person finds them adequate. It's very, very difficult to engage someone in critical examinations of interpretations that work for her or him, especially if approached with the suggestion is that those understandings might be naïve or indefensible. Perhaps for that reason, a great many people regard questions of epistemology as irrelevant and unproductive time wasters.

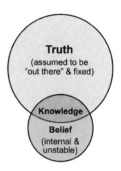

Truth (assumed to be "out there" & fixed)

Knowledge

Belief (internal & unstable)

The word *epistemology* was coined in the mid-1800s to mean "theory of knowledge," and there's more than a little irony in this definition. The word is derived from the Greek *episteme*, "know-how" – which, as detailed in Chapter 1.1, was part of a dyad. Its complement, *gnosis*, "deep knowledge of the universe," is the root of the word *knowledge*.

In other words, in defining epistemology as the theory of knowledge, *episteme* eclipses *gnosis*. Truths and facts are separated from and made superior to unvalidated beliefs.

Obviously we don't. We write from the perspective that those whose work in education – that is, whose careers are entirely about knowledge and learning – have an obligation to be aware of at least some of their epistemological assumptions. To ignore topics of knowing and learning is to consciously accept the risk of perpetuating out-of-date and perhaps-incoherent beliefs, along with similarly troublesome classroom practices, curriculum content, and schooling structures that are fitted to those beliefs.

What's *knowledge*?

Before you read our answer to the question, "What's knowledge?" we recommend that you take it on yourself, perhaps jotting down some of the words and phrases that come to mind.

We have two reasons for this suggestion. Firstly, it

may be useful to experience how difficult it can be to craft a response. In particular, it's not easy for most people to offer a definition of *knowledge* that doesn't invoke a cognate the word *know* – which, of course, sets up a less-than-useful circularity. Secondly, in those responses that don't rely on the word *know*, there may be some important clues about what's being taken for granted.

Metaphor is is a cognitive mechanism humans use to map insights from one domain onto another. It is particularly useful for making sense of highly abstract concepts.

For example, the concept of *knowledge* is difficult to define. Most commonly, it is described through the metaphor of a physical object that can be held, built, exchanged, consumed, and so on – even though there are major problems with these sorts of associations.

We recently engaged a group of teacher candidates in this task, asking them to record one another's definitions and descriptions before undertaking an analysis of the metaphors and images that were used. Some of the responses are summarized in the charts on the next page. (There were many more contributions, but we've omitted those that varied in minor ways from the entries listed.) As the left columns illustrate, most of the articulations involved a KNOWLEDGE-AS-CONSTRUCTABLE-OBJECT metaphor. Knowledge, that is, is most often characterized as some THING that is PICKED UP, GRASPED, ASSEMBLED, PASSED ALONG, TOSSED AROUND, and POSSESSED.

At first glance, it might seem like these metaphors are all over the place – a point that was underscored in statements that blended more than one association (e.g., "the *collection* of *insights* from across *domains*," which combines metaphors of OBJECTS, ILLUMINATION, and TERRITORIES). But they do have at least one important point of convergence: across all of them, knowledge is interpreted as some sort of nonmaterial form that is described as a physical entity.

It wasn't easy for class participants to arrive at the realization that English speakers tend to characterize knowledge as a THING. It actually took them close to an hour to come to it, along with the other core metaphors (i.e., LIGHT/ILLUMINATION, FOOD/LIQUID, BUILDING/CONSTRUCTION, and TERRITORY). Somewhat ironically, it turns out that the task of making such metaphors explicit is intellectually demanding – even though, on the implicit level, humans use metaphors constantly and with great ease.

The more interesting part of the exercise came through the balance of the term, during which class members were asked to pay attention to the metaphors that they and others were using in their everyday

KNOWLEDGE AS OBJECT/POSSESSION	
Explicit descriptions	**Implicit references**
The *things* you're sure of. The *things* you can do. The *stuff* you've learned. The *content* of a course What you've *picked up*. What's been *passed along*. The *collection* of facts and truths. Information that's been *gathered*.	*Toss* ideas around. She *holds* some pretty strange beliefs. I *have* an idea. I don't *catch* your meaning. Oh. I *get it*! Darn … I almost *had* it! Ram *it* in; cram *it* in. Knowledge-*broker*. Knowledge is cultural *capital*. I'm not *grasping* this. She knows *tons of things* about that. Why are we studying *this stuff*?

KNOWLEDGE AS LIGHT/ILLUMINATION	
Explicit descriptions	**Implicit references**
What you're able to see. Things that have been *brought to light*. The *insights* built up by humanity.	Oh, I *see*! She's still *in the dark*. Suddenly *the light* went on. Not getting the *complete picture* here.

KNOWLEDGE AS FOOD/LIQUID	
Explicit descriptions	**Implicit references**
What you've *taken in*. *Sustenance* for the mind.	Immersed in *a sea* of ideas. *Food* for thought. We're *drowning* in all the details. I just sat there and *soaked it all up*.

KNOWLEDGE AS BUILDING/CONSTRUCT	
Explicit descriptions	**Implicit references**
The *assemblage* of human truths. The insights *built up* by humanity.	*Getting* ideas *together*. *Solid foundations*. Mastering the *basics*. *Building* an understanding. *Put it together*!

KNOWLEDGE AS TERRITORY	
Explicit descriptions	**Implicit references**
A *domain*. A *field*; every *field* of study combined.	I'm *lost*. I don't see *how she got there*. *Where are you* with all this stuff? What's your *area*? This *course* covers *too much ground*. His thinking is *all over the place*.

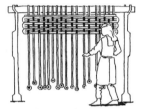

Metaphors used by educators are often drawn from the most sophisticated technologies of the time. For example, the word *order* was borrowed from the Latin *ordinem*, "a row of threads in a loom," which was metaphorically applied to social classes, ranks, positions, and other means to differentiate among statuses. Along similar lines, religious orders were well established in and through the Church.

The loom's output was also the inspiration for other metaphors associated with knowledge and learning. In particular, the words *text*, *test*, and *technology* all derive from the Latin *texere*, "to weave."

discussions. This task generated a *much* longer list, elements of which were included in the right-hand columns of the charts on the facing page.

This metaphorical understanding of KNOWLEDGE AS A CONSTRUCTABLE OBJECT is ancient and has became part of culture common sense long ago. With the Scientific and Industrial Revolutions, however, the metaphor was embraced with a new seriousness. The goal of the sciences, for example, came to be explicitly defined in terms of generating *objective truths* – that is, insights that stood like OBJECTS that were independent of personal biases, that could be shown to be true through repeatable demonstrations, and that could be assembled out of simpler truths. Within industry and business, such objective knowledge came to be treated as a COMMODITY. Through patents and copyrights, bits of knowledge came to be treated as items that could be OWNED, ASSIGNED A VALUE, and PURCHASED.

Within formal education, the KNOWLEDGE-AS-CONSTRUCTABLE-OBJECT metaphor meshed well with the assembly-line mentality that infused the structures of schooling. That detail continues to be evident in, for example, curricula that emphasize objective facts, marketable skills, measurable outcomes, and other learning *object*ives.

Again, we don't mean to suggest that the KNOWLEDGE-AS-CONSTRUCTABLE-OBJECT metaphor was the only one to influence thinking about formal education when modern schooling was invented. But it was the dominant one, and so we focus on it in this chapter in order to make the discussion manageable.

Order: a hidden geometry of knowledge

This perspective on knowledge – as something external, stable, and objectively real – has prevailed for centuries. For good reason. It meshes with more ancient, deeply engrained beliefs about the ordered and stable nature of the universe. That belief was bolstered in the 1500s and 1600s when an influential group of philosophers and scientists argued that *all* valid knowledge should be objective – by which they meant that it should align with a particular geometry.

This thinking was influenced by the **geometry of the plane** (or **Euclidean geometry**), developed in ancient Greece, and usually experienced in schools as the naming of shapes, classification of angles, and writing of formal proofs. Claims to truth came to be described in terms geometric forms – specifically, points, lines, and planes – and, following the model of the geometric proof, knowledge came to be understood as something that could be reduced to simpler bits, which could then be logically reassembled to generate more sophisticated truths.

Notions of basic parts, linear relations, and formal logic aligned well with the widespread belief that the universe was stable and ordered. They also connected well with new, factory-based modes of production, in which multistep projects (e.g., making a clock) were fragmented into tiny tasks and sequenced as points along a production line. It's probably not surprising, then, that the same line-based imagery was used to design curriculum in the 1700s – and, ever since, to direct and defend curriculum structures and content. It makes perfect sense if knowledge is understood as a CONSTRUCTABLE OR MANUFACTURABLE OBJECT.

But we're getting ahead of ourselves. Let us highlight some of the ways that the forms (i.e., points, lines, and planes) and processes (i.e., reduction of fundamental pieces, logical argumentation) of planar geometry have become commonsensical. We'll address these two topics in sequence.

Regarding the pervasiveness of planar forms, consider this situation: almost every educator has struggled with the expectations to be able to *plan* well, to ex*plain* clearly, and to speak in *plain* language. Clear planning, explaining, and plain speaking are popularly seen as reliable markers of real understanding.

But where do the concerns with planning, explaining, and plain speaking come from? In these cases, the etymologies are telling. They all derive from the Latin *planus*, "flat." That is, "plain language," "plain truth," "plain and simple" – along with common references to *laying things out*, keeping things *on the level*, ensuring that shares are *even*, and so on – are entangled in the same conceptual weave as planar geometry. The unit-

Rationalism and *empiricism* are two closely related approaches to knowledge production that rose to prominence at the start of the Industrial and Scientific Revolutions.

Often described as opposites, they are actually complementary. Rationalists turned inward and suggested that knowledge must be reducible to fundamental truths that might be logically combined into grander truths. Empiricists looked outward, arguing that theories must be grounded in evidence. In both cases, the key measure of validity is the extent to which a theory allows one to predict events.

ing theme across these ideas is that reality is seen to have an innate order, and the whole point of research is to de*line*ate the categories that define that order. (We also suspect that a reason that the metaphor of KNOWLEDGE AS TERRITORY is compelling may be tied to the notion of plains/planes, but we've been unable to find evidence to support or reject this hunch.)

We're actually hoping that you're a little skeptical of the claims in the previous paragraph. We certainly were at one point in our studies, and that skepticism prodded us to grapple with some of the knots of association in the English language. One of the most intriguing of these tangles is the one that has evolved around line-based images, some bits of which are presented in the following chart.

SOME NOTIONS ASSOCIATED WITH LINEARITY		
Term	**Derivation**	**Some current usages and cognates**
right	Proto-Indo-European *reg-*, "move in a straight line," via Latin *rectus*, "straight" and Latin *regula*, "straight edge"	right angle, righteous, right handed, right of way, right *vs.* wrong, human rights
rect-		rectangle, correct, direct, rectify, rector, erect
regular		regulation, regulate, regular attendance
rule		obey the rules, ruler, rule of law, rule out, rule of thumb, ruled paper, rule of order
line	Latin *linum*, "flax thread"	linear, time line, line of text, line of argument, line of thought, linear relation, sight line, linear causality, family line, toe the line
ortho-	Greek *orthos*, "straight"	orthodox, orthodontics, orthogonal, orthopedic
straight	German *streccan*, "stretch"	straight up, go straight, straight answer, straight talk, straight and narrow, straight laced, straight sexually

This chart is far from complete. The webs of association are also tied to images and meanings of *truth*, being *justified*, and other highly valued notions. Perhaps even more intriguing than this collection is the cluster of words that entered English meaning, literally, "not linear/straight," "bent/curved," or "wandering." The list includes *aberrant, bent, crooked, deviant, distorted, erroneous, hallucinated, kinky, meandering, perverted, queer, sick, tortured, twisted, vague, warped, weak, weird, worrying, writhing,* and *wrong*. For us, the contrast between the words in the left column of the chart above with the italicized words in the previous sentence is particularly telling. In English, linearity is strongly associated with Good, nonlinearity with Evil. It's no surprise that scientists and philosophers would see knowledge in such terms.

Nor is it particularly surprising that educators in the 1700s would adopt the word *curriculum* to refer to what children were to study. The noun form of the Greek verb *currere*, "to run," a curriculum is a running course. The image was ideal for blending together commonsensical metaphors of knowledge (as OBJECTS, LIGHT, TERRITORIES, etc.) and images of knowledge (as linear and logical). It also tied in very nicely with the metaphor of SCHOOLS AS FACTORY-PRODUCTION LINES.

Of course points, lines, and planes are represented in more than the structures of modern curriculum. They are also manifest in the physical organizations of most schools. As will be discussed in more detail in Chapter 1.3, this same geometry has a strong presence in the shapes of schools, in the organization of classrooms, in the ranking and ordering of learners, in the classifications of abilities and disabilities, in the structuring of the school day, in the work of teaching … the list goes on.

It's also strongly represented in popular beliefs about learning.

What's *learning*?

As already mentioned, the nature of learning is perhaps the most contested topic within the field of education, at least among theorists and researchers. To get a sense of the range of opinions and views, we urge you to do some searching online. It's not hard to locate websites listing 50 or more *categories* of theories – that is, not 50+ theories, but 50+ clusters (!) of theories.

To adapt an old saw, theories of learning are like toothbrushes: everyone has one and no one wants to use anyone else's.

We recommend engaging in the same sort of exercise as the one suggested above regarding knowledge. That is, chat about your understandings of learning

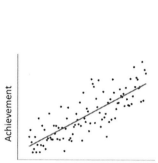

Time on Task

A *linear* model is one in which two phenomena are seen to have a direct and predictable cause-and-effect relationship – that is, one that obeys the laws of classical (Newtonian) physics. There is a popular belief that modern science is responsible for this conception because, until recently, scientific models of different phenomena tended to be linear.

In fact, most of linear models were proposed only as approximations because scientists lacked the computational power needed for more accurate descriptions (see Chapter 4.1). Beliefs in and desires for simple linear relationships reach much further back into history.

and jot down the words and phrases that you use. We recently asked a group of pre-service teachers to do this, and a portion of their responses is presented in the charts below.

LEARNING AS ACQUIRING	
Explicit descriptions	**Implicit references**
Picking things up. *Getting it.* *Wrapping* your mind *around things.*	I totally *don't get* what this class is about. I can *pick up* the minor details later. I'm not *grasping* your meaning.

LEARNING AS ILLUMINATING	
Explicit descriptions	**Implicit references**
Coming *to see* something. Turning *the light* on.	Totally not *seeing* it. I don't like being *kept in the dark.* Suddenly *the lights* went on. It's *clear* to me.

LEARNING AS CONSUMING/INTAKING	
Explicit descriptions	**Implicit references**
Taking things in. Getting concepts *into your head.*	*Soaking* up information. I must have *absorbed* that somewhere. *Ram* it in; *cram* it in. *Digesting* the facts. *Ruminating.* The concept is starting *to gel* for us.

LEARNING AS CONSTRUCTING/BUILDING	
Explicit descriptions	**Implicit references**
Building understandings. *Constructing* knowledge.	I'm having trouble *putting things together.* You have *to make* your own sense of things.

LEARNING AS JOURNEYING	
Explicit descriptions	**Implicit references**
Making *progress.* *Converging onto* an understanding.	Don't worry. I'm *getting there.* I'm not sure *where she's coming from.* It's not clear to me *how you got there.* There's a lot *to get through* in a single term.

Once again, these interpretations might at first appear to be all over the map. However, also once again, most of them share an assumption – namely that learning is a linear process of internalizing. In this frame, learning is seen to happen when something that starts on the outside of one's head somehow comes to be manifest inside one's head. In terms of visual metaphor, the underlying image might be depicted with the simple graphic:

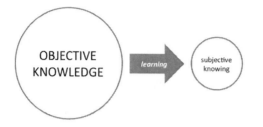

Those perspectives on learning that assume this sort of outside-to-inside process are known as **correspondence theories** of learning. In a nutshell, within this category, learning is understood in terms of creating a subjective internal model or map of an objective outer world – by which "truth" and "correctness" comes to defined in terms of the level of match (or correspondence). A more *accurate* inner model or map is more *right*.

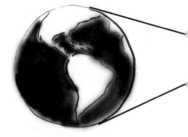

A *correspondence theory* is one in which learning is understood in terms of acquiring, projecting, or building an internal model that corresponds to an external reality. This category is also known as *representationism* – that is, learning is about constructing an internal representation an outer reality.

(Note: although the word *construct* is frequently used within these theories, they should not be construed as constructivist theories.

In other words, according to this way of thinking, truth or correctness can be measured. To do so, one need only compare subjective interpretations to objective truths – a line of thought that links to the notion of quality control on a production line. That is, a correspondence-theory mindset infuses the culture of *evaluation* – of scoring and grading – in schools.

It's important to draw a distinction between the practice of testing and the culture of evaluation. As will be revisited in later chapters, virtually every theory of learning embraces some manner of testing – that is, of creating opportunities to assess a learner's emerging interpretations in order to adapt teaching. In most frames for education, these information-gathering activities are not the same thing as assigning a value to a learner's performance. The conflation of testing and evaluation is unique to Standardized Education.

Another quality that is specific to Standardized Educational sensibilities, and a hallmark of correspondence theories of learning, is the presence of such radical dichotomies as internal *vs.* external, mind *vs.* body, thought *vs.* action, fact *vs.* fiction, true *vs.* false,

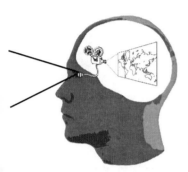

See Chapters 2.2 and 3.2 for a description of that category.)

The most commonsensical correspondence theories are known as *mentalisms* – which, as illustrated here, are built on an assumption that a knower has an internal model or map of am external reality. The most popular mentalism at the moment is the one that uses the specific metaphor, BRAIN AS COMPUTER, which is known as *cognitivism*.

literal *vs.* figurative, self *vs.* other, individual *vs.* collective, subjective *vs.* objective, nature *vs.* nurture, and theory *vs.* practice. If you find yourself believing there is a clear unambiguous boundary between the terms in any of these dyads, chances are you favor a correspondence theory of learning ...

... which would hardly be surprising. These theories are dominant in popular culture. To prove the point, try to describe learning without using any of the terms or images in the charts on pages 28 and 33. It's possible (as discussed in later chapters), but it's difficult to do without consciously avoiding KNOWLEDGE-AS-OBJECT and LEARNING-AS-ACQUIRING metaphors.

Before we leave the topic of correspondence theories of learning, it's worth mentioning that there are two subcategories: **mentalisms** and **behaviorisms**. These two subcategories are often described as opposites, but they are rooted in similar beliefs. In particular, both assume there is a radical separation between objective (external) reality and subjective (internal) constructs of that reality. The critical difference, as one might guess, is that mentalisms focus on what's going on in the mind and behaviorisms focus on observable and measurable behaviors.

Mentalisms are the default commonsensical model in western culture, and a common indicator of a mentalist theory is the strategy of using the latest technology to describe learning. Over the past millennium, metaphors for learning have included catapults, writing on a slate, a printing press, photographs, telephone switchboards, movie cameras, computers, and the Internet. While the underlying image has varied, the alignments with KNOWLEDGE-AS-OBJECT and LEARNING-AS-ACQUIRING metaphors have been very stable. Consider the metaphor of BRAIN AS COMPUTER, which rose to prominence in the 1950s. Its entailments include that KNOWLEDGE IS INFORMATION OR DATA, that LEARNING IS INPUTTING AND STORING THOSE DATA, that THINKING IS PROCESSING, that REMEMBERING IS RETRIEVING, and that COMMUNICATION IS THE TRANSFER OR EXCHANGE OF INFORMATION. (Critiques of mentalisms are offered in later sections, and so we don't want to get too deeply into them here. However, it bears mention that, now that brain activity can be observed in real time, what's going on does not at all resemble the inner workings of a digital computer. Nor are there indications of internalized maps or models of an external world. Yet mentalist theories continue to prevail.)

Behaviorisms, the other subcategory of correspondence theories, constitute an important topic for teachers for several reasons. In particular, they were the dominant theories of learning among researchers and policy makers for much of the 1900s and, even though they have been shown to be inadequate for making sense of the complexity of human learning, they continue to have a strong presence in curriculum documents, classroom practices, and evaluation schemes.

Among behaviorisms, learning is defined as CHANGES IN BEHAVIOR due to environmental circumstances. Note that, even though behaviorists are careful to avoid mentioning of internal states, these theories assume that learning is about creating correspondences between environmental stimuli (i.e., outer factors) and learned responses (i.e., inner connections). As such, these theories focus on manipulation and control of environmental conditions, which includes identification of desired ends (e.g., setting clear expectations, stating unambiguous learning objectives, specifying precise behavioral standards), engineering of situations (e.g., subdividing grand learning objectives into manageable bits, setting rewards and punishments), and ensuring that those ends are met.

Because behaviorisms are no longer prominent among the theories of learning that are used to inform teaching, we will say little more about them. However, it's vital to emphasize that they have by no means gone away. Behaviorist principles infuse a great deal of schooling practice, and so all teachers should have at least a preliminary knowledge of what they assert and how they have been taken up. There is an abundance of information on behaviorisms in education available online, from both advocates and critics.

To recap then, correspondence theories of learning – both mentalisms and behaviorisms – assume that learning is a matter of assembling an internal structure that in some way resembles, represents, maps,

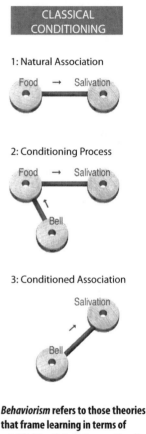

CLASSICAL CONDITIONING

1: Natural Association

2: Conditioning Process

3: Conditioned Association

Behaviorism refers to those theories that frame learning in terms of establishing links between stimuli and behaviors. Prominent in the early 1900s, these theories were strongly influenced by the imagery of telephone switchboards (and the activity of linking nodes together).

Two mechanisms for forming associations are illustrated. On the left is a case of *classical conditioning*. A neutral stimulus (a bell) comes to

or otherwise corresponds to an external reality. This notion, in turn, is associated with a particular view of what a *learner* is.

What's a *learner*?

Once again, we urge you to answer this question for yourself before checking out our response.

Given that learning is most popularly understood in terms of taking things in, it follows that learners are most commonly seen as the CONSUMERS, INGESTERS, SPONGES, or agents who otherwise acquire knowledge. This interpretation fits with our analyses of the definitions and descriptions that people tend to offer in response to the question, "What is a learner?" In particular, the people we ask consistently identify three qualities:

- The learner is a person, an individual, a hermetically sealed knower.
- That individual is deficient – that is, a learner is a learner precisely because there's something she or he needs to acquire.
- While each is unique, the learner can be understood in terms of norms – that is, relative to other, comparable learners.

We've already addressed the first quality in the preceding section. The assumption of **radical individualism** – of an inner self isolated from others and insulated from objective reality – is foundational to all correspondence theories of learning. These theories only make sense if such extreme separations are assumed.

The notion that the learner is deficient is aligned with the factory mentality within education, in which a learner is likened to a product being manufactured. Anywhere along the production line, the product is necessarily incomplete. Likewise, within a frame of Standardized Education, until the learner has demonstrated the competencies required for graduation, she or he is seen as lacking or deficient.

The notion of the "**normal** learner" is the most recent of the above constructs, having only pressed its way into the educational imagination about a century ago. It derives from the adoption of statistical methods

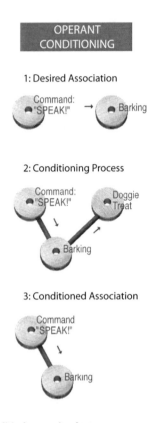

OPERANT CONDITIONING

1: Desired Association

2: Conditioning Process

3: Conditioned Association

elicit the same involuntary response (salivation) as a non-neutral stimulus (food). On the right, an instance of *operant conditioning* is shown. A reward (doggie treat) is used to increase the probability that a stimulus (the command, "Speak") will elicit a particular voluntary response (barking).

Such learning mechanisms can be used to create long and complicated chains of behavior in many species.

in the 1800s by psychological and sociological researchers. More specifically, it is linked to efforts to demonstrate that, just like height and weight, human qualities such as the ability to learn are distributed normally.

A **normal distribution** is a member of a family of mathematical models that is most associated with the familiar "bell curve." Normal distributions present two important pieces of information: the *mean* (i.e., the arithmetic average or the *norm*, at the center) and the *standard deviation* (i.e., an indication of how the data are spread out). The humped shape of the curve illustrates how, for many phenomena, most data points cluster around the mean and the number quickly drops off as one moves further from the mean. Many everyday phenomena – the sizes of potatoes in a field, human heights in a specific population, shoe sizes, gasoline prices – seem to obey normal distributions.

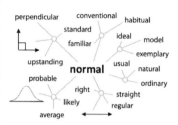

The original impetus for the development of the normal distribution, almost 200 years ago, was the study of errors made in astronomical measurements. When astronomers tried to plot their observations, they found they could not generate the smooth paths and curves that were predicted by the laws of physics. The reason turned out to be simple. All measurements have errors.

The word *normal* has become such a *familiar, natural, regular, likely, standard* part of everyday discourse that it's easy to ignore its baggage.

That's also true of a *normal distribution*. This commonly used mathematical model presents two important pieces of information: the *mean* (or *average* or *norm* or *standard*) at the center and the measure of divergence (or *standard deviation*) from the norm.

At the time, mathematicians assumed measurement errors to be random. However, after some focused analysis, it was shown that these errors were always distributed in the same way. Most are quite small (i.e., in terms of the normal distribution curve, under the bulging part of the bell), some are more serious, and a tiny few are whopping. The pattern turned out to match a distribution that probability theorists had developed a few decades earlier, which astronomers adopted and dubbed the "normal distribution of errors curve."

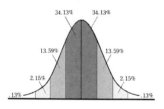

It was soon noticed that the same curve could be applied to manufactured products. The objects produced by a factory will deviate from the desired standards in a highly predictable manner. It was in this way that the notion of *production standards* was tied to the notion of *normal distributions*. Standards within industry were, in effect, the ranges of acceptable deviation from the mean/norm. In fact, within industry, the *normal distribution* was renamed the *standard distribution*.

Standards and *norms* actually have a deeper association than this one based in industry. Both words entered English as references to right angles – that is, they are also parts of the family of terms drawn from the geometry of the plane. The chart below highlights other members of this particular cluster:

SOME NOTIONS ASSOCIATED WITH RIGHT ANGLES		
Term	**Derivation**	**Some current usages and cognates**
standard	Latin *stare*, "stand" (i.e., make a right angle to the ground)	standardized tests, standard from, setting standards, raising standards, meeting standards, standard time, standard unites, standard deviation, standard of living
normal	Latin *norma*, "carpenter's square"	normal curve, normalize, normative, normality, normalcy, normal child, achievement norms, normal development
perpendicular	Latin *pendere*, "to hang" (i.e., vertically)	pendulum, depend, pending, independent
upright	"up" + Latin *rectus*, "straight"	morally upright

Extending this list, other commentators have suggested there are etymological connections between *vertical* and *verity*, as well as between the notion of right angles and *truth*. We've been unable to confirm the etymological connections, but there are strong associations in contemporary usages (e.g., a builder wants a wall to be true – or perfectly vertical). As well, antonyms to the words in the chart are telling: *abnormal, askew, nonstandard, odd, slanted, substandard* – all derived from terms meaning, literally, "not vertical" or "leaning."

When the normal distribution began to move from the physical sciences into the social sciences in the early 1800s, it was first applied to social statistics (e.g., birth rates and death rates) and, later, human dimensions (e.g., height and age). These applications were rooted in the assumption, borrowed from the sciences, that variation is linked to error. That is, differences in height weren't seen in terms of natural diversity, but in terms of error or deviation from what was normal.

That same sensibility was carried into efforts in the mid-1800s to apply the normal distribution of errors curve to mental qualities. This work started with the assumption of a "normal man" (and, yes, the bulk of this research was conducted on men, typically undergraduate students) whose physical dimensions, moral attributes, aesthetic sensibilities, intellectual capacities, and so on were seen to represent a level of perfection to which all should aspire – just like the standardized, normal product from a factory.

Sensibilities have changed somewhat since then. Today, the "normal" is seen less in terms of an ideal standard and more in terms of average. As well, some deviations (e.g., above the mean for height and intelligence, below the mean for waist size and introversion) are commonly seen as superior. At the same time, deviations in the other direction continue to be seen as flawed, in error, deviant, or undesirable.

Such extensions of notions of normal are pervasive in schooling – where individual intelligence has been subjected to a normalist sensibility more than any other phenomenon.

What is intelligence?

As might be expected, there is no unified definition of intelligence. However, it's fair to say that definitions and descriptions tend to be hinged to assumptions about knowledge and learning. For example, the notion that intelligence is a measurable capacity flow out of the following stream of metaphors:

Intelligence is defined in many different ways. All of these images serve as visual metaphors for intelligence within a frame of Standardized Education, where the phenomenon is most often characterized in terms of MEASURABLE CAPACITIES – including abilities to retain facts, to perform skills, and to notice similarities.

KNOWLEDGE IS AN OBJECT.

⬇

LEARNING IS TAKING THINGS IN.

⬇

THE LEARNER IS A CONTAINER.

⬇

INTELLIGENCE IS THE CAPACITY OF THE CONTAINER.

More descriptively, within this metaphoric field, intelligence is a MEASURABLE CAPACITY – where the measurable dimensions include size, speed, and accuracy. Unsurprisingly, these assumed dimensions are reflected in popular metaphors of intelligence, some of which are presented in the charts on the next page.

INTELLIGENCE AS SPEEDINESS	
Explicit descriptions	**Implicit references**
Quickness.	Not the *quickest* deer in the forest. *Slow* learner. *Retarded* (i.e., literally, "delayed").

INTELLIGENCE AS ACUITY	
Explicit descriptions	**Implicit references**
Sharpness. *Smartness* (i.e., originally, "sharp," as is "smarting"). *Cleverness* (i.e., related to *cleaver*). *Discernment* (i.e., originally, "to separate").	He's not the *sharpest* knife in the drawer. She's a little *dull*.

INTELLIGENCE AS MEASURE/CAPACITY	
Explicit descriptions	**Implicit references**
Talent. *Potential.*	She has an incredible *capacity* for math.

INTELLIGENCE AS ENDOWMENT	
Explicit descriptions	**Implicit references**
Giftedness.	Use the *gifts* you were given.

INTELLIGENCE AS LUMINOSITY	
Explicit descriptions	**Implicit references**
Brightness.	Not the *brightest* bulb in the marquee. She's *brilliant*. He's a little *dim*.

With regard to the meanings of intelligence that dominate within a frame of Standardized Education, the critical element across these interpretations is the assumption of measurability – which, in turn, is tethered to the mathematics of normality and normal distributions. Indeed, a significant industry has burgeoned over the last century around the measurement of intelligence, almost all of it oriented by the conviction that intelligence is normally distributed.

So far, no one has been able to create an intelligence test that confirms that conviction. The most common explanation for this troubling fact has been that the tests are inadequate. Few in the field wonder if the assumption might be flawed – but that's a topic for a later chapter, along with other critiques of a capacity-based interpretation of intelligence. Our present interest is to look at how object-oriented beliefs about knowledge and acquisition-oriented beliefs about teaching are embodied in the teaching practices of Standardized Education.

Suggestions for delving deeper

1. Chat with others and quiz them about their meanings of *knowledge* and *learning*. What metaphors do they use? How do their understandings fit with yours? How do they fit with the metaphor of KNOWLEDGE AS CONSTRUCTABLE OBJECT? Speculate on possible entailments for meanings of learning, learner, and intelligence.

2. As mentioned, the dominant theories of learning in the 1900s were behaviorisms. Do a little research on them. In particular, why do educators now broadly reject behaviorist theories? And how are they still manifest in schooling?

3. Copying – that is, precisely mimicking the work of someone else – is often scorned as an activity that oppresses creativity and individual expression. Yet it is a prominent and core emphasis in the education and training of artists, athletes, and others at the top of their fields. Is copying restrictive or enabling? How might the tension of "copying *vs.* free expression" be resolved within the practice of teaching?

1.3 Teaching and Standardized Education

One of the most ubiquitous images associated with Standardized Education is a triangle that links teacher, learner, and subject matter:

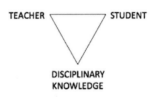

First, find a common denominator. Then make equivalent fractions . . .

By far the most popular synonym for teaching within Standardized Education is *instructing*. Literally meaning "giving instructions," in its most basic sense instructing refers to a collection of educational practices that are teacher-centered, skill-based, outcome-oriented, and minimally interactive.

To be honest, we've never been able to discern much explicit insight in this figure, beyond the rather mundane suggestion that teaching has something to do with linking knowers and knowledge.

However, there is some important implicit information. For example, a commitment to the simplicities of planar geometry is obvious. As well, the image only makes sense if the three vertices are treated as "things," tying into deeply engrained metaphors of KNOWLEDGE AS OBJECT and LEARNER AS CONTAINER. From that it follows that teaching must be some sort of DELIVERING or RELAYING process.

In terms of more subtle insights, as with knowledge and learning, popular beliefs about teaching are revealed in the terms chosen to describe it. For example, one major influence on teaching in the first public schools was the **medieval university**, from which the following emphases were borrowed:

- TEACHING AS LECTURING – from the Greek *legein*, "to orate, tell, or declare," originally, "to pick out, choose, collect";

- TEACHING AS PROFESSING – via the French *professeur*, from Latin *professor*, "expert in some domain of art or science," from *profiteri*, "lay claim to, declare openly."

Associated notions include TELLING, PRESENTING, CONVEYING, and INFORMING – which collectively highlight two key aspects of this conception of teaching. Firstly, the teacher was understood to be an expert in a domain, one who selected and preserved what was important to know. Secondly, teaching was a matter of RELAYING that knowledge, principally by oral means. Importantly, notions of TEACHING AS LECTURING and TEACHING AS PROFESSING are far more ancient than the medieval university. Their roots extend at least into ancient Hellenist (Greek) and Semitic (Jewish and early Christian) traditions.

To be clear, these TELLING conceptions of teaching weren't new when public schooling was invented. Rather, what was novel was their extension to *all* levels of education – so they were new to the teaching of younger children. Prior to then, there were few resemblances between the church-based school and the medieval university, save for the fact that they were places where people were collected to learn.

Indeed, terms for teaching associated with religion and church-based schools point to quite different emphases and approaches. The following were among the metaphors adopted from this precursor to the public schooling:

- TEACHING AS ENLIGHTENING – an entailment of the biblically prominent metaphor of KNOWLEDGE AS LIGHT, and part of a large cluster of vision-based associations (e.g., ILLUMINATING, HIGHLIGHTING, SHOWING, DISPLAYING, ILLUSTRATING, DEMONSTRATING, CLARIFYING, REVEALING);
- TEACHING AS EDIFYING – adopted from the from Old French *edifier*, "build up, teach, instruct (morally, in faith)," from Latin *aedificare*, "to construct";
- TEACHING AS DISCIPLINING – aligned strongly with notions of self-control and obedience to sacred rules, the meanings of *discipline* also include physical punishment, direct instruction, and a discrete

A *conduit model of communication* is assumed in almost all metaphors and synonyms for teaching within a frame of Standardized Education. This model asserts that communication is a process of packing thoughts into word-objects that and conveying them (through some sensory channel/conduit) to a receiver who unpacks the meaning.

The model clearly aligns with KNOWLEDGE-AS-OBJECT and LEARNING-AS-ACQUISITION metaphors. However, as discussed in much more detail in Chapter 2.2, it has some serious conceptual flaws.

domain of knowledge – and so perhaps more than any other, this word is suggestive of core aspects of early religious education.

Notice that these metaphors are very different from those borrowed from the medieval university, which were principally concerned with oral communication. These ones are more about directing behavior and ordering thought, consistent with key religious principles of the time.

That is, there is an implicit linearity in the metaphors borrowed from religion, based as they are on vision (e.g., "LINES of sight"), construction (e.g., SEQUENCED assembly), and order (e.g., RIGHTness and RIGHTeousness). This quality made such metaphors easy to align with brand new descriptions of teaching that drew explicitly on images associated with planar geometry. Examples that sprang into common usage in the earliest stages of industrialization were:

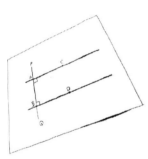

In much the same way that it shows up in popular understandings of knowledge and learning, *Euclid's geometry of the plane* is a strong theme in conceptions of teaching associated with Standardized Education. It is sometimes explicit (e.g., TEACHING AS DIRECTING), sometimes veiled (e.g., TEACHING AS EXPLAINING), but most often implicit (e.g., TEACHING AS TRAINING).

- TEACHING AS EXPLAINING – originally *explane,* derived in the early 1400s from the Latin *explanare,* "to plane, to level, to smooth";
- TEACHING AS DIRECTING – taken up in the late 1300s, from the Latin *di + rectus,* "put straight."

Of course, EXPLAINING and DIRECTING are seen more as aspects of teaching than full-blown descriptions. Other words that were part of the same wave of metaphors and synonyms included:

- TEACHING AS TRAINING – first used within education in the early 1500s, likely borrowed from the gardening technique of "training plants" (i.e., by tying them to lines and lattices);
- TEACHING AS DRILLING – borrowed from the military in the 1600s, where it referred to directing practice maneuvers to develop precision and automaticity.

Considered together, this collection of metaphors and images inherited or borrowed from medieval universities, religion, and planar geometry paints a portrait of teaching as very CONTROLLED and very CONTROLLING.

A few other descriptions of teaching captured notions of order, efficiency, and related ideals of the newly industrialized world, notably TEACHING AS DELIVERING

CONTENT and TEACHING AS INSTRUCTING. Unlike the metaphors already listed, these two were explicitly derived from an objectified sensibility toward knowledge:

KNOWLEDGE IS AN OBJECT/THING.

⬇

LEARNING IS TAKING KNOWLEDGE-THINGS IN.

⬇

THE LEARNER IS A CONTAINER OF KNOWLEDGE-THINGS.

⬇

TEACHING IS DELIVERING CONTENT TO THE CONTAINER.

KNOWLEDGE IS A CONSTRUCTABLE OBJECT.

⬇

LEARNING IS PUTTING THINGS TOGETHER.

⬇

THE LEARNER IS A BUILDER.

⬇

TEACHING IS INSTRUCTING

These metaphors were also suggestive of a sort of teaching that was all about technique, proficiency, efficiency, measurability, and accountability.

The metaphor of TEACHING AS INSTRUCTING is of particular interest because of its continued prominence, especially at higher grades and in post-secondary institutions where it tends to be used as a neutral and preferred synonym for teaching. When it was first picked up in the 1400s, it literally meant "providing instructions" – telling someone what to do, giving orders, directing practice, and so on. In brief, it captures key aspects of all the metaphors mentioned above, and so it's perhaps not surprising that it rose to and maintained such prominence.

By the 1800s, as the first teacher-training institutions began to appear, the work of teaching had come to be understood almost entirely in terms of INSTRUCTING – that is, as a set of the sorts of learnable skills associated with giving instructions. This simplified construal made it possible to create lists of sub-competencies and to impose quantitative research methods onto an

A *profession* is a service-oriented, non-business-based career. In principle, decisions to enter a profession are motivated by the reward of being of service, not by quest for personal or financial profit.

All professions have entry requirements in the form of specialized educational preparation. As well, all have specialized vocabularies and formal credentialing procedures from self-governing bodies.

otherwise complex and unruly occupation. In the process, by presenting teaching in terms of discernible and measurable skills alongside a distinct and learnable knowledge base, the prospect was opened of elevating teaching to a profession alongside medicine and law.

In much of Europe and North America, many of the first institutions created for teacher education were known as **normal schools**, so named because "norm" was roughly synonymous with "model" at the time. The normal school was a place for student teachers to encounter the modeling of teaching practices in model classrooms in a model school. It was where prospective teachers were expected to learn the rather narrow and rigid norms of behavior deemed appropriate for educators. The title of "normal schools" persisted for more than a century, and it was only in the mid-1900s that names of teacher education institutions began to change to "schools (or faculties) of education," as they were incorporated into universities.

The metaphor of TEACHER AS AN AGENT OF NORMAL meshed well with the standardized approach to schooling. With the official expectation that every child's educational experience should be uniform/level/even/planed, it fitted to the ideals of the era, such as order, linear cause-and-effect, efficiency, predictability, uniformity, and precision. The goal of uniformity was the major impetus for now-massive textbook and examination industries, as standardized resources were necessary to ensure similar treatments of topics and uniform progress through them. As well, there have been multiple attempts across recent centuries to, in effect, "teacher proof" the curriculum – that is, to impose structures and resources that would minimize the variations in experience from one classroom to the next, one school to the next, one jurisdiction to the next, and so on.

The first teacher education institutions were known as *normal schools*, so named because their purpose was to provide a standardized/normal model of teaching practice. The first normal schools were established in Europe in the 1800s.

This sensibility is alive and well. One of its more recent instantiations is the **Common Core Curriculum**, a movement in the United States aimed at leveling out the teaching of core disciplines across the nation. Another instance is international comparison testing (such as **TIMSS**, **PIRLS**, and **PISA**), which compels participating nations to adhere to very specific programs of study. While these projects are perhaps the most visible examples at the moment, they are merely two of many mechanisms to ensure uniformity.

Such presses toward normality and standardization further highlight the ORDER- and CONTROL-oriented qualities of modern education. As the above metaphors suggest, the teacher is expected to be the dominant person in the classroom, MANAGING learning experiences, SUPERVISING behaviors, and so on. At the same time, the teacher is subject to similar controlling structures – and, in fact, has considerably less autonomy than a classroom-level view might suggest.

Within this culture of management and control, particular obsessions have emerged among educators. We look at the more prominent of these in the next section. Before going there, however, we want to collect together the metaphors, synonyms, and images of teaching discussed in this section, bearing in mind that these words are not simple *descriptions*. They are also *prescriptions*. Each announces both a way of looking at teaching and a way of approaching teaching – both a theory and a practice.

The list of synonyms for teaching to the left reveals that the main sources of metaphors of teaching within the frame of Standardized Education are physics and engineering. Those domains fit with the sensibility that teaching and learning have a cause–effect relationship, that curriculum should follow a linear trajectory, and ultimately that teaching is a predictable, mechanical undertaking.

AGENT OF NORMALITY	EDIFYING	MANAGING
CLARIFYING	ENLIGHTENING	PRESENTING
CONVEYING	EXPLAINING	PROFESSING
DELIVERING CONTENT	HIGHLIGHTING	RELAYING
DEMONSTRATING	ILLUMINATING	REVEALING
DIRECTING	ILLUSTRATING	SHOWING
DISCIPLINING	INSTRUCTING	SUPERVISING
DISPLAYING	INFORMING	TELLING
DRILLING	LECTURING	TRAINING

Teacher competencies

As mentioned at the start of Chapter 1.2, there is no shortage of "how to" manuals for teachers. To our reading, almost all are firmly situated in a frame of Standardized Education, and they offer a model of INSTRUCTION that is well captured in the above list.

In our experience, the most forceful encounters with this mode of teaching are not in school classrooms, but within teacher education programs. And the most adamant push toward it is not from faculty members, school boards, parents, or practicing teachers, but from a large portion of people enrolled in the programs. Year after year, there is always a significant subgroup of pre-service teachers who demand they be instructed in the instrumental methods of Standardized Education.

Such a demand, of course, should be expected. For many teacher candidates, virtually all of their formal education has been structured by standardized textbooks and punctuated by standardized exams. It makes perfect sense that they'd see teaching in such terms and that they would insist on a curriculum that prepares them for it. As if looking to intensify the situation, teacher education programs often support these anxieties. In particular, practicum expectations are frequently articulated as checklists of competencies that are to be demonstrated, including planning a lesson, evaluating student work, managing a classroom, and demonstrating appropriate disciplinary knowledge – that is, of enacting a TEACHING-AS-INSTRUCTING metaphor.

We offer brief descriptions of each of these clusters of concern below. Our intention here is not to offer instruction on how one might develop these categories of competence, but on foregrounding how these obsessions are entangled with the assumptions of Standardized Education. While we don't expect they'll cease to be obsessions any time soon, we are hopeful that awarenesses of their self-referential, self-supporting natures might help to open perceptions to other perspectives on teaching, taken up in the other moments presented in this book.

The word *lesson* has the same distant roots as the word *lecture*, tracing back to the Latin *lectionem*, "a reading." It was first used in English in the early 1200s in the context of religious education to refer to an oral reading from the Bible.

Planning lessons

When does teaching start and end?

It might sound silly, but this is a serious question. Teaching always spills beyond the boundaries of class times, as it draws on experiences that happen before students enter the classroom and can have influences extend well after they leave.

Within a frame of Standardized Education, however, teaching is understood to happen in self-contained chunks called "lessons" and, for the most part, the major consideration in a lesson plan is *what* is to be taught. (The who, where, when, and why are generally treated as secondary concerns, if considered at all.) There are many models of the linear lesson and many examples of **lesson plan templates**, but typically a standardized lesson comprises clearly stated learning objectives, some sort of direct instruction, appropriate practice exercises, and an evaluation strategy to determine whether the pre-stated objectives have been met. Further, the specific objectives addressed should fit tidily into a larger unit of study, which should fit tidily into a complete course or year plan.

Perhaps the most common criticism of this pervasive mode of planning is that its rigid and mechanistic structure usually goes hand-in-hand with a curriculum of facts and skills – by which, for example, mathematics comes to seen as calculation, reading as decoding text, and history as facts. This tendency is likely supported by the very notion of learning objectives, which forces fragmentations and compartmentalizations of knowledge. In most jurisdictions, learning objectives are already cleanly parsed and clearly articulated, and so the teacher can usually pull them directly from mandated curriculum guides and programs of study. Often they are stated as **behavioral learning objectives** – that is, as observable and measurable outcomes.

There was a time that the teacher was fully responsible for translating learning objectives into an actual lesson. Over the past half-century, however, there has been a proliferation of teacher resources to assist in planning. To make things even easier, publishers often tailor these resources to match a jurisdiction's curriculum. As well, there's an abundance of premade lesson plans available online for virtually every topic covered in a standard curriculum.

There are both plusses and minuses to this wealth of pre-planned material. On the one hand, some have argued, it reduces the teacher's work to mere implementation and thus contributes to a deskilling of the profession. On the other hand, used wisely by a discerning teacher, they can free up mind space that might then be devoted to other demands of teaching.

Regarding the direct instruction component of the standardized lesson, one piece of advice that has

Lesson Section	Face-to-Face
1. OBJECTIVES	
• Inform learners what they will be able to do by end of lesson • Purpose Why is this important? • Where will this be used?	By the end of this able to respond c 8 out of 10 test
2. ANTICIPATORY SET	
• Focus learners' attentions • Practice or review of previous learning • Mental set through interesting activity	Students will be favorite video ga connecting the geometric shape
3. REVIEW	
• What has already been learned? • How does it connect to the	Classifying tria and calculating

The phrase "lesson plan" combines two dominant themes of Standardized Education – namely the lecture/delivery emphasis inherited from the Church and the planar geometry influence inherited from the ancient Greeks (via the Industrial and Scientific Revolutions).

Not surprisingly, then, standardized lesson templates are geared toward a thoroughly engineered, fully predictable experiences for teacher and students alike.

endured for more than a century is that explanations should be kept under 10 minutes or so. Various rationales have been offered for this brevity. A popular one is that it is roughly the attention span of a moderately engaged learner. A more compelling reason is that a great deal of information can be stated in 10 minutes, and even the most attentive learner will be hard-pressed to retain all of the salient details if things go on much longer.

In any case, the next component of a typical standardized lesson is directed practice, in which learners read, print, calculate, experiment, and engage in tasks that are intended to support the lesson objectives. As with teacher resources, there is usually an abundance of published exercises for students and so the work of setting appropriate practice is often very straight-forward. As well, the practice exercises often serve as an in-built means to monitor students' progress and comprehension – that is, as the necessary evaluation component.

Given its firm position in schooling practices, you would think there'd be strong evidence for assigning homework. In fact, there isn't that much, especially at the younger levels.

Many factors appear to be at play, including types of learning support outside the classroom, the structures of assignments, and parental attitudes. One persistent (and somewhat commonsensical finding) is that students who struggle in class with concepts will continue to struggle outside of class, potentially amplifying problems rather than easing them.

Most commentators recommend that directed practice be followed with feedback on those exercises, a terse review of key points of the lesson, and a look forward to the next topic. This portion of the lesson might also include the assignment of homework, although perspectives on the value and effectiveness of out-of-class assignments vary dramatically. (A **homework debate** is raging on the topic at the moment.)

Whatever the components and their specific order, the parts of a lesson are expected to be allotted discrete chunks of time – not because the teacher is supposed to stick to a fixed itinerary but because a properly planned lesson should occupy students for the allotted block of time. There are different schools of thought on the extent to which a teacher might deviate from these plans, owing to more recent insights into how people learn (see Chapter 2.2). However, the original expectations were clear: the whole point of the well-defined lesson and its accompanying timeline was the efficient attainment of objectives – that is, to *avoid* deviations. This was as true of unit and year plans as it was of lesson plans. Indeed, it continues to be the case in many schools, where teachers are expected to have all quiz and exam dates set at the start of the school year.

Another relatively recent innovation for the lesson plan is a section in which the teacher lists possible accommodations for learners' varied abilities, interests, needs, and styles. As with license to deviate from plans, this aspect is rooted in non-standardized ways of thinking about learning and knowledge (which we look at in later moments). The expectation actually represents quite a departure from standardized lesson and its tendency to "teach to the middle" – that is, to aim explanations and exercises to those students imagined to constitute the bulge of a normal distribution of learning ability.

One category of accommodations merits special mention in this section: **learning styles**. This pop theory is often presented as a strategy for **strengths-based learning, individualized instruction** or **personalized learning** (a major contemporary emphasis, discussed in Chapter 2.3), but which is in fact rooted in the same naïve theory of learning as most standardized practices. According to this perspective, each learner shows preferences for particular sensory modalities; some are "visual learners," some are "auditory," some are "tactile," and so on. The idea springs from the uncritical embrace of the metaphor, LEARNING IS TAKING THINGS IN, by which it follows that knowledge must enter by one portal (i.e., sensory system) or another. Accordingly, teachers should structure lessons to appeal to all styles, ensuring that each learner can employ their preferred modality.

One of the most popular contemporary "theories" is *Learning Styles*.

It's also one of the most problematical. The perspective is based on the assumptions that KNOWLEDGE IS INFORMATION and LEARNING IS INPUTTING – which means that teachers must find the best conduits to input information.

There is no empirical support for these ideas. Knowledge and learning are more complex, as is teaching. (See Chapter 2.2 for a more thorough critique of the underlying principles.)

Not only is there is no empirical support whatsoever for this notion, its advice may actually constrain learning as it caters to familiar habits rather than challenging underdeveloped abilities.

Returning to the components of a "good" lesson within a frame of Standardized Education, the vital aspects are seen in terms of clarity of presentation, appropriateness of practice, and accuracy of evaluation. In the spirit of mass production, its purpose is not to meet the particular needs of each learner, but to offer uniform instruction geared toward meeting a pre-stated level of expertise by most learners.

Evaluating students

Once again, there is no shortage of resource texts offering advice on the how's of setting assignments and determining grades. We're more concerned here with the origins and intentions of these practices. On that count, a quick analysis of the roots of the most common words associated with interpreting student performance is useful.

An important note before going there: one of the more common phrases within this frame is "evidence based," meaning that all practices and claims should be supported by some manner of data or proof. Student achievement is one of the phenomena commonly mentioned alongside the phrase. As discussed below, another is "teacher effectiveness," which is treated as synonymous to student achievement in much of contemporary research.

That point is vital to understanding contemporary evaluation emphases and practices, which are rooted in notions of accountability and quality control – of learning and teaching alike. These are entailments of the SCHOOL-AS-FACTORY metaphor, and the same sensibility is reflected in usages of the words *evaluation* and *assessment*. While the words are sometimes used differently in contemporary educational discourse, both were imported into schooling from the world of business where they referred to processes of determining monetary value or worth. As it turns out, almost all of the terms associated with student achievement are anchored to this emphasis. Others include:

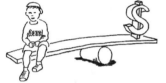

The word *evaluation* is derived from from Old French, *é + value*, "out + worth = appraise." The notion was first used in commerce and later picked up as a metaphor by educators. That is, assigning a mark was originally understood as analogous to naming the worth of a product. That meaning is now one among many, along with "portion of answers correct," "rank in relation to peers," and "progress toward completion."

The word *assessment* derives from the Medieval Latin *assessare*, "set a tax upon," and so its original meaning in English was very similar to that of *evaluation*.

- GRADING – adapted from the practice of ranking manufactured goods according to quality (i.e., how well they meet pre-defined standards). It is derived from the Middle English *gree*, "step or degree in a series," which traces back to the Latin *gradus*, "step."
- SCORING – similar in meaning to *grading* within both education and business, it derives from the act of making notches or incisions (i.e., to signal different levels of quality). It traces back to the Proto-Germanic *skura*, "to cut," which is also the root of *scar* and *shear*.

- MARKING – adapted from the practice of placing prices on items for sale. The word traces back to and across a range of European languages, originally referring to specifying borders and indicating margins.

The industry- and science-inspired sensibility of ordering and ranking at work here is clear, and it extends well beyond this particular cluster of words. Consider, for example, the many cognates of *grade* used in education – heard in such phrases as "grade levels," "gradual progress," and "graduation requirements." As for the means of translating student performance into a score/grade/mark, there are two main schools of thought within this frame: **norms-based** evaluations and **standards-based** (or **criteria-based**) evaluations.

Determining a norms-based grade, or "grading on the curve" in more popular terms, involves comparing students to one another. This practice rests on the assumption that learners are normally distributed, and so the expectation is that the bulk of students would get average scores, with many fewer earning lower or higher grades. Although only a little more than a century old, in terms of making explicit use of a normal curve, norms-based grading picks up on a long history of differentiating among students by comparing them. This practice, in fact, is where the notion of *grades* (i.e., "steps") comes from.

Norms-based scoring has been widely criticized, largely because it doesn't say much about what has been learned. It indicates only where the learner sits relative to classmates. In addition, there is evidence that competition increases and cooperation declines with norms-based grading, as students tend to see one another more as hindrances than positive influences on their own learning.

Standards-based grading systems are purported to respond to these concerns. With this approach, expectations are clearly stated up front, often in the form of **grading rubrics** in which each score corresponds to specific criteria. The grade earned is thus an indication of individual performance, not collective ranking.

It might appear that norms-based and standards-

	EXEMPLARY	PROFICIEN
CONTENT	Facts are validated; sources are cited	Facts are val sources are c
ASSERTIONS	Conclusions are well supported/justified	Conclusions/ further justi
ORGANIZATION	Arguments are easy to follow	Flow of argu not always c

Grading rubrics **are now a common part of the educational landscape. Ideally, they present clear expectations, information on how grades will be distributed, and qualities used to assign grades.**

The word is derived from the Proto-Indo-European *rudhro-*, **"red," and is a reference to the red ink used to record the directions in religious services.**

First published in the 1950s, *Bloom's Taxonomy of Question Types* is used to classify questions according to difficulty and frequency. The simplest (knowledge recall) are the most common and the most complicated (evaluation) are the rarest. Within this model, it's assumed one must build to higher-level questions incrementally – and so it is a prominent tool for planning within Standardized Education. The suggestion is that lessons should begin with many low-level tasks and move up systematically to arrive at one or two, high-level culminating questions.

based grading strategies are worlds apart since they offer different types of information. However, they are rooted in the same sort of industry-inspired grading/scoring/marking sensibility. This detail comes through clearly in the common practice of determining class averages of standards-based grades – which, in effect, converts standards-based grading into norms-based grading. Small wonder that grading represents one of the most contested elements of schooling, for students and teachers alike.

In later sections we'll cover some strategies designed to address frustrations around grading. Unfortunately, it's virtually impossible to broach this topic within a frame of Standardized Education – for the reasons discussed over these first three chapters. When the project of education is defined in terms of standards, when normal distributions are imposed, and when the interpersonal dynamic that drives humans is assumed to be competition, then grading/scoring/marking is an inevitable entailment. A further, frequently cited reason for grading is as a source of motivation for students. In this case, the metaphor of GRADES AS REWARDS – or, closely related, GRADES AS RENUMERATION – is often invoked.

Questioning is another evaluation-related topic that will be explored in greater depth in later chapters. It tends to be treated rather shallowly within a frame of Standardized Education. Most often it is taken up in terms of classifications different question types, the most common of which is known as **Bloom's Taxonomy**. In terms of a teaching tool, the advice that springs from such schemes of categorization is that the teacher should make sure to ask questions from all levels, ranging from recall and comprehension, through application and analysis, to synthesis and evaluation. As it turns out, however, questioning is considerably more complex than a taxonomy can capture.

Managing classrooms

While not a concern shared by all pre-service teachers, classroom management is easily the most common anxiety encountered in teacher education programs.

Once again, there are hundreds of manuals devoted to the details on strategies that might be used to control groups of learners. And, once again, we're less concerned with means to manage and more interested in where this obsession comes from.

The metaphor of MANAGEMENT gives this one away immediately. Consistent with the cause–effect mindset of science and industry in the 1600s and 1700s, the teacher is expected to have complete control of student learning and behavior. In brief, within a frame of Standardized Education, an engaged classroom is a classroom filled with quietly attentive students who do what they're told when they're told.

The main device for managing classrooms is to be found in the manner in which they tend to be organized. Borrowing a model of surveillance developed in prisons and asylums, students in the first public schools were organized in rows and the teacher was situated on an edge so that learners could be observed at all times.

The recommendations for managing classrooms tend to be similar to the advice for planning and evaluating. They typically revolve around clear rules and clear consequences for breaking rules. Behaviorist theories – and particularly principles of **behavioral modification** based on those theories – have had a strong influence. With their focus on rewarding good habits and discouraging bad ones, they show up as advice that emphasizes consistency, repetition, praise for correct outcomes, and immediate correction of deviations from desired behaviors.

Master is an ancient term for *teacher* that derives from Latin *magister*, "chief, head, director, teacher." Its usage in English dates back to at least the 1100s. By the 1300s, it was being used to refer to the teaching certification (i.e., a master's degree) that was required to join the faculty of a university.

This topic will be revisited in other moments, in which alternatives to a COMMAND-and-CONTROL mindset on teaching are discussed. These include, for example, developing personal relationships, structuring meaningful tasks, supporting individual mindfulness, and thinking in terms of collective dynamics rather than personal behavior – all of which fall outside the frame of Standardized Education.

Knowing your stuff

What do you need to know in order to teach a discipline?

The word *doctor* referred to teachers before it was taken up as a title for physicians, which is why it continues to be used to refer to the highest level of university degree across disciplines. It traces back to classical Latin *docere*, "to show, cause to know," originally "make to appear right" (a meaning that lingers in phrases such as "doctor the results").

Until very recently, the assumption was that teachers need to have taken more advanced courses than the courses they're teaching, which is precisely the thinking behind the common requirement for university-level credits in, say, calculus for prospective high school math teachers.

The practice is based in an ancient assumption, as evidenced in the meaning of MASTER, a synonym for teacher from the 1300s. At that time, the master's or magisterial degree was the credential needed to teach in the university. That degree was entirely discipline based and involved no study whatsoever in how learning happens or how teachers can support it.

It probably won't come as a surprise that this is still the case in most universities, although the necessary credential is now a *doctoral* degree.

The same assumption – that is, that the only necessary preparation for the teacher is more advanced study in a discipline – was picked up and maintained by the public schooling system. Of course, this changed gradually as teacher education institutions emerged and evolved over recent centuries. However, it remains the major emphasis in most teacher education programs for prospective high school teachers. (Typically a disciplinary baccalaureate degree, and often a master's degree, is required prior or concurrent to an education degree.)

We mention this detail at this point for two reasons. Firstly, it's useful to know why most teacher education programs require advanced study in discipline areas. Secondly, as developed in later chapters, the evidence supporting such a requirement is thin to non-existent – which is not to say that a more advanced knowledge is unimportant. Rather, it appears that "knowledge of a discipline" and "knowledge of how a discipline is learned" are two very different things. More later.

And what does the research say?

Given that Standardized Education has centuries of history and is explicitly aligned with the physical sciences, one might expect that there would be a deep evidence base for its signature structures and practices.

One would certainly get that impression from current interest in **best practices**, a decades-old notion within business that has recently migrated to education. In business, best practices are understood in evolutionary terms, as the systems and routines employed by the highest-performing companies – and, as might be expected, one of those habits is the capacity to adapt to changing circumstances.

Within education, the notion is far less clear and subject to many, often-conflicting definitions. That said, most interpretations are geared toward improved student performance and demand some sort of empirical evidence.

Unfortunately, with regard to the demand for evidence, educational research is often mixed and conflicted, owing in large part to widely varied assumptions about knowledge, learning, teaching, and the purposes of schooling. That said, there is a reasonably common agreement on the notion of "teaching effectiveness" in a large portion of published research. Specifically, as mentioned earlier, teaching effectiveness tends to be defined in terms of student achievement on standardized tests.

A *meta-analysis* is a comprehensive review of many – usually hundreds – of published research articles on a specific question. The meta-analysis is a relatively recent phenomenon in the educational research literature because the field is relatively young and many of its constructs are still evolving.

One might be justified in assuming that this definition would skew research results in favor of entrenched structures and practices associated with a TEACHING-AS-INSTRUCTING attitude. Its geared-for-the-test emphases should give it a massive advantage in a research culture that pays such heed to the standardized test.

However, what the evidence seems to suggest is that the obsessions of Standardized Education do not correlate significantly with effective teaching. That is, the foci on planning lessons, evaluating students, managing classrooms, and knowing your stuff – while important – pale in significance beside some elements that receive relatively little air time. A tool that has recently emerged in research – the meta-analysis– has helped to lend some clarity to the situation.

One of the persistent frustrations of educational research is that virtually any change in teaching practice can have an impact on student performance, and usually in a positive direction – even when completely opposite strategies are attempted. This persistent result

The meaning of the word *evaluation* has evolved in the last century, as revealed in the distinction between *formative* and *summative evaluations*. A summative evaluation is *an assessment of learning*. It is conducted at the end of a teaching sequence, and is intended as a final appraisal – aligning with the original meaning of *evaluation* in education. (And so "summative evaluation" would've been a little redundant 100 years ago.)

A formative evaluation is an *assessment for learning*. It can occur at any time during the learning process, with the goal of enabling that learning.

has given credence to the suggestion that the critical element in educational practice is likely the sort of attentiveness and renewed engagement that goes along with deliberate change, not the change itself.

Meta-analyses consistently highlight this point. They also highlight that there are a handful of practices and structures that really do make a difference. For example, there is now broad consensus that the single most important "factor" in a child's educational success is not the child's school, social-economic status, or measured ability, but the child's teacher.

John Hattie has published more meta-analyses in education than anyone else. Based on his extensive reading and analyses of others' research, he suggests the following strategies are the top 10 (from his list of 138) influences on student achievement:

1. Student self-reported grades – The most accurate predictors of learner performance turn out to be learners themselves. Asking students about their self-expectations and then pushing them to exceed those expectations can support confidence, which in turn will increase self-expectations. And so on.

2. Piagetian programs – Jean Piaget was a learning theorist who was highly critical of Standardized Education. One component of his work dealt with stages of cognitive development, and it turns out that programs that pay attention to his insights – that is, programs that break from the standardized mindset – tend to support increased achievement. More in Moment 2.

3. **Response to Intervention** – RtI refers to a strategy for providing systematic support to students who are experiencing difficulty. Its two defining components are frequent assessment and early response.

4. Teacher credibility – Students who think their teacher is credible tend to perform better. Four key aspects of credibility are trust, competence, dynamism, and immediacy.

5. Providing formative evaluation – A **formative evaluation** is an assessment of learning during the learning. Its purpose is not to assign a score, but to

provide information on progress that might be used to adapt subsequent activities. (The practice of assigning grades after learning or teaching is assumed to be finished is called **summative evaluation**.)

6. Micro-teaching – Micro-teaching was once a mainstay of teacher-education programs, but has declined in popularity over the past few decades. It involves video recording a short lesson and debriefing that lesson with colleagues. The participation of a well-seasoned teacher can enhance the experience.

7. Classroom discussion – A discussion involving the whole class, in which the teacher not only stops lecturing but releases some control for the topics and direction of the lesson, is associated with improved achievement as it presents opportunities for students to learn from one another, supports personal engagement, and compels more critical thought.

AUTHENTIC EDUCATION

8. Comprehensive interventions for learning-disabled students – While there is much debate around the nature and prevalence of learning disabilities, there can be no argument that some students endure differences in perception and cognitive process that make it difficult if not impossible to learn in standardized settings. Working individually with the student to identify strategies and support reflection can greatly enhance achievement.

9. Teacher clarity – Clear communication of intentions, of explanations in lessons, of results in evaluations, and so on are correlated to student achievement on tasks in which that clearly communicated information is evaluated. Go figure.

10. Feedback – Achievement can be supported by inviting descriptive feedback *from the student to the teacher* on matters of task (What am I supposed to do?), process (What am I doing?), and self-regulation (How am I doing?).

(Note that a major issue with meta-analyses is that they are generally focused on older ideas, since a critical mass of research is needed before such an analysis can be undertaken. That can take decades in some cases.)

One of the main barriers to educational change is that the tools devised within a dominant sensibility (such as the use of standardized tests to assess the effectiveness of Standardized Education) give a home-court advantage. It seems unlikely that pedagogical approaches rooted in other ways of thinking will be able to compete.

Even so, as meta-analyses have demonstrated, other ways of teaching seem to be beating Standardized Education at its own game.

Value-added modeling is a relatively new method of teacher evaluation that is fully aligned with the sensibilities of Standardized Education.

Rooted in a metaphor of LEARNING AS INCREASE IN NET WORTH, within VAM a teacher's contribution is measured by comparing their students' current test scores to their scores in previous school years *and* to scores of other students in the same grade. Statistical methods are used to isolate the teacher's contribution (that is, the *value added* by that teacher).

It is a useful exercise to review the above list against the backdrop of Standardized Education. To our reading, *only one* (!) of these 10 strategies – namely "teacher clarity" – is commonly identified as a core element of TEACHING AS INSTRUCTING. The rest represent modest-to-significant departures from this pervasive sensibility.

This sort of result isn't unique to meta-analyses. Similar findings have been produced from **value-added modeling**, an approach to research imposed from economics. With this method, a teacher's contribution is defined and measured by comparing students' test scores from the previous year to their scores after having studied with that teacher. The approach has been used to identify teachers who contribute "greater value" – that is, whose students consistently progress further than the students of their colleagues. The methods and the findings of value-added modeling are a topic of intense debate right now, in part because of worries they might eventually be used for credentialing and merit pay – which, in turn, might further entrench the narrow fact-oriented, skills-heavy, and efficiency-driven teaching emphases. Even so, in terms of teaching strategies, emerging results of value-added research are turning out to be similar to the results of meta-analyses. In general, teachers who pay more attention to their students' learning – who, in effect, break from the model of Standardized Education by doing less telling and more listening – get better results.

That should give pause. To re-emphasize, across both meta-analyses and value-added research, Standardized Education has a home-court advantage. Learning, effectiveness, achievement, and success are all defined in its terms. As well, research questions and methodologies are aligned with its purposes. One might thus expect its privileged modes of teaching to come out ahead. The simple fact that they don't suggests that there are some significant issues with this mindset.

In the remaining three moments, we address these and related issues, aiming to unpack divergent approaches to teaching and their associated perspectives on knowledge and learning.

Suggestions for delving deeper

1. We've offered brief traces of the metaphors and entailments that connect OBJECT-based conceptions of knowledge to DELIVERY- and INSTRUCTION-based conceptions of teaching (see p. 46). What metaphors of knowledge might be behind other prominent metaphors of teaching, such as DIRECTING? ILLUMINATING? PROFESSING?

2. Over the past few decades, a new trend of referring to students as CLIENTS or CUSTOMERS has emerged, coupled to a broader movement of interpreting formal education in terms of a business. What are some of the entailments of this shift in metaphors with regard to the role of and the expectations on the teacher?

3. One of our local school boards has a "No zero grades" policy. A few years ago, a math teacher assigned a grade of zero to a student who had turned in no work and completed no exams. When he refused to change it, he was fired. Clearly conflicting understandings of the meanings and purposes of grades were at work. What might these have been? If you were appointed to mediate the disagreement between the teacher and the board, how would you approach the task?

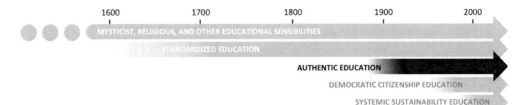

MYSTICIST, RELIGIOUS, AND OTHER EDUCATIONAL SENSIBILITIES
STANDARDIZED EDUCATION
AUTHENTIC EDUCATION
DEMOCRATIC CITIZENSHIP EDUCATION
SYSTEMIC SUSTAINABILITY EDUCATION

MOMENT 2 •
authentic education

In brief ...

The term "Authentic Education" refers to those approaches to schooling rooted in the human sciences that emphasize personal engagement, learner difference, developmental stages, and personalized learning aligned with individual curiosities and goals. Classroom approaches are based in reality, focused on understanding, and rich with inquiry.

2.1 • The context ...

While some of its sensibilities trace back to ancient times, Authentic Education only emerged as a strong movement in the early 1900s. Major triggers included a shift in focus across the physical sciences (toward studies of transformation), rigorous research into human learning, and the emergence of a middle class that demanded more of schooling.

2.2 • On knowledge and learning ...

Drawing inspiration and metaphors from biology and structuralism, personal knowing came to be framed as EVOLVING NETWORKS OF IDEAS. Correspondingly, learning was reframed in terms of ADAPTATION and MAINTAINING COHERENCE.

2.3 • On teaching ...

With a shift from teacher-centered classrooms to learner-centered settings, teaching was recast in terms of GUIDING and FACILITATING. It involves attentiveness to each learner's unique history and is oriented toward the development of each individual's potentials.

Take a glimpse ...

Suggested YouTube searches: [child-centered approach] [inquiry-based learning] [progressive education] [authentic education]

AUTHENTIC EDUCATION		
DESCRIBING & PRESCRIBING TEACHING		
KNOWLEDGE & LEARNING		
HISTORY & CONTEXT		
active learning		
cooperative learning	accommodation	
deep/surface learning	adaptation	antipositivism
deliberate practice	assimilation	deconstruction
differentiated learning	associative learning	education for all
facilitating	body-based knowing	evolutionary theory
fixed/growth mindsets	coherence theories	existentialism
formative assessment	conscious/unconscious	genetics
inquiry approach	constructivism	Gestalt psychology
manipulatives	developmentalism	human sciences
metacognition	dual-process theory	neurology
PCK	explicit/tacit knowing	phenomenology
Piagetian tasks	genetic epistemology	pragmatism
problem-based learning	multiple intelligences	psychoanalysis
reflective practice	progressivism	rise of middle class
self-regulated learning	schema theory	romanticism
wait time	variation theory	structuralism

iconic visual metaphor:
INDIVIDUAL'S BRANCHING
POTENTIALITIES

2.1

The Emergence of Authentic Education

authoritative
credible
legitimate
reliable
trustworthy
original
convincing
accurate
unquestionable
real
genuine
truthful

authentic

Among its common definitions, the word *authentic* means true, real, unforged, verified, trustworthy. It is derived from the Greek *autos* + *hentes*, "self doing, self accomplishment," suggesting that the measure of authenticity is to be found in one's own experience. During the 1900s this emphasis on self-verification and self-direction – that is, on the individual's perceptions and interpretations – was taken up as a central theme in schooling and is a hallmark of Authentic Education.

By 1900, the project of standardizing education was very much complete. In most industrialized nations, curriculum contents and teaching methods had become stable and predictable.

In fact, with the use of standardized textbooks, grading structures, lesson plans, teaching practices, and – most importantly – examinations, by the early 1900s, one could expect to find reasonably similar curricula almost anywhere in the industrialized world. These trends have continued. Today, such resemblances can be found almost anywhere on the planet, along with similar-looking school buildings, similar classroom resources, and similar grading strategies – many of which bear uncanny resemblances to the buildings, resources, and strategies of a century ago.

That's not necessarily a good thing. A common criticism today is that formal education is more and more out of step with the world. Whereas society has changed dramatically with the transition from the Industrial to the Information Age, schooling has remained entrenched in an industrialized sensibility. Its content, its purposes, its methods, its structures – the entire project – is increasingly out of sync with the world's evolutions.

In some ways, such criticisms are valid. For example, mathematics textbooks from the late 1900s very much resembled those used in the late 1800s. To lesser extents, programs of study in most other subject areas have remained remarkably stable over the last century – at least in comparison to the dramatic changes in their parent disciplines over that time.

Despite such similarities and stabilities, there have been some profound shifts in thinking around the project of education. Some of these transformations were signaled by challenges to traditional schooling that started to be raised in the early 1900s and that were raging by the middle of the century: Should schooling be focused on technical proficiency or on conceptual understanding? Might education be structured in ways that nurture individual strengths rather than imposing common standards of performance and achievement? Does the notion of generic education still make sense?

Such debates were heavily influenced by new thinking on learning – or, more specifically, by the emergence of a robust science of human learning and personal development through the 1900s. Prior to that, models of schooling tended to be oriented by the assumption that people aren't much different from one another. After all, it makes no sense to standardize education unless everyone learns in the same way and follows the same developmental trajectory. And those were precisely the assumptions targeted by researchers and educators intent on more sophisticated understandings of of human learning and personal development.

Regarding human learning, the dominant metaphors of ACQUISITION and INTERNALIZATION were gradually recognized as misleading and inadequate. Given that no THING actually moves from the outside to the inside in moments of learning, these OBJECT-based metaphors don't actually make much sense. As detailed in Chapter 2.2, the new science of learning thus recast the phenomenon in terms of ADAPTATIONS and TRANSFORMATIONS rather than PICKING THINGS UP.

Progressive Education is a near-synonym for Authentic Education. The word *progressive* in this phrase was chosen to differentiate the movement from *traditional* (standardized) sensibilities. Among key markers of Authentic/Progressive Education are an emphasis on experiential learning, organizing units of study around themes, and highly personalized learning aligned with individual curiosities and goals.

Regarding personal development, researchers of the new science of learning paid attention to both the similarities and the idiosyncrasies among learners, breaking away from the statistics-driven construct of the "normal child" that was assumed to occupy the desk of Standardized Education (as discussed in Moment 1).

These shifts were actually reflective of a radical change in emphasis that unfolded across the physical sciences through the 1800s, as researchers refocused their attentions onto *change* – that is, on how such phenomena as geological formations, living entities, species, and so on transformed through time.

Emphases on transformation and adaptation – and, in particular, on fine-grained analyses of what triggers change and how forms maintain fitness – were soon informing theories of learning. Those new theories, in turn, were the main impetus for the emergence of Authentic Education – that is, a progressive form of schooling that was in many ways the opposite of a traditional, standardized one. This moment in formal education came to be characterized by real/*authentic* problems, to be structured through genuine/*authentic* inquiry, to afford students transformative/*authentic* feedback, and to nurture the learner's unique/*authentic* being. In brief, then, the three chapters in this moment delve into the emergence of *authenticity* as a fundamental orienting principle in education. This chapter focuses in particular on the historical and conceptual developments that sparked the movement.

The word *science* is derived from the Latin *scire*, "to know" (in the sense of *episteme*-knowledge, not *gnosis*-knowledge), which is derived from the Proto-Indo-European root *skei*, "to cut, to split." The association with rational thought and empirical research dates to the early 1400s, when it was picked up to describe an emphasize on naming and classification (i.e., splitting phenomena into categories).

New perspectives on how things change

As emphasized throughout Moment 1, the invention of modern, mass schooling was associated with a shift in emphasis on the sorts of knowledge that was important to teach – away from deep understanding of the universe (*gnosis*-knowledge) and toward fact-based information (*episteme*-knowledge). Along with this change, curricula shifted away from liberation through the arts and toward instruction in the sciences.

For nearly half a millennium, then, programs of study have been dominated by the sciences and teaching has been subsumed within instruction. Challenges to these two facets of formal education emerged in the early 1900s, and those challenges were rooted in a dramatic shift in thinking about what science is all about.

To appreciate the shift, it's useful to be aware of the original meaning of the word *science*. A hint of this can be gleaned from its derivation: it comes from the same Indo-European root as *scissors*, *incisor*, *shed*, and *schism*. That is, its original meaning had to do with cutting apart, separating, dividing, splitting, categorizing – in a nutshell, with parsing up and classifying all forms and phenomena. In other words, science was focused on discerning the universe's *natural order* – literally, its innate or inborn organization, which was assumed to be stable and eternal.

This assumption of an unchanging cosmos extends back at least to the ancient Greeks and to a sensibility that the physical world is merely a flawed reflection of an ideal, perfected realm. An implication of this sensibility is that whatever change is observed in the physical realm must be either a movement toward the Ideal (in which case it is "good") or a deviation from that line (in which case it is corrupt – hence the equating of "bad" with bent, skewed, and meandering lines, discussed in Chapter 1.2). For instance, with regard to human development over a lifetime, changes due to maturation and learning were seen to fall into the natural-and-good category, whereas changes caused by disease or injury were seen as unnatural-and-bad.

In other words, the focus in the early stages of the Scientific Revolution was on the imagined-to-be ideal forms rather than the actual material objects and physical events encountered in the real world. So oriented, scientists were focused on the ways things *were supposed to be* instead of the way things actually were – an emphasis that was anchored to the ancient assumption that all worldly forms are flawed reflections of their ideal instantiations. (Indeed, the conception of education as DRAWING OUT one's natural being is rooted in exactly this sensibility, and it continues to be represented in everyday discussions of helping children "reach their potentials," learn about "who they really are," and "be who they're supposed to be.")

This detail highlights that modern science, in its early stages, was greatly influenced by ancient mysticism. In particular, the inherited conviction that the cosmos is unchanging was realized in a science that was centrally concerned with taxonomies and typologies – that is, with naming things and classifying them. An exemplar from this era is the **Linnaean taxonomy**, developed by Carl Linnaeus in the 1730s, to classify animals, plants, and minerals. A regularly modified version of the system he devised for animals is still in

The terms *class* and *classification* trace back to the Latin *classis*, "a division" (most often used in reference to the military). The notion thus aligns well with the emphases on naming and categorizing in early western science.

use and is a required topic of study in most high school biology programs. Other, similarly minded systems were proposed at roughly the same time by chemists, meteorologists, astronomers, and geologists. In fact, the modern classification of scientific disciplines used to separate university departments (i.e., Physics, Chemistry, Biology, etc.) froze into place in that era.

Somewhat ironically, it was the sorts of fine-grained analyses conducted by Linnaeus and his contemporaries that prompted a shift in what science was all about in the 1800s. While attempting to identify clean distinctions among minerals, species, landforms, celestial bodies, and so on, researchers began to realize the task was fraught with problems. Some of the forms they studied seemed to be strangely related to one another, and so scientists began to refocus their efforts on relationships and developmental trajectories rather than fixed traits and hard-and-fast distinctions. To be clear, this transition was a titanic one. By way of illustration, the question of how an orange is related to a lemon is much more complex than the matter of how they are distinct. Researchers had to go beyond description of obvious features into questions of history, context, genetics, and so on. More pointedly, it raised issues of how forms might have common ancestors and how lineages might converge and diverge.

	Human	Giant Kelp	Wild Geranium
Kingdom	Animalia	Protoctista	Plantae
Phylum	Chordata	Phaeophyta	Tracheophyta
Class	Mammalia	Phaeophyceae	Magnoliopsida
Order	Primates	Laminariales	Geraniales
Family	Hominidae	Lessoniaceae	Geraniaceae
Genus	*Homo*	*Macrocystis*	*Geranium*
Species	*sapiens*	*pyrifera*	*sericeum*

The change in focus across the sciences in the 1800s is reflected in the shift in visual metaphors, away from rectangulated typologies and taxonomies (i.e., that assumed things were fixed and that foregrounded differences) and toward branching images (i.e., that focused on development and that highlighted relationships).

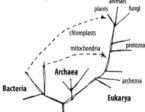

This shift in emphasis began to unfold in the 1700s and gained momentum in the early 1800s. By the early 1900s, the new metaphor of *evolution* had been taken up in virtually every area of science and the presence of the word flagged attentiveness to transformation and interrelationship. Coined in the mid-1600s, the word *evolution* is derived from the Latin *evolvere*, "to unroll" – which signals a very different way of thinking to the then-prevalent emphasis on naming and classifying. By the start of the 1900s, this sensibility came to dominate the sciences, owing in large part to the compelling contributions of Charles Lyell in geology, August Schleicher in linguistics, Jean-Baptiste Lamarck and Charles Darwin in biology, and Gregor Mendel in genetics.

However, it wasn't until well into the 1900s that the shift in focus began to register in the theories that informed schooling. Perhaps surprisingly, the first influences weren't in curriculum content, where they might have been expected. Rather, they showed up initially in new ways of thinking about differences among learners, which in turn impacted thinking about teaching.

Learning as an evolving coherence

As noted in Chapter 1.2, commonsense ways of thinking about learning tend to assume some sort of gap or deficiency – between inside and outside, between where one is located and where one should be, between what one has and what one must acquire, or between personal models of the world and the way the world really is. Across these images, learning is understood metaphorically as a process of BRIDGING THE GAP or MENDING THE DEFICIENCY, and thus a matter of JOURNEYING, ACQUIRING, MASTERING, or ASSEMBLING.

Historically, until the late 1800s, there were very few challenges to such perspectives, and the ones that did arise tended to come from philosophers who were far removed from life in the school. They had little educational impact. That began to change with the emergence of a science of learning that drew on the images and metaphors of the new science of change.

Before diving deeper into this discussion, it's important to draw a distinction between emergent research into human learning and the field of behavioral psychology, which appeared at roughly the same time. As noted in Chapter 1.2, behavioral psychology was tethered to cause–effect thinking and oriented toward articulating laws and principles that might be used to transform teaching into a precise enterprise. The new science of learning rejected this mechanistic attitude, looking instead at the complex ways that experience and language play into the emergence of understanding. In fact, this domain of inquiry began by rejecting the assumption that learning was about TRAVERSING or CLOSING SOME SORT OF GAP, as assumed both within commonsense perspectives, or as ESTABLISHING STIMULUS–RESPONSE LINKS, as assumed by behavioral psychologists. Rather, the new proposal was that learning is a

Many 20th-century theories, including *structuralism* and *constructivism*, are built around particular meanings of *structure* and *construct*.

In English, *structure* is a core notion in both architecture and biology, but the meanings are quite different. In relation to buildings, structure is associated with preplanning, logical connection, deliberate sequences. In biology, it is a reference to the complex history of an emergent form – always unique, always unfolding, never fully predictable.

Similarly, the French verb

an ONGOING ADAPTIVE DYNAMIC, which is a fundamental life process.

This difference is perhaps most obvious in the contrasting views of the body across the two schools of thought. In commonsense terms, the *body* is usually seen as a problem. It's the thing in the way – that's blocking, that must be traversed, that's lacking, that must be directed and trained, that must be filled. So understood, knowledge that begins on the outside of the body has to work its way to the inside. This view of the body as "something in the way" was implicit in approaches to teaching that held it still in a fixed desk, that forced it to conform to rigid schedules, and that sought to manipulate it through structures of reward and punishment.

As will be discussed in more detail in the next chapter, in the new science of learning and development, the body was rethought as the *means of* learning, not as a *barrier to* learning. In this frame, BODILY ACTION is more than a way to demonstrate knowledge or understanding; action is in fact a fundamental aspect of learning and knowing. Your body is not something you *have*, but an integral and un-ignorable part of who you *are*. Moreover, it is something that is transformed through the process of learning – an insight expressed by psychoanalysts, phenomenologists, and pragmatists in the first half of the 1900s, and later revisited by neuroscientiests at the end of the century. The new science of human learning and individual development, that is, rejected such naïve and simplistic dichotomies as mental *vs*. physical and mind *vs*. body.

This shift was actually part of a broader cultural movement known as **structuralism**, which swept through linguistics, mathematics, sociology, and other domains in the early 1900s. Seeking to explain how complex, dynamic forms evolved, structuralists focused on the internal coherences of these forms – that is, on the always-changing structures that defined and enabled them. For example, in linguistics, it was suggested that language is not a collection of labels but an evolving ecosystem. It gains its coherence from the interconnections among words, the way they are woven together. The word *structure* itself can be used

construire **can be translated as either "to construct" or "to construe" – words that have quite different webs of association.** *Construct* **presses attentions toward preplanned buildings;** *construe* **points toward the role of interpretation, association, and emergent possibility.**

Structuralism and constructivism invoke the latter meanings, which are truer to the original sense. Both derive from the Proto-Indo-European *stere-*, **"to spread, extend, stretch out." The associations with spreading and growth are better preserved in cognates** *strew* **and** *construe*.

to illustrate this point. As just noted in the margins, it is most commonly used in reference to planned and rigid objects, but it can refer to more contingent and fluid forms. Which meaning is taken depends on the context in which the word is used, the intentions of the speaker, the expectations of the hearer, and a complex and deeply historical web of linguistic associations.

The same is true of all words according to structuralists. We've aimed to illustrate this point throughout the book, particularly around the word *teaching*. This term is clearly not a simply a label for a particular social role or a category of activity. What the word *teaching* means depends on the context of its use, the histories of its users, and the network of associations of the language. It's an evolving form.

It is precisely this attitude toward structure that was intended by educational innovators and learning theorists in the 1900s with the development of a **constructivist theory of learning**. This theory is focused on the manner in which the individual construes her or his world by creating coherences among diverse experiences. The meaning *construct* within the theory *constructivism* means something more toward "construe" than "build." It is not a reference to assembling an internal edifice of knowledge, but to an endless process of organizing and updating one's associations as new experiences and new interpretations are encountered. So understood, learning is not about ACQUIRING INFORMATION or CLOSING A GAP or ESTABLISHING A STIMULUS–RESPONSE BOND. Rather, learning is a process of MAINTAINING COHERENCE. And knowing is not a matter of HAVING AN INTERNAL MODEL THAT MATCHES AN EXTERNAL REALITY, but of ENSURING THAT ONE'S CURRENT WEB OF CONSTRUALS IS VIABLE AND COHERENT.

This new focus on INTERNAL COHERENCE in theories of personal learning is one of the major reasons for the emergence of *authenticity* as an orienting principle in education. Authentic Education begins with honoring the individual's unique history and proceeds with the nurturing of that individual's potentials.

Coherence is derived by Latin *com-* + *haerere*, to "stick together." It is a fitting image for structuralist discussions of bodies, knowledge, and learning as it orients attentions toward how parts of a whole are held together, how their interconnections change, and how grander forms emerge in webs of association.

The pairing of *assimilation* and *accommodation* is fundamental within Authentic Education. *Assimilation* comes from the Latin *ad-* + *similis*, "to resemble." Its most familiar cognate is *similar*. In developmental theories, the process of assimilation is associated with modest changes (in mental structure, emotional response, etc.).

Accommodation comes from the Latin *ad-* + *commodore*, "to make fit." That is, an accommodation is an adjustment, a recategorizing. In developmental theories, it is associated with the emergence of markedly different ways of thinking.

Development as a coherence evolving

Along with a new way of looking at learning, science's shift in focus away from identifying distinctions and toward understanding change also prompted new interests in human development among educators.

Development through the lifespan wasn't a topic of particular interest prior to the 1900s. In fact, it could be argued that such "stages" in life as infancy and adolescence are recent inventions. As evidence, life stages are parsed very differently in many non-western cultures. In fact, it may have been parsed differently in pre-modern Europe. For example, prior to the 1600s children were often portrayed as miniature adults in paintings, their clothing was a scaled-down version of adult fashions, their furniture was adjusted for size but not function, and so on. That began to change dramatically in the 1600s, at the same time as the creation of public schooling. The child began to be seen and discussed as a distinct type of being, one that required the protection and intervention of adults. On this count, the 1762 publication of Jean-Jacques Rousseau's *Emile, or On Education* was a significant cultural marker in which a radically new model of education – one based on the developmental stages of a child – was proposed. Critiquing schooling's near-exclusive focus on the learning of facts and skills, Rousseau advised that physical, emotional, social, and other dimensions of development must also figure into the structures of education.

This advice, of course, coincided precisely with the re-focusing of science. The stage was thus set for the emergence of a science of human development. This domain began to unfold through the 1800s, concerned mainly with infants and young children. In the 1900s, paralleling the emergence of "education for all," the field expanded to include adolescence. In the latter half of the 1900s, coinciding with the **life-long learning** movement, the range of interest expanded to include adult development and aging.

Developmental research tends to be hubbed in psychology and medicine, and the range of **developmental theories** now spans motor skills, psychophysiological processes, cognition, consciousness, problem solving, moral understanding, language, social competence, sexuality, personality, emotion, self-concept, and identity formation. A common feature of these theories is the distinction between continuous, gradual change – **assimilations** – and more significant transitions from one mode or stage to another – **accommodations**. Education is, of course, concerned about both sorts of change, but as explored in more detail in Chapters 2.2 and 2.3, developmentalists argue the distinction is vital.

Indeed, having a sense of whether an event of learning is an assimilation of an accommodation is a core element to *authentic* teaching, as informed by constructivism. A situation similar to the one illustrated in the sidebar, for example, was recently presented to a group of about 400 pre-service teachers. They were first shown a series of chair images and then shown other pictures of other artifacts that are used for sitting – including a stool, a bean bag chair, a wheelchair, a dentist's chair, and auditorium seating.

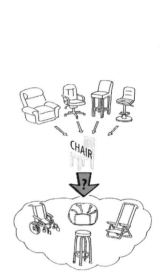

Opinions were split in various ways. For instance, about half the group readily agreed that a stool is a chair. That is, for them, stools were assimilated into their concept of CHAIR. For the other half, it didn't belong. For individuals in that group, an accommodation to their CHAIR concept would have been needed in order to see the stool as fitting. (You can probe your own CHAIR concept by monitoring your reactions to the other non-normal-chair images in the sidebar. Do you recognize them immediately as chairs, or do you pause and wonder?)

This example cuts to the heart of Authentic Education and distinguishes it from the model of generic preparation that prevails in modern, Standardized Education. In brief, the driving sensibility is that it is ridiculous to think that two learners – much less each person in a class of 30 learners (!) – will be at the same developmental stages (conceptual, emotional, physical, etc.). A schooling that is structured around assumptions of normal development, normal ability, and so on, then, is decidedly inauthentic.

Within Authentic Education, a *concept* is understood as an ever-evolving coherence that arises out of a mass of experiences. It is a means used to collect and compress events and encounters that have shared qualities. Once created, that coherence becomes a tool for organizing one's world as it is applied to interpret new experiences according to their fitness with the current version of the concept.

Authentic Education is attentive to both processes of coherence-making and phenomena that prevent it.

The metaphor of *epistemological obstacle* has thus arisen, referring to a resilient preconception that can frustrate a learner's efforts to understand a concept. Much of teaching in Moment 2 revolves around recognizing and challenging such constraining phenomena.

From the ideal to the real

Many interpret the 20th-century shift in educational discourse from the language of standardization to the language of authenticity as a move toward an education that is supposed to be specifically tailored to each individual, and therefore a pie-in-the-sky notion that will never be practical.

In fact, it isn't that at all. Authentic Education isn't strictly about individualized learning or personalized teaching. It's about a mode of schooling that is based on the realization that learning is a complex, dialogical phenomenon that can't be caused. Or, from the eyes of the pedagogue, learning is not *determined* by teaching.

However, learning is *dependent* on teaching.

What the Authentic Education movement is, then, is a shift in thinking about the role of the teacher, away from an *implementation* mindset and toward and *improvisational* attitude. In an implementation mindset, the teacher is cast as an assembly-line worker of sorts – a functionary responsible for implementing a curriculum, a management strategy, and an evaluation regime that meets imposed standards. In contrast, an *improvisational* attitude is more organic and about attending and adapting to the specifics and the needs that actually present themselves in the classroom.

As will be explored in Chapter 2.3, there are huge, practical differences between these sensibilities. For example, an implementer's attentions will be largely focused on being *planned* (since plans are what get implemented) – and this obsession continues to dominate many teacher education institutions. The improvisational attitude will be much more concerned with being *prepared* – that is, with being ready. That, of course, entails some planning, but also involves a readiness to depart from plans when one's imaginings about what might happen don't actually fit with what unfolds in a classroom.

This particular difference is evident in a rather remarkable shift in metaphors used to describe schooling and teaching through the 1900s. At the start of the century, the images and metaphors tended to be drawn from physics and engineering, with major emphases on planning, implementing, causing, managing, efficiency, measuring, and so on. By the end of the century, the prevailing language had shifted to a vocabulary that is more aligned with biology and ecology, reflected in notions of adapting, fitness, viability, coherence, and structure. (To be clear, the rhetoric of Standardized Education is still powerful, and continues to dominate in some contexts. It hasn't been replaced by any means. It is simply less prevalent in some situations.)

More coarsely, the change in sensibility between Standardized Education and Authentic Education is reflected in the following sorts of shifts:

The difference between Standardized Education and Authentic Education is analogous to the contrast between a human-made canal and the natural path of a river. The canal is built for efficiency and inattentive to the particularities of landscape (hence as straight as possible). The river's path is a function of its context and history; it is *authentic* to its situation.

- from a model of education that is based on an *ideal* (typical, normal, standardized) learner to one that is based on *actual* learners, in all their variability;
- from a teaching that is about *optimization* to one that is *good enough*;
- from a conception of the learner that is *deficient* (in need of completion, correction, etc.) to one that is *sufficient* (adequate for the situation, but evolving).

These shifts are anything but subtle. They point to a completely different sort of educational experience and to a dramatically different type of teaching.

Suggestions for delving deeper

1. Chances are that most of your schooling was within a frame of Standardized Education. Can you identify elements of your experience that were influenced by (or teachers who were more inclined toward) Authentic Education?

2. Think about something that you do really well and that you enjoy doing. How did you learn it? What sorts of teaching might have contributed to its development? How were those experiences similar to the structures of Standardized Education? How might they reflect the sensibilities of Authentic Education?

3. The distinction between *assimilation* and *accommodation* is an important one. Using the list of 100 synonyms for teaching on page 1, discuss with colleagues which terms are readily assimilated into your conceptions of teaching and which would require accommodations of your conceptions of teaching. Are there any significant differences among your conceptions of teaching?

2.2 Knowledge and Learning in Authentic Education

A frustration with traditional teaching is that it never seems to produce uniform results. Different learners inevitably make different senses of what's taught – no matter how well planned the lesson, how consistently delivered the explanation, how uniformly structured the practice, how precisely engineered the evaluation.

One might think that advocates of Standardized Education would see this outcome as a problem. But they usually don't. Instead it tends to be swept under the carpet, either by pointing to measurable differences among learners or by blaming the situation on "noise."

In the first case, as this line of thinking goes, learners subjected to the same lesson might end up in different places because of differences in ability, aptitude, and other quantifiable personal qualities.

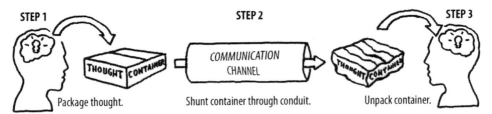

STEP 1 — Package thought.

STEP 2 — COMMUNICATION CHANNEL — Shunt container through conduit.

STEP 3 — Unpack container.

Even though there is no evidence to support the "conduit model" of communication, it is so entrenched that most English speakers take if for granted.

The second explanation is rooted in a commonsensical but scientifically ungrounded theory of communication, popularly known as **the conduit model**, as mentioned in Chapter 1.3. Premised on a KNOWLEDGE-AS-OBJECT metaphor, this model describes a three-step process: firstly, a sender packs knowledge-objects into containers known as "words"; secondly, those containers are shuttled through a communication channel;

thirdly, a recipient unpacks the meaning from the word-containers as they arrive. This model is usually implicit, and it's the one invoked in such common phrases as "putting thoughts into words," "relaying information," "channels of communication," and "unpacking what's been said." With respect to the issue of learners making different senses of the same lesson, this perspective suggests it's about miscommunication, which can be caused at any one of the three steps – the packing, the transmitting, or the unpacking.

Over the last century, researchers into communication and learning offered some serious challenges to these explanations. But before we describe the crux of those critiques, it might be useful to analyze an instance of communication. How you would respond to the following request?

> Turn down the air conditioning, please.

A too-cold passenger recently uttered this statement. She was was asking that the conditioner be adjusted to pump out less cool air (i.e., the "down" of the request referred to a "reduction in output"). The driver cranked up the output (i.e., he interpreted the "down" in terms of a "decrease in temperature").

Now imagine a slightly different scenario. What if it had been a cold day and the car's heater had been turned on – and a too-hot passenger had requested:

> Turn down the heater, please.

Assuming both communicants used "down" in the same senses as before (i.e., respectively, to refer to a "reduction in output" and to a "decrease in temperature"), the driver would have responded in the desired way – even though two very different meanings were at play. Despite the dissonance, it would appear as though the driver and the passenger had communicated perfectly.

Such examples of conflicting interpretations prompt the suggestion that communication is not about packing–transmitting–unpacking information. There are simply too many possible interpretations of any utterance for that perspective to be plausible. Just consider the many possible meanings of the first two words of the request, *turn* and *down*, some of which are illustrated in the webs from visualthesaurus.com:

With regard to visual metaphors, discussions of Authentic Education revolve around some very different images and frames to those invoked in discussions of Standardized Education. Most obviously, references to Euclid's geometry of the plane are much less frequent.

More subtly, knowing is typically characterized in terms of sprawling, interlinked networks rather than tidy, well-bounded categories, learning as ever branching paths rather than linear trajectories, and teaching in terms of triggering rather than causing.

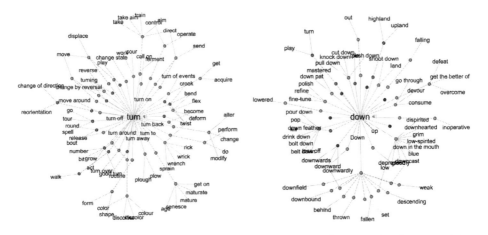

In brief, there are literally thousands of ways of interpreting, "Turn down the air conditioning." (Most would be decidedly wacky in this context – such as the meanings associated with "Turn down the offer," "Turn down the bed," and "Turn down the sidestreet.") When one considers the fact that *every* word is at the center of its own web of association, communication is revealed to be incredibly complex. It simply doesn't make sense to think in terms of a straightforward process of packing meaning into words.

Rather than a packing–transmitting–unpacking process, then, it would appear that communication is more about triggering or activating associations. When compatible webs are triggered for both speaker and hearer, clear communication is assumed to have occurred. When the dissonant webs are triggered, it's miscommunication.

Perhaps the most important detail to notice here is the shift in the *location* of the communicative activity. The conduit metaphor suggests that most of the activity of communication happens between people (hence the emphasis on the conduit), whereas an activating-networks-of-association perspective locates virtually all of the activity in minds.

Insofar as theories of knowledge and learning go, there are many issues tangled together here. Let us frame our strategy for unraveling some of them by highlighting a few of the key differences among the images above. The visual representation of the conduit metaphor reveals an assumption of linearity, underscoring its alignment with a KNOWLEDGE-AS-OBJECT metaphor. In contrast, webs of association are non-linear: their links move in multiple directions, they branch, they will have different weights for different people, and so on.

Further, there are no centers to these sorts of network. Each word is its own hub in a grand web of association – that is, pressing on any of the terms in the above image will explode into a similar web of associations. (Check out visualthesaurus.com. That's literally what happens on that site.) This sort of structure is known as a *decentralized network*, which is not really a network without a center. Rather, it is a network where almost any node might be construed as a center, depending on the how the network is activated.

A different geometry is being invoked here. It is not about the orderly geometry of the plane, but shapes that are more unruly, more dynamic, more complex.

What, then, is *knowledge*?

The word *knowledge* is used to refer to at least two distinct phenomena in discussions of schooling. Firstly it is used to refer to collective knowledge – that body of broadly endorsed facts and beliefs from which curriculum is drawn. Secondly, it is used to refer to individual knowledge – PERSONAL UNDERSTANDINGS, SUBJECTIVE INTERPRETATIONS, IDIOSYNCRATIC BELIEFS.

The latter – that is, individual knowledge – was the particular concern of a cluster of theories of learning that emerged at the start of the 1900s. These new ways of thinking weren't much concerned with collective knowledge (e.g., curriculum contents or the parent disciplines of school subject areas). Rather, they were mainly focused on individual knowledge.

Or, more precisely, individual *knowing*.

About a century ago, theorists of learning began to use the gerund *knowing* instead of the noun *knowledge* in a deliberate effort to challenge some deeply entrenched entailments of the KNOWLEDGE-AS-OBJECT metaphor. Three of these challenges are of particular relevance, summarized in the following table:

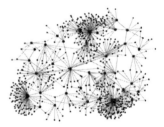

As its name suggests, a *decentralized network* is a structure with no specific center. However, it may be useful to think of it more as a network with many centers than one with no centers – that is, a network in which each node is in a sense the center of its own network. Examples of decentralized networks include languages, social networks, the Internet, and neuronal structures (see Chapter 4.2).

SHIFTING VOCABULARY FROM "KNOWLEDGE" TO "KNOWING"	
Qualities highlighted by the gerund *knowing*	**Rejected entailments of the KNOWLEDGE-AS-OBJECT metaphor**
dynamic character – i.e., fluid, constantly being revised as new experiences unfold	**stable** – i.e., real "truth" is assumed to be eternal and unchanging
inseparability of *knower* and *knowledge* – i.e., there must be some*one* to know some*thing*	**detached** – i.e., assumed to stand alone, independent of context, systems of interpretation, etc.
associated with action – i.e., knowing can't sit on a shelf; all knowing entails some sort of action/activity/activation	**inert** – i.e., knowledge itself is assumed to be free from entailments; it's what people do with knowledge that can raise issues

Knowing, then, points to the always evolving, intricately networked, inevitably unique, and necessarily engaged nature of personal knowledge. To cut to the chase, a very different conception of what it means to know something was being proposed.

Several academic movements contributed to the emergent discussions of knowing, including **phenomenology**, structuralism, **existentialism**, and **psychoanalysis**. With specific regard to education, the two most prominent influences were **John Dewey**'s **pragmatism** (discussed in Chapter 2.3) and **Jean Piaget**'s **genetic epistemology**.

KNOWING

KNOWLEDGE

The word *knowing* (vs. *knowledge*) is used in discussions of education to flag the dynamic, idiosyncratic, and situated qualities of personal understandings.

The phrase "genetic epistemology" means, literally, "origins of knowing." It was coined by Piaget and is strongly associated with constructivist theories of learning (discussed later in this chapter). Genetic epistemologists reject the commonsense belief that personal knowing is a matter of correspondence – that is, about an internal, subjective model that corresponds to an external, objective reality. Rather, individual knowing is argued to be about the coherence – the ONGOING CREATION AND RE-CREATION OF WEBS OF ASSOCIATION, where the measures of personal meaning and truth are the extent to which components of the web hang together. The two emphases of genetic epistemology are, first, to make sense of how knowers assemble and maintain these webs of association and, second, to describe the sorts of developmental stages that emerge across a lifetime as knowing grows more sophisticated.

The distinction between correspondence and coherence is so important that it bears repeating. Roughly a century ago, a new wave of theories emerged that rejected the commonsense *correspondence theories* – that is, the belief that personal knowledge is about CONSTRUCTING AN INTERNAL MODEL that corresponded to the external world (see Chapter 1.2). Instead, these **coherence theories** suggested that knowing is an ONGOING PROCESS OF CONSTRUING A WORLD BY CONSTANTLY REVISING WEBS OF ASSOCIATION in order to maintain a personally coherent sense of reality. In this frame, a word or concept is meaningful not because it maps onto an object or event in the real world, but because it occurs in an intricately woven web of associations.

The power of this idea for educators was obvious. In particular, it provided a plausible explanation for the people's tendency to interpret similar experiences in different ways. If the sense one makes is more about one's history than the immediate situation, it doesn't matter how well a lesson is structured or how clear an explanation might be provided. Each student is going to have a unique interpretation.

Accompanying this shift from describing personal knowing in terms of coherence rather than correspondence was a shift from a vocabulary rooted in physics to a vocabulary drawn from biology. For example, rather than talking about cause–effect, efficiency, and validity when describing the learning process, educators began to talk about ongoing adaptation, adequacy, and viability. And rather than using the image of a pristine edifice with firm foundations and a logically ordered structure, genetic epistemologists began to characterize personal knowing in more evolving, organic terms that were more attentive to the diverse origins of different knowers' knowings.

We mentioned this point in Chapter 2.1 in relation to two conflicting definitions of the word *structure*. Once again, the meaning of structure – and, with it, the meanings of *construct* and *construction* – is critical here, because the word is subject to nearly opposite interpretations. The metaphor of KNOWING AS STRUCTURING was taken up by genetic epistemologists because a biological structure, such as a cell or a tree or an ecosystem, is a living history – a dynamic physical trace of a lifetime of experiences and interactions. The

(Imaging a Correspondence Theory)

In Chapter 2.1, we offered the above image as a visual metaphor for commonsense theories of knowledge and learning associated with Standardized Education. This graphic is intended to be suggestive of a metaphors of KNOWLEDGE AS OBJECT and LEARNING AS ACQUISITION.

Crafting a visual metaphor of the theories of knowing and learning associated with Authentic Education is a much more difficult task. Few images call to mind notions of dynamic coherence, ongoing adaptation, and ever-increasing levels of sophistication.

metaphor, then, was intended to suggest vibrant forms, deep histories, intricate webs of association, constant evolution, and ever-mounting complexity.

In other words, the metaphor was a direct challenge to commonsense assumptions within Standardized Education. For example, it was offered as an alternative to images of tidy and orderly edifices of knowledge. As well, it was a refutation that learning is a matter of linear accumulation, suggesting rather that personal knowing is a multi-directional, adaptive process that can only be understood in terms of the individual's *entire* history. In pragmatic terms, the sense a student makes has vastly more to do with that student's past than anything the teacher might say or do.

More profoundly, the KNOWING-AS-STRUCTURING metaphor was intended as a challenge to deeply entrenched beliefs about what it was to be human. It entailed a rejection of the pervasive assumptions that humans are principally conscious and logical creatures. On the contrary, genetic epistemologists argued, most of human knowing occurs beneath the surface of consciousness, where analogy is a vastly more important and more prevalent process than logic.

(Imaging a Coherence Theory)

Even so, we find the above graphic useful for highlighting some key elements. In it, the jagged line represents learning, and is intended as a reminder of the non-linear movement associated with the development of a concept. The nested circles reflect levels of knowing, as moments of assimilation (motions inside a particular level) and accommodations (crossing a boundary into a qualitatively different way of thinking) contribute to a more encompassing, more powerful schema.

Can you know what you know?

Perhaps the biggest shift in thinking about knowing that unfolded through the 1900s was the realization that most of what you know you don't know you know.

To make sense of that statement – that "most of what you know you don't know you know" – two different meanings of *know* must be invoked. A more comprehensible rephrasing might be, "Most of the coherent sense you have about the world is not available to immediate conscious awareness." That is, *knowing* involves both nonconscious and conscious aspects.

One of the major developments in psychology over the 1900s was a demonstration that most cognitive activity is nonconscious. In terms of sensory perception, for example, a human body has more than 10 million sensory receptors, yet at most a few dozen sensations can bubble into awareness at any instant. (All the other information of the senses is still active in the brain;

it just doesn't consciously register.) Similarly, and as illustrated with the visual metaphor of decentralized networks, humans can only be aware of the "surface" of concepts and are oblivious to the vast webs of association that render them meaningful. (It would be utterly debilitating to have to consciously trace out webs of association in order to assemble coherent meanings. Nonconscious processes do that for you.)

The suggestion of powerful unconsciousnesses sprang into popularity in the early 1900s, owing in large part to the work of Sigmund Freud and other proponents of psychoanalysis. In more current terms, theories focused on these conscious and nonconscious aspects of knowing are dubbed **dual-process models**. These perspectives suggest that each human has two interacting-but-distinct knowing systems, often referred to as "System 1" and "System 2."

Think about something you're really, really good at. Your facility with whatever you're thinking about is a matter of System 1 knowing. System 1 is fast and may feel automatic – mostly because it is rooted in memory and strengthened by extensive practice. When called to act, System 1 draws on honed skills, rehearsed lines, and experienced situations. System 1 is analogical – associative, metaphorical, impressionistic. It can take on great amounts of information and can present actions and interpretations that are so immediate, relevant, and accurate that it might feel like intuition or instinct.

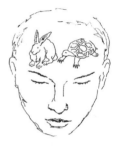

A *dual-process model of knowing* is a one that suggests humans have two distinct-but-entangled knowing systems, one that is conscious (explicit) and one that is nonconscious (tacit).

In contrast, System 2 is slow – mostly because it is thinking based. It's called into action when facing a situation that is unfamiliar or overly confusing – that is, when the knower has no practiced procedures or pre-rehearsed interpretations to call on. System 2 is deliberate and requires effort, and is therefore slow and easily tired. And assuming that there are no major problems with the brain's executive functions, System 2 can more-or-less take responsibility for initiating and persisting with the task at hand.

The chart on the next page summarizes some of the contrasts between these simultaneous and co-entangled knowing systems. In the process, it underscores that most of what you know you don't know you know … because most of what you know is System 1 knowing.

SIMULTANEOUS KNOWING SYSTEMS		
(Automatic) System 1	SYSTEM	(Reflective) System 2
memory based (rehearsed) • associative and analogical • oriented to whole (able to chunk) • highly attuned to context •	MODE	• thought based (dealing with novelty) • rule seeking and logical • analytic (focused on aspects) • not particularly sensitive to context
mostly not conscious • can feel intuitive, even instinctive • in charge (lead actor), but "silent" • can be hampered by biases •	"FEEL"	• mostly conscious • can be frustrating, often excruciating • feels in charge (but a supporting actor) • able to recognize pre-judgments
always at work in the background • rapid, automatic, and low effort • massive capacity •	DEMAND	• typically demands full attention • slow, deliberate, and high effort • constrained by working memory

But here's the kicker: System 2 – the conscious knowing system – likes to think of itself as being in charge. Your conscious self tends to believe it's the lead actor, but it's really a supporting character. Most of the time, System 1 – the nonconscious knowing system – is running the show. That usually turns out to be appropriate. System 1 is highly skilled and usually knows what to do, which frees up System 2 to step into the game when it must.

As far as modern schooling goes, for centuries discussions and programs have been mainly focused on System 2: conscious, thinking-based, slow knowing. That has happened in large part because it's much easier to objectify, represent, and examine details that are explicit and immediately available to consciousness. In contrast, tacit System-1 knowing is highly personal and can be hard to symbolize. That makes it difficult to share with others. (This is why being highly skilled at something doesn't necessarily make someone a good teacher.) More fundamentally, however, it also makes it more difficult to share it with oneself – that is, to bring it to explicit awareness. Tacit knowledge is simply knitted into one's being – ENACTED, EMBODIED, PERFORMED, TAKEN-FOR-GRANTED. This category thus encompasses personal insights, intuitions, hunches, convictions, values, and morals.

Importantly, this dyad is not a dichotomy. Systems 1 and 2 are not sealed off from each other. They work in tandem, each influencing the other – and that means that there are at least four distinct categories of knowing, depending on how these systems are activated. The following table lists these four categories, which are often identified as a developmental sequence from not knowing that you don't know (the first category in the chart) through to a competence that is fluid and automatic (the bottom category).

ENGAGEMENTS IN DIFFERENT SORTS OF KNOWING			
Category of knowing	Description	(Automatic) System 1 engagement	(Reflective) System 2 engagement
unconscious unskilled	Knower is not aware s/he lacks a competence.	**active**, seeking possible patterns or relationships, but not oriented by a coherent concept	**inactive**, or focused on other, unrelated matters
conscious unskilled	Knower is aware a competence is lacking.	**active**, developing proto-concepts based on newly recognized coherence	**active**, focusing attentions on and deliberately analyzing features of the situation
conscious skilled	Knower is aware a competence has been developed.	**active**, honing and streamlining the concept or skill	**active**, focusing on more fine-grained elements of the situation
unconscious skilled	Knower has a competence that operates without conscious attention.	**active**, taking charge and presenting the illusion of effortlessness	**inactive**, but available for new challenges

We've already mentioned that modern schooling has been mainly focused on the conscious, System 2-type knowings. To put a finer point on this statement, the target level of knowing for formal education is almost always the conscious-skilled category, where students are aware that they have (hopefully) developed a competence and, therefore, prepped for testing. Put in different terms, schooling is not typically geared to supporting the development of deep expertise.

It's important to note that this rubric isn't complete. For example, another popularly discussed category of knowing is **metacognition** or **self-regulated learning**. Literally, metacognition refers to awareness of awareness. More descriptively, it is a reference to awareness of different aspects of one's knowing – what one knows, how one learns, what one is prone to take for granted, and so on. In terms of Systems 1 and System 2, metacognition might be described as a disposition (i.e., grounded in System 1) toward being aware (i.e., activating System 2) of the habits of one's knowing. (We revisit metacognition in Chapter 2.3, as this construct is associated with some useful advice for teachers.)

Learning

As we noted in Chapter 1.2, the one definition of *learning* that works across every theoretical perspective is that it has something to do with transformations in knowing.

Within a frame of Standardized Education, in which knowledge is seen mainly in terms of OBJECTS, learning is understood mainly in terms of ACQUIRING THOSE OBJECTS. In contrast, within a frame of Authentic Education, in which personal knowing is a dynamic, multifaceted phenomenon, learning is construed in terms of such diverse processes as BECOMING AWARE, PRACTICING, HABITUALLY DOING, IGNORING, FORGETTING, REPRESSING, and so on (see the figure below). In brief, every act is an act of learning, since every act affects knowing.

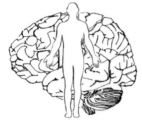

The word *embodied* is used across many current discussions of knowing and learning to refer to the notion that the capacities of the human mind are determined by the body's structure, actions, sensorial capacities, and contexts. The most radical versions of this perspective assert that all human knowledge, no matter how abstract, is rooted in bodily action.

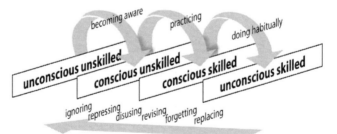

This point – that every act is an act of learning – entails a completely different way of looking at the body, not as form through which one learns but as the structure that is learning. That is, within Authentic Education, the human body is not seen as a form that houses a mind, but as an integral part of one's being. The adjective **embodied** (as in **embodied cognition** and **embodied learning**) is commonly used to signal this sensibility, and the word is encountered in many contemporary theories of learning. A shared element across these theories is that physical experience – the body's movements through space, its encounters with other forms, and so on – are the origins of understanding.

Consider, for example, the concept, IN.

According to the perspectives on knowing and learning associated with the Authentic Education movement, your understandings of the world are rooted in your earliest physical experiences. The concept IN, for example, likely began with activities involving some sort of containment, such as holding a soother in your mouth and, slightly later, dropping Cheerios into a cup. These unrelated experiences started to pull together into a coherent concept as you noticed others use the word *in* to refer to situations with well-defined insides and outsides.

As your repertoire of experiences grew and as you developed more language to organize and connect those experiences, the concept of IN expanded to include such diverse meanings as "at work," "fashionable," and "having powerful friends" – that is, instances that only have metaphoric insides and outsides.

Several processes are at work here, including some key ones that are not identified in the graphic on page 87. In particular, learning a concept would appear to involve three main sorts of process:

A *schema* is a concept. The word was introduced to interrupt commonsense understandings of a concept as something universal, stable, and isolated. In contrast to these notions, a schema is typically described as idiosyncratic, evolving, and entangled with other schemata.

- actions associated with in-ness – the development of a repertoire of concrete, physical experiences (e.g., putting objects in one's mouth),
- uses of the word *in* – the connecting of experiences with similar qualities through a common referent (e.g., hearing "in" used to refer to different objects inside different containers), and
- elaboration of the concept IN – the metaphoric extension to other aspects of existence (e.g., being informed that "3 is in the set of natural numbers" and "bright colors are in this season").

Borrowing on the work of earlier thinkers, Piaget used the word **schema** to refer to such emergent personal concepts. A schema is a structure, in the dynamic, adaptive, biological sense. It is simultaneously a reference to the experiences that might be collected together in a concept by an individual and to the connections that individual makes to other schemata.

Piaget is the person most frequently associated with the *assimilation* and *accommodation* pairing presented in Chapter 2.1. In effect, these two processes refer to the different dynamics of System 1 and System 2. Assimilation – when new experiences are easily knitted into an existing schema – is a System 1 process. For example, in a young child's development of the schema for IN, references to "in your bedroom" or "in the book" might be readily assimilated, since the references have to do with objects inside well-defined spaces.

Accommodations – those experiences that require conscious reworking of a schema in order to make sense of them – are System 2 processes. For example, "in the yard" (which might trigger a dissonance between understandings of IN-side and OUT-side) or "in the moment" (which requires a major leap of abstraction) may demand some conscious effort to create new connections and/or revise old ones.

There are many, many *constructivist theories*, and some have little in common with others. In this book, the phrase is used to refer to those theories of individual cognition in which learning and knowing are understood in terms of ongoing processes of construing and maintaining coherence in one's network of associations.

These processes of assimilation and accommodation are analogical, not logical – meaning that the most important processes of abstract learning are figurative and associative reasoning. When faced with having to make sense of a new situation, human minds usually don't proceed with deep analysis, but by rapidly generating many diverse interpretations and then homing in on ones that are adequate to maintain coherence.

It is because of these penchants for generating diversity and favoring analogy over logic that Piaget and other learning theorists in the 1900s emphasized processes of CONSTRUING – including NOTICING patterns, INVENTING connections, BLENDING schema, guessing and testing, generalizing … the list goes on. In brief, learning is not a singular process of progressing toward some target knowledge; it is a DIVERSIFIED ENGAGEMENT OF GENERATING MORE EXPANSIVE UNDERSTANDINGS. Once again, it seems a pity that the associated theories of learning are most commonly known as *constructivisms*. While the notion of constructing can be hijacked to refer to the creation of networks of association (rather than edifices of knowledge), it rarely seems to support appreciations of the diversities and complexities of the processes associated with learning.

The developing learner

In highlighting the many and diverse processes associated with learning, constructivist theorists have also helped researchers and educators make sense of a long-recognized, but poorly understood quality of human development: individuals seem to progress through distinct stages as they grow older. These stages appear to be quantum-leap sorts of moments, where preferred modes of thinking, habits of association, pressing concerns, and other aspects of one's being can shift dramatically. Why does that happen?

There was once a widespread belief that these leaps occur as part of a natural biological process, but this notion was debunked when anthropological research demonstrated that stages, trajectories, and timings can differ massively between cultures. Piaget offered an alternative suggestion, anchored to the notion that learning is an unending process of revising one's network of associations. He proposed that moving from one developmental stage to the next is an instance of extreme accommodation, a moment when one's accumulated experiences and the mounting sophistication of one's webs of knowing both compel and enable a new, more powerful way of organizing one's thinking.

The table on the next page, which provides a quick glance at the stages of Piaget's theory of cognitive development, elaborates this point. Notice how each stage emerges out of and encompasses, but completely transcends, the preceding level. This chart offers only a cursory summary of Piaget's extensively researched and much more elaborate model. Each stage comprises substages, each of which in turn reveals its own particular subtleties and complexities.

Piaget's theory of cognitive development is easily the best-known and most researched **developmental stage theory**. However, it's important to note that there are a great many others in the current literature, covering such elements of personal development as cognition, morality, sociality, emotions, agency, and

A *developmental stage theory* is one that presents human growth in terms of a sequence of stages through which a person, under normal circumstances, might be expected to progress through a lifetime. Foci of these theories include cognitive, moral, social, and ego development, among other personal capacities or qualities.

PIAGET'S THEORY OF COGNITIVE DEVELOPMENT		
Stage	**Typical Ages**	**Some of the key preferences and achievements**
Sensorimotor	0–2 years	• motor responses and senses coordinate with one another • curiosity about the world with active sensory exploration • language used to catalogue objects and to make demands • learns that objects continue to exist, even when not observed ("object permanence")
Preoperational	2–7 years	• proper syntax and grammar used to express concepts, showing evidence of symbolic thinking • strong imagination; growing intuitions • concrete abstract thought begins to appear, but is difficult • learns that some qualities of objects are conserved, even when others (e.g., shapes) change ("conservation")
Concrete Operational	7–11 years	• problems are solved in a more logical fashion, although limited to concrete objects and events • abstract concepts of time, space, and quantity emerge, but understood only in terms of concrete applications, not as independent concepts
Formal Operations	11+	• able to think abstractly, theoretically, hypothetically, and counterfactually • abstract logic and reasoning appear, and are no longer tethered to concrete situations • concepts learned in one context can be adapted or extended to be applied in another

ego/identity. Collectively these theories have had major impacts on curriculum structures and teaching strategies – which is a point that perhaps merits some pause. It means, for instance, that it has only been over the last century that educators have been paying close attention to the very, very different competencies and habits that different age groups bring to the classroom.

There are, of course, many criticisms of an overly religious application of developmental theories. The most common one is that these models are based on statistical averages. That means that in a typical classroom children are likely to be distributed across multiple levels, and so one cannot assume that age is a sufficient indicator of stage. Another is that these models are almost always based on studies of middle class children in large western cities (or some other distinct subpopulation), and so there can be issues with generalizing to, say, children in remote communities.

Of course, these concerns are not condemnations of the theories or their associated research. Rather, they are more in the category of cautions. The core tenet of the movement, that each person is a unique being, should serve as a reminder that these theories aren't intended as universally applicable generalizations.

Ability

Within the frame of Standardized Education, intelligence is centrally defined in terms of capacities for formal reason. It is typically described as composites of information storage, symbol manipulation, linear logic, abstract thought, and analytic processing.

A devastating challenge to this conception arose in the mid-1900s, and it came from a surprising place. In the 1950s, computer scientists working on artificial intelligence ran up against an unexpected problem. Buoyed by early successes in programming computers to perform tasks that humans find enormously difficult – in particular, those demanding logical thought and repetitive processes – researchers confidently predicted that electronic brains would soon surpass human brains.

They quickly realized, however, that many of the tasks that are simple and routine for humans are enormously complex, such as recognizing faces, parsing words in sentences, expressing novel thoughts, wending through crowds, interpreting metaphors, and so on. And so, somewhat ironically, artificial intelligence research highlighted that human intelligence is about vastly more than facility with logical and symbolic tasks.

This insight set the stage for more nuanced and varied definitions of intelligence. It would be impossible to survey them here, but a few commonly cited qualities bear mention:

- intelligence is multi-faceted;
- intelligence varies massively, depending on wakefulness, distractions, interest, practice, and many, many other conditions – an implication of which is that you can make yourself smarter.

Apart from general agreement that intelligence is neither a fixed nor a singular competence, the only point of emergent consensus on its nature seems to be that it is enormously complex.

A century ago, the consensus was that training for athletic events was tantamount to cheating. It was considered an unfair way to enhance performance, because it made it impossible to measure one's *natural* (from the Latin *naturalis*, "by birth") ability.

Until very recently, discussions of intelligence have tended to share a similar attitude about innate ability. Evidence is mounting, however, that commonsense beliefs on in-born intelligence are problematical.

Several theories have arisen around the multi-faceted character of intelligence. For example, in his **Triarchic Theory of Intelligence, Robert J. Sternberg** has foregrounded analytic, creative, and practical aspects as he defined intelligence in terms of achieving context-sensitive goals. Taking another tack, **Howard Gardner** has identified several types of intelligence. To qualify as a distinct intelligence in his **Theory of Multiple Intelligences**, a competence must be associated with a specific brain region, unfold through a distinct developmental progression, be measureable, and there must be prodigies and geniuses. So far he has identified nine distinct sorts of ability that satisfy these and other criteria (see the sidebar). We discuss some of the practical implications of Gardner's theory in Chapter 2.3.

With regard to the variable nature of intelligence, studies of extraordinary performance have indicated that there are some common elements among "geniuses." Typically they

- began early in life,
- were immersed in a setting that valued and nurtured their specific competence,
- had a good teacher,
- practiced deliberately, and
- practiced extensively.

We provide more detail on the elements, as they relate to teaching practice, in Chapter 2.3.

Research into the development of exceptionality has helped to reframe a popular **debate on nature *vs.* nurture**. For most of the last century, this debate was taken up in a this-or-that sort of argumentation, driven in large part by a deeply ingrained belief that ability is genetically rooted (i.e., it is a *gift*). Research into extraordinary performance reveals that this dichotomous thinking is a gross simplification. Nature and nurture aren't opposed; they're two tightly interwoven elements that contribute to personal possibility. In fact, and coming as a surprise to many, humans are born on a surprisingly level playing field when it comes to ability, and so the "nature" part of the dyad is more a matter of setting the stage for emergent possibility rather than a defining of eventual ability.

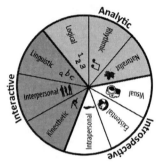

According to Howard Gardner, intelligence is not a fixed capacity but an always-evolving cluster of potentials that enable a knower to make contributions that are valued in a culture, to solve problems in life, and to produce new knowledge. His current list of intelligences includes musical-rhythmic and harmonic, visual-spatial, verbal-linguistic, logical-mathematical, bodily-kinesthetic, interpersonal, intrapersonal, naturalistic, and existential. Each individual is seen to have a unique blend of all the intelligences.

Another way of saying this is that, within a frame of Authentic Education, the notion of personal *potential* is understood as something that is created rather than something that is predetermined. No doubt there are limits on what humans are able to do, but no one really knows what those are. Within the frame of Authentic Education, part of the educator's role is to ensure the conditions are present to grow potential.

That emphasis perhaps represents the greatest contrast between Standardized Education and Authentic Education. Standardized Education ignores individual difference as it seeks to offer uniform experiences leading to a generic set of competencies. Authentic Education seeks to amplify possibilities by attending to and nurturing each individual's unique interests and competencies.

Within Standardized Education, the word *potential* is usually discussed as something pregiven and therefore unleashed. Within Authentic Education, it's more often framed as emerging possibility – and therefore grown.

Suggestions for delving deeper

1. Personal memory seems to be structured in a decentrally networked manner. You can illustrate this point for yourself by drawing out part of a web of memories. Start by selecting an experience from your past and represent it with a word or two on a page. Then in a style similar to the word networks near the start of this chapter, send out spokes to some other memories triggered by this one. Then do the same thing for some of the memories at the end of those spokes, and so on.

2. Your conception of teaching is strongly shaped by your experiences with teachers. Returning to the images, synonyms, and/or metaphors (listed in the Prologue) that might have resonated with you, do those notions summon associations with favorite teachers? Whether they do or not, what were some of the qualities of those teachers that made them memorable. How do those qualities align with some of the tenets on knowing and learning presented in this chapter?

3. Your System 1 is busily at work right now, enabling you to read this text without having to sound out words, summon definitions, make connections to other topics, and activate other subskills that had to be painstakingly developed with the assistance of System 2. Regarding your area of teaching specialization, what topics might fall into System 1 competence for you? And what might you do to ensure that those mastered competencies don't get in the way of helping novices grapple with the subskills needed to get where you are?

2.3 Teaching and Authentic Education

Priming **is a process of orienting perceptions and readying expectations by drawing attentions – often implicitly – toward particular aspects of a situation. As simple as it sounds, it can have profound influences on perceptions, actions, and learnings – including negative ones if a disabling thought is triggered.**

What do you see in the image to the left?

Obviously this is a question about subjective perception rather than objective representation. There is no right answer; every observer will see something different. For precisely that reason, psychologists have used such tasks for more than a century: your interpretation reveals aspects of your past, your desires, your obsessions, and so on. Your perception, that is, is about projecting your history onto a present event.

With your brain's power to generate diversity, it's easy to summon different projections. Suppose, for example, that we'd begun by mentioning that this particular image was deliberate, portraying two people crouching, back-to-back, cradling ducks in their laps. Can you see it?

Our stating this interpretation is an instance of **priming** – that is, of biasing your perceptions in a particular direction. Of course, the image is just a blotch that can be read in countless ways, But, once perception is primed, it tends to wander in that direction.

This demonstration illustrates some important details around teaching within a frame of Authentic Education. It shows, for instance, how teachers might influence learners' understandings as they engage in the endless process of maintaining conceptual coherence by connecting experiences and updating those connections. The teaching here isn't about CONVEYING INFORMATION; it's about REORIENTING PERCEPTION and TRIGGERING ASSOCIATION-MAKING. It is an attempt to trigger different elements of your past that might be imposed on a current experience. It's about an approach to teaching that begins with the realization that perception isn't a passive process of taking in, but a dynamic, complex, and participatory phenomenon. Let us underscore this point with another demonstration:

With the book about 30 cm (12 inches) from your face, cover your left eye and place a fingertip on the gray dot at the center of the image on the side. Stare at that fingertip with your right eye and maintain that focus as you slide your finger toward the triangle below.

Without shifting your gaze from the moving fingertip, pay attention to what happens to the dot. It should disappear from view. (If it persists, try sliding your finger a bit more to the left. It might also help to turn the book a few degrees clockwise or to vary the distance between your eye and the page.)

Why does this happen? The physiological explanation is simple. Everyone has a blind spot where the optic nerve passes through the back of the eye, leaving a zone with no light-sensitive cells. But that's not the most interesting part.

Try the experiment again, this time attending to what happens with the black line in the middle when the dot falls into your blind spot. For most people, the "missing" part of the line is seen as filled in – that is, conscious perception (System 2) doesn't perceive the gap in the visual field because it sees what nonconscious processes (System 1) suggest is likely there. So the critical detail is not that there's a blind spot, nor that that spot usually goes unnoticed. It's that the brain is projecting something that isn't on the page.

The point? Perception is not merely about gathering information and channeling it to the brain. If that were the case, gaps would be noticed. Rather, perception is more a matter of negotiating a relationship between current and past events. Experience has "taught" that there are no holes in the fabric of space, and so nonconscious processes fill in the gap with what should probably be there. **Optical illusions** work for similar reasons as they trigger conflicts between System 1's expectations and System 2's analyses.

In other words, eyes aren't cameras, ears aren't

microphones, and so on. The situation is actually far more complex. Nerve cells run in *both* directions between sense organs and the brain – and *there is more communication from the brain to the sense organ than from the sense organ to the brain.* Far from being passive processes of TAKING IN, then, perception and learning involve active FISHING FOR INFORMATION.

So what does this complexified insight into perception and learning say about teaching?

How might we teach authentically?

It would be an understatement to say that proponents of the Authentic Education movement have offered fuzzy advice to teachers – on how to teach, on what to emphasize, on when to do what …

The problem stems from the fact that the theories driving the Authentic Education movement are about learning, not teaching. They present nuanced accounts of what it means to know something and how individuals make sense of their experiences, but they offer little commentary on teaching apart from emphasizing that *teaching doesn't cause learning.* As already emphasized, learning is of course *dependent on* teaching. But it is not *determined by* teaching.

The preceding sentences might be taken as a harsh criticism of the project of Standardized Education. In effect, the assertion is that the ideas of a uniform pedagogy, a universal curriculum, and standardized outcomes are misguided. At the same time, the theories that propelled Authentic Education don't dictate against lecturing, direct instruction, or any other of the prominent strategies of Standardized Education. Rather than rejecting such methods, these theories are critical only of the naïve assumption that such strategies will have their desired effects. They can't. Every learner will construe their experiences in their own way.

As frustrating as this realization might be for those who want simple, straightforward advice on teaching, it is immensely useful for making sense of the meta-analyses of educational research mentioned at the end of Moment 1 (in Chapter 1.3). Why is student self-

A defining quality of teaching within Standardized Education is that it be *predictable*. Plans are oriented by clear outcomes, lessons follow a regular sequence, and so on.

Within Authentic Education, which aims to wrap teaching around the needs and curiosities of children, the more important quality is that learning events be *postdictable* – that is, able to be rendered sensible in retrospect.

reporting such a powerful learning technique? What is a Piagetian program, and why is it more effective than one rooted in an instructional mindset? And so on. In this chapter, we aim to answer these and other questions raised by those meta-analyses.

Before proceeding to these matters, an important qualification must be made. It's deceptively easy to construe the Authentic Education movement as being the opposite of the Standardized Education movement – and, in fact, many of the grand debates around schooling in the mid-1900s were rooted in this imagined opposition. For example, in the **Reading Wars**, **Whole Language**'s concern with meaning was pitted against the mechanical foci of phonics instruction. Similarly, in the **Math Wars**, the comprehension-oriented emphases of **Reform Mathematics** were presented as a challenge to the rote-calculation foci of traditional instruction. Similar tensions have arisen around most subject areas.

However, Whole Language, Reform Mathematics, and other trends associated with Authentic Education were never intended as *opposites* to more traditional approaches. Rather, they were offered as *complements* – that is, as additional elements that might support deeper understandings and more engaged learning. For this reason, it's important to re-emphasize that the Authentic Education movement does not prescribe content or dictate methods. Rather, its concern is more with approaches that might support learner agency and interest through more profound connections to the subject matter. Sometimes the best way to do that is to permit student-centered free exploration, and other times it may be through a teacher-centered lesson and accompanying practice exercises from a textbook.

Whole Language **is an approach to teaching literacy that emphasizes comprehension and meaning alongside traditional strategies for decoding (e.g., phonics, spelling, grammar).**

Reform Mathematics **is an approach to teaching numeracy that emphasizes conceptual thinking and problem solving alongside procedural competence.**

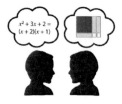

Surface learning *vs.* deep learning

The original impetus for public schooling was a need for a literate and numerate workforce, which is why the "3 R's" (reading, 'riting, and 'rithmetic) featured so prominently. On a cultural level, the original aim was to meet the needs of a newly industrialized society by equipping prospective workers with generic, instrumental literacies.

By the early 1900s, however, major economies had become more based in service than industry. As well, an emergent middle class was starting to demand more from schooling than a one-size-fits-all style of preparation. With these shifts, there was a dawning realization that mass schooling was overwhelmingly focused on what might be called "surface learning" – ends-driven, competence-focused, utilitarian, procedural, rote. This recognition, in turn, served as an impetus to parents, politicians, policy makers, and educational theorists, who began to call for more authentic approaches that might contribute to deeper learning. Some shifts in sensibility, from **surface learning** to **deep learning**, are summarized in the table below.

SURFACE LEARNING *vs.* DEEP LEARNING		
Surface Learner	QUALITY	**Deep Learner**
Learner is inattentive to why content might be important or how it might connect to what she or he already knows.	PERSONAL CONNECTION TO CONTENT	Learner consciously RELATES course material to past experiences, current understandings, and personal interests.
Learner sees course material as disconnected bits of knowledge – that is, as impersonal facts to be memorized or skills to perform.	VIEW OF CONTENT	Learner seeks to INTEGRATE knowledge, looking for patterns, connections, generalizations, and underlying principles – within and across disciplines.
Learner has no agency and regards facts and procedures as fixed – ceding authority to a teacher, textbook, or other external source.	ATTITUDE TOWARD AUTHORITY	Learner is open to new ideas, but willing to ENGAGE in critical exchanges with external authorities when incoherences or inconsistencies arise.
Learner memorizes and performs without reflecting on purposes of and strategies for learning.	SELF-AWARENESS AS A LEARNER	Learner is aware of her or his own understandings and able to REFLECT on her or his own processes of learning.

Of course, the frustration with these sorts of distinctions is that it would seem that the teacher has very little control over a learner's habits and dispositions. What do you do with a student who is lodged in a mindset of surface learning?

In fact, teachers can have a significant influence, and it all begins with an awareness that no one emerges from the womb as a surface learner. Every human is born with an aggressive desire to know more. In other words, surface learners aren't born; they're made. In particular, the objectified knowledge and depersonalizing methods associated with Standardized Education seem to be tailored to nurture surface learning. In response, many of the structures and practices associated with Authentic Education are intended to revive the innate drive to learn.

Perhaps the most researched contribution in this regard is **Carol Dweck**'s constructs of **fixed and growth mindsets**. Dweck was interested in the psychology of success and studied the beliefs and attitudes that different people bring to their learning and performance. She noticed two broad categories, persons with fixed mindsets and persons with growth mindsets. Some of their distinguishing qualities are summarized below:

FIXED MINDSET *vs.* GROWTH MINDSET		
Fixed Mindset	QUALITY	**Growth Mindset**
Ability is pregiven, gifted, static. Potential is defined at birth.	BELIEF ABOUT ABILITY	Ability is mutable, experience dependent, learned. Potential is created.
A challenge is a test where one must prove or validate one's abilities. They are threats that are better avoided.	ATTITUDE TOWARD CHALLENGES	A challenge is an opportunity to test and stretch one's abilities. They are to be sought out and embraced.
A failure or obstacle triggers resignation and withdrawal.	RESPONSE TO OBSTACLES	A failure or obstacle teaches about current levels of expertise and triggers persistence and increased effort.
Poor at estimating abilities, partly because unused to "trying" (which is seen as demonstrating inability).	AWARENESS OF ABILITIES	Accurate at estimating abilities, in large part because of constant self-testing of those abilities.
Correction is avoided, scorned, and ignored. Others are blamed for poor performances. Tendency to lie about poor outcomes.	RESPONSES TO CORRECTION	Correction is sought out and heeded. Accepts responsibility for successes and failures. Honest about evaluations.
Others are seen as competitors and their successes are taken as threats.	RESPONSES TO OTHERS' SUCCESSES	Others are seen as indicators of possibility and their successes are taken as inspirations and challenges.
Tendency to reach early plateaus.	TRAJECTORY TO SUCCESS	Tendency to manifest consistent growth.

Comparing this table to the previous one, it's apparent that a student with a fixed mindset is more likely to engage in surface learning and someone with a growth mindset will be more inclined toward deep learning.

For educators, perhaps the most important row in the above chart is the bottom one. Growth-mindset learners continue to improve, whereas fixed-mindset learners often stall in their development. Tracking learners over time, Dweck and others have accumulated evidence to show that the critical element in extraordinary performance is not innate ability, but mindset. Very "average" people can pull off some amazing feats if they can maintain a belief in their own possibilities.

That realization raises the issue of how teachers might contribute to learners' mindsets. To that end, Dweck and others have demonstrated that specific practices can significantly affect students' attitudes. For example, tasks and emphases that focus students' attentions on the dynamics of learning and knowing (rather than on themselves and their abilities or inabilities) are more likely to contribute to growth mindsets. As well, the teacher's own mindset is influential, as it will manifest itself in teaching. Some of these strategies are described in more detail in the chart:

TEACHER INFLUENCES ON FIXED MINDSET *vs.* GROWTH MINDSET		
Contributing to a Fixed Mindset	PRACTICE	**Contributing to a Growth Mindset**
Praise the ability. (Implicit message: "You have fixed traits, and I'm judging them.")	THE FOCUS OF PRAISE	Praise the effort. ("You are a developing person and I'm interested in your growth.")
Emphasize *objectified knowledge* – present static, right/wrong, fixed facts and procedures, without any indication of context and history. (Implicit message: "This information has nothing to do with you.")	THE NATURE OF THE CONCEPTS PRESENTED	Emphasize *emergent knowing* – include insights into the authors/artists/scientists behind the knowledge along with their situations, struggles, and triumphs. (Implicit message: "Someone, somewhere worked hard to come up with this, and that matters.")
Organize activities in uniform, graduated, and logically sequenced steps, and invite no learner input. (Implicit message: "You have no agency in the structure of your own education.")	STRUCTURE OF LEARNING TASKS	Create tasks that permit learners to adapt the level of difficulty and that afford opportunities to diverge or elaborate. (Implicit message: "You are an active agent in your own education.")
Permit statements that identify firm limits in ability – e.g., "I don't understand how to balance a chemical equation." (Implicit message: "My abilities end at that point.")	USE OF "YET"	Encourage the use of "yet" whenever limitations are identified – e.g., "I don't understand how to balance a chemical equation … yet." (Implicit message: "I am capable of figuring this out if I stick with it.")
Don't pause after a question is posed, communicating an expectation for immediate responses. (Implicit message: "I expect you to know already.")	USE OF WAIT TIME	Wait a minimum of 3 seconds after posing a question that demands thought. (Implicit message: "This question is important. I expect you to put some effort into thinking about your answer.")

The contents of this table hint at a burgeoning area of educational research – namely, the sorts of tasks, repetitions, and attitudes that contribute most significantly to enhanced understandings and performances.

Deliberate practice and metacognition

"Practice" is one of the most contested topics within Authentic Education. Unfortunately, the word is often associated with a hallmark of Standardized Education: uniform, rote, repetitive exercises designed to support automatized performance of routine procedures. It is thus not uncommon to hear blanket condemnations of practice from advocates of Authentic Education.

Those who argue against practice seem to be conflating an outcome (accurate, automatized performance) with a process (repetition) – and that's unfortunate, given that every learned competence across every category of ability can be improved through practice. The issue is not whether or not practice is useful (it is!), but the qualities of practice that contribute to enhanced possibilities.

The phrase **deliberate practice** has been taken up to refer to activities that are developed specifically to enhance awareness and improve performance. Significantly, deliberate practice is not geared toward mindless application and rote competence. Quite the opposite, in fact: it is a cognitively demanding engagement that supports deeper awareness and insight into what one is doing.

Deliberate practice is a mode that both increases fluidity and supports mindful attention to what one is doing. It is often contrasted with the rote practice of Standardized Education, which is intended to develop automaticity but not conceptual insight.

That is, the purpose of deliberate practice is *not* just fluidity, but an awareness of the nuances that enable and amplify a capability. Deliberate practice supports the knowing of both System 1 (memory-based) and System 2 (thinking-based). Deep, growth-oriented learning is dependent on an ongoing conversation between these two aspects of one's being. In blunt terms, the sort of repetitive practice that is geared only toward System-1 automaticity can arrest development by making it difficult or impossible for the learner to be consciously aware of the elements that contribute to a competence. Conversely, attempting to be explicit about everything involved with a knowing can be just as constraining. System 2's working memory is just too limited to be aware of every detail associated with expert performance.

So, how does one develop both System-1 fluidity and System-2 acuity?

A first step in answering this question is the realization that System 1 is easily bored and System 2 is easily frustrated. (These opposing responses of Systems 1 and 2 – that is, boredom and frustration – help to make sense of many children's conflicting reactions to Standardized Education.) Effective practice must present enough variation and complexity to be arousing, and yet not so much as to be overwhelming.

To accomplish this, the learner must be involved in defining the practice, and that practice must be **effortful**. That is, there has to be a genuine risk of failure (which keeps things from being boring), but a likelihood of success (which helps to minimize frustration). Learners must be encouraged to push to the edges of their abilities so that they can be aware of where those edges are. Critically, "failure" here is not being used in the sense that is typically associated with schools. Failures within effortful practice are not demeaning or defeating; they are informative and formative. Effortful practice also has a high cognitive demand, and so may require breaks and diversions to be maintained.

Effortful practice **is a mode of engagement where there is a genuine risk of failure. Properly structured, the failures associated with effortful practice are informative, not discouraging.**

A second important element for ensuring that failures are experienced as positive and informative is the presence of a teacher who can provide honest, constructive, and personally sensitive feedback on performances. All three elements are vital. Brutal honesty supports awareness of one's evolving competence; constructive advice helps the learner to channel attentions; appropriate sensitivity will ensure the learner continues to be engaged and challenged.

A third quality of deliberate practice is that there should be a lot of it. Across domains – academics, performing arts, sports – the single most significant factor that separates poor, average, and exceptional performances is the extent of effortful, supported rehearsal. Different studies have generated different numbers so there is no certainty over exactly how much deliberate practice is needed to achieve exceptionality, but the following are commonly reported:

- 1st-tier (world-class) performers: 24+ hours/week (~10,000 hours by age 18);
- 2nd-tier (masterful) performers: 15 hours/week (~5,000 hours by age 18);
- 3rd-tier (recognized expert) performers: 9 hours/ week (~3,500 hours by age 18).

Of course, few educational institutions are structured in ways that afford the extensive practice needed for the top two tiers. However – and perhaps shockingly – there is ample opportunity to support 3rd-tier levels within the 30+ hours that children spend at school each week.

There are also some important qualifications to be made on aspects of expert performance that are well outside the influence of the teacher or institution. For example, two common qualities of persons who develop outstanding expertise are that they typically begin early in life and that they are usually immersed in settings that value and support their emergent competencies. Additionally, while it is clear that exceptionality is vastly more a matter of extensive, supported practice than genetic endowment, there are elements of innate personal disposition that make a huge difference. In particular, the capacity to focus (and even to obsess) is broadly associated with extreme expertise.

To be clear, then, the suggestion is not that all teaching should be geared toward exceptional performance. Rather, it is that there are insights to be gained from the sorts of practice associated with outstanding performance. Three in particular merit emphasis:

Chunking refers to the expert's ability to make immediate sense of a complete scene. For example, a novice will see the above image as a series of notes, whereas the expert will recognize it at a glance as the start of Beethoven's *Für Elise*.

- System 1 and System 2 can be simultaneously educated, a realization that has relevance to all areas of human learning and all levels of expertise;
- deliberate practice enhances perception by supporting the ability to **chunk** – that is, to read a whole situation (a musical score, a hockey play, a classroom dynamic, etc.) rapidly and accurately as a single unit, enabling an expert response;
- deliberate practice enhances memory, as stronger, more extensive, and more intricately networked associations are established.

These sorts of enhanced competencies are all aspects of a learnable disposition known as **metacognition**, a knowing about knowing or awareness of awareness. In particular, they illustrate two main components to metacognition: knowing about cognition and regulation of cognition. The former encompasses attentiveness to study skills, patterns of attention, reasoning strategies, memory capabilities, and other aspects of learning. The latter includes such abilities as self-monitoring, self-assessing, self-challenging, and self-pacing – and, importantly, it is quite different from the focus on one's own ego known as self-consciousness. Metacognition is about awarenesses of one's learning processes, not the sort of acute identity-centeredness that overwhelms learning by consuming working memory with thoughts about one's self.

Metacognition **refers to an awareness of cognitive processes. Within education, it is often seen as a valuable competence, enabling one to be aware of (and therefore able to modify and enhance and regulate) strategies for solving problems, engagement in learning, understandings of key principles, and so on.**

So … what's a Piagetian task?

Jean Piaget is perhaps the most-cited researcher and educator within the Authentic Education movement, which is why his name is so prominently associated with task structures and pedagogical strategies aligned with this moment in education.

Before delving into some of the key features of a Piagetian task, it's appropriate to mention other prominent authors of the Authentic Education movement. Notables include:

- in France, **Jean Jacques Rousseau**, whose book *Emile, or On Education* (1762) is still required reading in many education programs;
- in Germany, **Friedrich Fröbel**, who initiated the experience- and exploration-rich Kindergarten in the early 1800s;
- in Italy, **Maria Montessori**, whose insights into human learning continue to be employed in schools around the world that bear her name;
- in England, **A.S. Neill**, whose 1960 book *Summerhill: A Radical Approach to Child Rearing* was one of the most influential texts in education in the 1900s;
- in the United States, **John Dewey**, who was easily the most influential educational thinker in North America in the 1900s.

Many others could be mentioned. Unfortunately space prohibits us from doing that, and from discussing particular contributions and divergences.

Instead we highlight four major points of agreement that, considered together, offer a strong description of what has come to be called a Piagetian task.

Firstly, learning experiences should be **developmentally appropriate**. That means, for example, that thinking strategies and pedagogical methods should be different between primary schools and middle schools, between middle schools and universities, and so on.

Secondly, efforts should be made to coordinate concepts with the bodily activities that align with them. This advice is perhaps best developed within mathematics education, with its current emphasis on the timely use of manipulative tools, but it extends to all disciplines. The underlying principle, as developed in Chapter 2.2, is that all abstract knowing is rooted in bodily experience – and while educators must be careful not to reduce sophisticated concepts to physical actions, attending to the embodied elements of understanding can contribute greatly to insights. (Further details can be found by searching **active learning, manipulatives, gesture studies**, and **embodied learning**.)

Thirdly, learning tasks should introduce new variation to learners, but care should be taken to limit the extent of variation at any single step. Compare, for example, the following exercises designed for a first lesson on equivalent ratios:

According to popular belief, people generally remember ...

10% of what they **read**
20% of what they **hear** — PASSIVE LEARNING
30% of what they **see**
50% of what they **see & hear**
70% of what they **say & write** — ACTIVE LEARNING
90% of what they **do**

Active learning refers to modes of structuring lessons that place responsibility for learning on learners. Distinguished from the largely passive learning of Standardized Education, active learning involves activities that go beyond listening and watching. These include reading, writing, discussing, and problem solving along with higher-order thinking tasks that demand analysis, synthesis, evaluation, and the creation of new knowledge.

APPLYING VARIATION THEORY	
Varying one aspect	**Varying many aspects**
$2:2 = 1:1$	$2:2 = 1:1$
$16:16 = 1:1$	$4:8 :: 1:2$
$a:a = 1:1$	9 to 7 can be written $9:7$
$\pi r^2 : \pi r^2 = 1:1$	$15/3 = 20:4$

In the instances on the left, it's obvious what the teacher hopes the learner will discern. By contrast, on the right there is so much variation it's not at all clear what is being taught. Humans are naturally inclined to look for difference and change, but that tendency can be overwhelmed by too much variety. (Further details can be found by searching **variation theory**.)

Finally, perhaps the strongest point of agreement of the educators mentioned above is that schooling should be *learner-centered* – which is not the same as *learner-directed*. While it is important to remember that the learner determines the meanings of experiences, the inexperienced learner should not be expected to define an educational trajectory. The teacher is more culturally aware, and so has a greater responsibility for selecting and structuring learners' experiences in ways that prompt learners toward knowings that are useful and fitting in society. The following are among the qualities of a learner-centered task:

- Learning tasks should be *differentiated* for learners.
- Learning tasks should be *variable entry* – that is, differentiable by learners, enabling them to adjust levels of challenge and depths of engagement.
- Learner-specific abilities and difficulties should be taken into consideration and addressed as early as possible. (Further details can be found by searching **Personalized Learning**, **Individual Learning Plans [ILP]**, **Response to Intervention [RtI]**, **Differentiated Instruction**, and **Multiple Intelligences Theory**.)

These sorts of suggestions are often collected together in advice for learner-specific educational programs – that is, strategies for engagement structured around strengths, weaknesses, interests, and so on.

No doubt, such expectations will appear onerous at first glance. Structuring and monitoring plans for 25–30 learners at a time is considerably more demanding than organizing and delivering a series of standardized lessons. However, there is an additional detail to consider. The shift from Standardized Education to Authentic Education is more than a shift in what the teacher does. The learner also has responsibilities. No longer seen as a passive agent to be controlled, the learner who is presented with choices, challenges, and appropriate supports is expected to play an active role in defining the structures and outcomes of schooling experience. That is, not all of the responsibility falls on the shoulders of the teacher. Rather, the teacher is expected to

Differentiated Instruction **is a framework for providing different routes through learning, usually within the same classroom. There are different versions, some of which align better with Standardized Education than Authentic Education, but all are based on the conviction that learners should be able to participate in selecting and structuring aspects of their learning experiences.**

design tasks in ways that enable and compel learners to select, define, and adjust possibilities.

This approach to teaching is built on the realization that humans have natural penchants for questioning, experimenting, and theory making. If curiosity can be ignited and conditions for investigation provided, learners are likely to engage. For that reason, **inquiry** is one of the more prominently encountered strategies within the Authentic Education movement. (Further details can be found by searching **Inquiry-Based Learning**, **Problem-Based Learning**, **Project Method**, and **Guided Discovery**.)

The inquiry method begins with authentic questions and problems – where "authentic" entails both genuine relevance to learners and substantial learning in order to arrive at some manner of resolution. The teacher's role in inquiry-based learning is most commonly described as FACILITATING – that is, literally, "making easy" – the inquiry process by helping to clarify questions, hone strategies, gather resources, and interpret results. Somewhat ironically, the more vital aspect of inquiry-based teaching is the task of CHALLENGING – that is, the opposite of "making easy." In the spirit of deliberate practice, teachers must be available to contest assumptions, reframe interpretations, present contradictions, and so on. The currently popular metaphor of GUIDING is intended to capture both the FACILITATING and CHALLENGING dimensions of this attitude.

Such GUIDING is not an "anything-goes" approach to classroom experience. On the contrary, there are disciplinary rules to be followed and there are established insights that must be honored. The teacher is responsible for assisting learners to appreciate these elements by, for example, involving them in structured critiques of one another's writing, presenting defensible arguments of mathematical insights, or executing empirical experiments. In this way, students simultaneously learn about the processes and the content of a living discipline. As well, ideally, they come to see themselves as agents in their own learning and in the grander project of knowledge production.

The *inquiry method* is focused on student-driven questions, in which the teacher avoids giving direct answers. Rather, the teacher aims to keep the questioning going by orienting learners to relevant sources of information, helping structure experiments, helping to interrogate assumptions, and so on.

Authentic assessment

The inquiry approach highlights a key orienting principle of Authentic Education – namely that learners should be understood in terms of their sufficiencies rather than their deficiencies. They are not CONTAINERS that require filling or INCOMPLETE HUMANS that need to be finished. Rather, they are ACTIVE AGENTS in the creation and maintenance of their worlds. Within this frame assessment is not at all about identifying shortcomings or ranking learners. Rather, assessment is understood as an ongoing formative process.

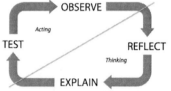

For many, the phrase **authentic assessment** is a reference to real-world situations that are relevant to the learner. More broadly, however, it is used to distinguish standardized evaluations from tasks designed to support learner agency, engagement, and metacognition. As such, the vital feature of an authentic assessment is that it be aimed toward upcoming learning experiences, not summing up past ones.

Guided discovery (or *discovery learning*) is another name for *inquiry learning*. Unfortunately, the use of "discovery" in the title has resulted in many errors in interpretation – because, when viewed through a Standardized Education lens, it looks like children are expected to rediscover insights that took humanity millenia to develop.

Owing to such confusions, advocates tend to opt for phrases such as "guided inquiry" and "problem-based learning."

One of the major challenges of Authentic Education is around what a teacher should do when there is evidence that a learner's understanding of a necessary concept is inadequate to move to more sophisticated topics. A popular example in discussions of this issue is illustrated with the image below. If a ball is rolled off a cliff, which path will it follow (ignoring air resistance)?

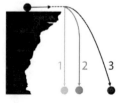

Across ages, *most* people select Path 1, a significant minority opts for Path 2, and a smaller minority chooses Path 3. For the purpose of understanding core concepts in introductory physics, it's important that learners appreciate why they should select Path 3. If they don't develop that appreciation, physics may become more a matter of rule following than a rich and powerful means to make sense of many aspects of the physical world.

Unfortunately, telling people their answer is wrong is rarely an effective way of helping them rethink the phenomenon. Too often, that response prompts learners to select Path 3 when in science class, even while maintaining a belief in their first response – in effect, forcing segregations rather than integrations of their knowing.

Once again, beliefs and understandings are derived from deep histories. That makes them highly resistant to change. They will persist as long as they're personally viable, which means that an important part of the assessment process is to anticipate the sorts of experiences that might invite desired accommodations to existing schema. (In this case, a student-directed inquiry into the trajectories of falling objects might be a good way to go.)

As this example illustrates, assessment activities are so central to teaching within the frame of Authentic Education that the words *teaching* and *assessing* might be considered synonymous. More descriptively, perhaps, teaching might construed more in terms of LISTENING than TELLING in the inquiry-based classroom – where the reference is a LISTENING TO the associations and construals that contribute to a learner's actions and articulations rather than a LISTENING FOR specific details. It is an attitude oriented toward appreciating the complexities of a learner's understandings for the purposes of designing experiences that invite elaboration.

This mode of teaching might be aptly described in terms of ORIENTING THE LEARNER'S AWARENESS. By POINTING and REMINDING, the teacher helps the learning to focus attentions, hold details in consciousness, explore implications of new associations – in brief, to notice possibilities that might not have been previously noticed.

Portfolio-based assessment involves a purposeful collection of student work that presents a record of efforts and development over time. (Portfolio means, literally, "carrier for leaves of paper.") The student takes part in choosing, explaining, and regularly updating the contents. The intention is to offer a nuanced portrait of insights and growth while supporting self-directed learning.

Teacher disciplinary knowledge

In the early stages of public schooling, teacher education consisted entirely of more advanced study in a discipline. To teach one simply needed to know more of the subject than the one being taught.

The inadequacy of that perspective was soon obvious. In their factory-like classrooms, teachers also had to be managers who oversaw and controlled the learning outcomes, behaviors, and other aspects of efficient functioning. Consequently, lesson planning, classroom management, and other skills were soon central parts of teacher education programs.

Both these emphases – that is, on more advanced disciplinary knowledge and on management skills – are seen as ill-informed and misdirected within the frame of Authentic Education. The issue is not so much that they're "wrong"; it's more that they are patently inadequate for understanding the complexity of teaching. An emphasis on management skills, for example, ignores the nature of human relationships, generally, and the **pedagogical relationship**, in particular. Regarding disciplinary knowledge, an exclusive focus on more advanced study betrays an ignorance of the fact that most disciplines are developed to be used, not to be taught. In the process, meandering paths toward difficult insights have been edited out, leaving abstract formulations that conceal their real complexity. In other words, there is a huge difference between *knowing a discipline* (a System-1 competence) and *learning a discipline* (mainly a System-2 undertaking).

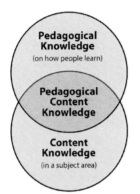

Pedagogical content knowledge (PCK) refers to an awareness of the metaphors, images, and other associations that are most likely to enable a learner to make coherent and appropriate sense of a concept. It is distinct from disciplinary mastery, which is more about automaticity with tightly packed concepts (System 1) than explicit awareness of the elements that constitute those concepts (System 2).

With emerging appreciation of the profound differences between experts and novices, it is now recognized that the effective teacher is AN EXPERT WHO CAN THINK LIKE A NOVICE. That is, the teacher has developed some of the qualities of an expert's knowledge, including intricate connectedness, deep automaticity, and chunking ability. At the same time, these System-1 skills are still available for conscious (System-2) analysis and application, so that the teacher has ready access to the metaphors, analogies, images, examples, exemplars, demonstrations, and other instantiations that render a subject comprehensible to others. This realm of **pedagogical content knowledge** is one of the most vibrant topics within current educational research.

As for the traditional obsessions with classroom management, the Authentic Education movement responds that needs to control children only arise when they are compelled to engage in activities that are not meaningful and productive. Very, very few children lack the capacity for deep engagement – in fact, the ones identified as being the most misbehaved are often the ones who can muster the most focus. Consequently, teacher education programs are seeing an increased emphasis on designing Piagetian tasks and a diminished concern with classroom control (much to the chagrin of some teacher candidates whose sensibilities are lodged in Standardized Education).

Given the vastness and dynamic character of teacher knowledge, teacher education in this frame is typically understood more in terms of nurturing an open disposition than acquiring mastery. This is not to say there are not well-defined things to learn; it is merely an acknowledgement that a teacher's education is career long. An initial certification program can orient, but it can't begin to pre-equip anyone with everything needed to teach. Common emergent themes in teacher education thus revolve around what might be understood as the deliberate practice of teaching – that is, educating both System 1 and System 2. (Further details can be found by searching **Reflective Practice**, **Lifelong Learning**, and **Teacher as Researcher**.)

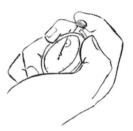

Just-in-Time Teaching **refers to another set of strategies aimed at encouraging the learner to take responsibility for learning. It revolves around structured feedback that links in-class work to work done at home, with the intention of enhancing motivation, improving focus, and supporting the teacher's efforts to adapt tasks to the student's needs and interests.**

Back to the research

As already noted, one of the grand ironies of Authentic Education is that it stands as a challenge to virtually every defining element of Standardized Education – and in particular to its rigid curriculum, its uniform pedagogy, and its culture of examination. Yet, as noted at the end of Chapter 1.3, even when constrained by these structures and evaluated by these standards, meta-analyses of educational research indicate that strategies and emphases associated with Authentic Education are more effective.

Of course, that's not surprising, given its attentiveness to the way that humans actually learn.

That emphasis on learning is certainly the strength of the Authentic Education movement. However, it is also one of its weaknesses. A focus on learning has eclipsed a critical awareness of the actual content of schooling – and so, at the same time we have witnessed dramatic improvements to strategies for teaching, the content of formal education has grown more and more out of step with societal evolution.

As we explore in Moments 3 and 4, more recent educational movements have arisen around this matter, in the process reframing formal school as an enterprise fraught with deep and difficult ethical issues.

Suggestions for delving deeper

1. The phrase "back-to-basics" is, most often, a call to return to the emphases and practices of Standardized-Education. Such movements are common, especially when standardized test results reveal slippages in rankings or scores. From a perspective of Authentic Education, what sort of response might help invite back-to-basics advocates into a more nuanced consideration of the issues?

2. Several descriptions and metaphors of teaching have been mentioned in this chapter – among them, FACILITATING, CHALLENGING, GUIDING, LISTENING, ORIENTING THE LEARNER'S AWARENESS, and EXPERT THINKING LIKE A NOVICE. How do these notions fit with your conception of teaching? Has your understanding shifted since your answered a similar question at the end of Moment 1?

3. As mentioned, pedagogical content knowledge is one of the most prominent foci of current educational inquiry. For an area of your teaching interest, do some research into the distinction between disciplinary content knowledge and pedagogical content knowledge.

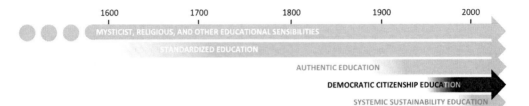

| 1600 | 1700 | 1800 | 1900 | 2000 |

MYSTICIST, RELIGIOUS, AND OTHER EDUCATIONAL SENSIBILITIES

STANDARDIZED EDUCATION

AUTHENTIC EDUCATION

DEMOCRATIC CITIZENSHIP EDUCATION

SYSTEMIC SUSTAINABILITY EDUCATION

MOMENT 3 •

democratic citizenship education

In brief ...

The term "Democratic Citizenship Education" refers to those approaches to schooling that are attentive to collective process and cultural inequities. Informed mainly by the social sciences, its principal aims are to promote social justice and productive collective action, in part through recognizing and (where appropriate) subverting hegemonic structures.

3.1 • The context ...

Starting in the 1800s and culminating in the mid-1900s, a series of civil rights movements helped to awaken public awareness to a range of social inequities rooted in popular ideologies and mythologies. Schools were implicated as they were shown to do more to perpetuate social conditions and uncritical prejudices than to challenge them.

3.2 • On knowledge and learning ...

With major influences coming from Marxism and antipositivism, knowledge was framed as SOCIAL CONSTRUCTIONS that are unavoidably partial – that is, as both incomplete and biased. Learning was recast as PARTICIPATION in and INDUCTION into a culture's discourses.

3.3 • On teaching ...

Paralleling the assertion that knowledge is partial, teaching took on two emphases, on participation and conscientization. That is, teaching is seen as a process of EMPOWERING by involving learners in participatory projects and through RAISING AWARENESSES of situations.

Take a glimpse ...

Suggested YouTube searches: [sociocultural theory] [participatory culture] [critical theory] [critical pedagogy]

activism	activity theory	civil rights movements
apprenticing	actor–network theory	critical theory
conscientization	anticlassism	cultural studies
coopetition	antiracism	feminism
critical pedagogy	antisexism	globalization
critical reflection	critical discourse theory	information age
dialogic learning	distributed cognition	knowledge economy
diversity education	Frankfurt School	Marxism
emancipating	hegemony	participatory democracy
empowering	hidden curriculum	postcolonialism
free schools	participatory culture	postmodernism
networks of practice	power	poststructuralism
peer critique	situated learning	social sciences
praxis	social constructionism	semiotics
PLCs	social contracts	technical revolution
scaffolding	sociocultural learning	
ZPD		

HISTORY & CONTEXT

KNOWLEDGE & LEARNING

DESCRIBING & PRESCRIBING TEACHING

DEMOCRATIC CITIZENSHIP EDUCATION

iconic visual metaphor:
COLLECTIVE COHERING
AROUND A SHARED FOCUS

3.1 The Emergence of Democratic Citizenship Education

Social justice refers to the fair treatments of all persons, irrespective of ethnic origins, gender, possessions, race, faith, sexual orientation, and so on. While a modern notion, it appears to be rooted in a conviction, encountered in many ancient belief systems, that all are created equal.

During the 1800s, **social justice** emerged as a topic of intense concern and widespread discussion among the citizens of the industrialized world, and for good reason. While a great deal of wealth had been created through the expansion of trade markets, the exploitation of new territories, and the streamlining of manufacturing, very little of it had worked its way to the working class. Instead, it was almost entirely held by the nobility along with a new social class of capitalists, which included merchants, industrialists, bankers, and other entrepreneurs. The distribution was so inequitable that the living conditions of many citizens actually worsened as wealth accrued.

Other reasons for the mounting interest in social justice included the emergence of mass communication (enabled by printing presses and postal services) and the rise of nation states that were founded on such democratic principles as equality of citizens, freedom of speech, and justice for all. In the United States, the French Republic, and other countries, monarchies were displaced and laws were enacted that reduced the privilege of the already advantaged and gave new rights and protections to the disadvantaged.

The plight of many children was a topic of particular prominence within these transformations of governmental structures, as is abundantly evident in the most popular source of entertainment at the time. Novels from the era, such as Charles Dickens' (1838) *Oliver Twist* and Victor Hugo's (1862) *Les misérables*, brought readers into the worlds of children who were exploited by the labor market, recruited into criminal activities, and otherwise abused – sometimes through the very institutions designed to protect them.

With the raising of public consciousness to such matters, governments responded with legislation to protect children. As might be expected, formal education figured prominently in these efforts. In the process, understandings of the role of schooling began to undergo subtle elaborations in both popular and political arenas, as its established purpose of preparing children for work life was extended to include some responsibility for social justice. It was argued that schools must do more than provide access to knowledge; they should also provide access to opportunity. Formal education quickly came to be described as an equalizer, a means by which the disenfranchised-but-diligent could gain access to cultural capital and raise their station.

Since being introduced, the notion that education can level the economic playing field by enabling individuals to transcend their situations has become ubiquitous and commonsensical. The belief is so prevalent that it has almost completely eclipsed an immense transformation in thinking about the nature of social class that unfolded through the 1800s. Two hundred years ago in the industrialized world, social class was widely regarded as part of the natural order – that is, the way things were supposed to be. In essence, the belief was that the universe had decreed that some people (and their descendants) were naturally superior and thus destined to have advantage. Within this mindset, the social class into which one is born is the class to which one belongs. Rigid cultural barriers were erected to block interclass movement. And even though this attitude is now considered foreign and nonsensical to most in developed nations, it continues in force in many locations in the world.

The erosion of this belief in most of the wealthy, industrialized world can be attributed in large part to formal education, which has indeed proven to be an effective means for some individuals to transcend the conditions of their youth. Such successes, however, are uneven. In fact, they remain more the exception than the rule. For the most part, children grow up and inhabit the same socioeconomic classes as their parents.

The word *equal* is derived from the Latin *aequus*, "level, even, just." Ironically, it is also a meaning that is entangled in the web of normality and linearity, critiqued in Chapter 1.2, and this realization has prompted many commentators to opt for the notion of *fairness* over *equality* as the principal aim of social justice. *Equal* ("same for all") and *fair* (from roots meaning "unblemished," as in fair skin, and hence "morally pure") invoke quite distinct networks of association, one very mechanical and the other decidedly more organic.

For the huge majority, schooling has not proven to be a great equalizer in any way.

As discussed in more detail in the next few chapters, it has been argued that public schooling actually operates as a barrier to the aspirations of most. Among educators, this realization began to rise to prominence in the mid-1900s, paralleling a series of civil rights movements that helped to raise public awareness of social inequities tethered to race, class, and gender.

A hope of these movements was to bring public policy in line with the well-established rhetoric of equality and justice. As one might expect, once again the public school was seen to have an important role to play. Schools should do more than prepare children for adult life and to afford opportunities for the diligent to transcend their circumstances. They should also, it was argued, help to nurture social mindedness. They must educate for democratic citizenship.

Partiality, ethicality, diversity

As former public school teachers, all three of us are deeply familiar with the seemingly endless sequence of educational fads, often characterized in terms of a swinging pendulum.

There's a good reason for that characterization, and it has to do with the tension set up in the 1900s between Standardized Education and Authentic Education. With its emphasis on preparing appropriately skilled and compliant workers, Standardized Education is most focused on serving the needs of society. By contrast, the emphasis within Authentic Education is on supporting each learner's interests and potentials. The movement is geared toward serving the needs of the individual.

In a nutshell, then, virtually every trend over the past century that has been experienced by teachers as an oscillating pendulum can be traced back to the fundamental dichotomy of society *vs.* self that resides in the tension between a Standardized Education and an Authentic Education.

An education that is focused on Democratic Citizenship steers around this empty and endless debate in the recognition that society unfolds from and is enfolded in

While the contrasts between Standardized Education and Authentic Education serve to foreground an individualist–collectivist tension, this conflict isn't new. It was already a topic of debate among the ancient Greeks, and was particularly apparent in the very different educational systems of Sparta and Athens.

Rather than letting itself oscillate between the poles of this debate, Democratic Citizenship Education reframes its terms, foregrounding that societies unfold from and are enfolded in selves.

individuals. In this frame, the this-or-that, individual-*vs.*-collective, self-*vs.*-society dichotomies that keep the educational pendulum swinging are argued to be empty and unproductive. Culture arises in the interactions of selves, and so even if one wanted to do so, it would be impossible to create an educational system that completely ignored individuality or collectivity.

The discourse of Democratic Citizenship Education thus reframes the role of the school. Long seen as an institution designed to perpetuate cultural needs and social values, this movement has helped to reveal how the school actually participates in the creation of values and possibilities. The school is not a cog in the machinery of society; it is a vibrant part of the body politic.

That means that schooling is a participant in shaping culture, and this realization means that the educational project is entangled in ethics. As explored through Moment 3, this sensibility has many implications – including the transformation of structures that give advantage to some while disabling others, curricula that privilege the beliefs of a dominant culture, and teaching methods that are fitted to the habits and expectations of specific groups.

More accurately, Democratic Citizenship Education expands the conversation to include both what is explicitly taught and what is implicitly taught within schools. Perhaps the most significant contribution of this movement is the realization that there is a **hidden curriculum** associated with every official, state-sanctioned curriculum. That is, students are taught far more than the content listed in programs of study. While they are learning about such explicit topics as their nation's history, how to structure an essay, how to factor quadratics, and why the sun appears to rise every morning, they are also steeped in an implicit curriculum on how to behave, how to relate to one another, and what to expect in life. These learnings are embodied in the ways desks are arranged, in the sorts of classroom resources used, in assessment tools, in teaching practices, through course offerings, and in every other structure that is enacted in the school.

In concise terms, *what* one is taught can't be separated from *how* one is taught.

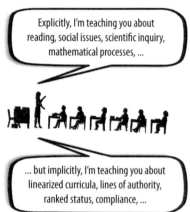

Explicitly, I'm teaching you about reading, social issues, scientific inquiry, mathematical processes, ...

... but implicitly, I'm teaching you about linearized curricula, lines of authority, ranked status, compliance, ...

A *hidden curriculum* is a side effect of a formal education. The term refers to lessons that are learned but not openly intended. These include norms, values, and beliefs that are implicit in curriculum foci, classroom resources, institutional structures, grading practices, and teaching methods.

In popular parlance, *discourse* usually refers to modes of communication. Within academic domains associated with Democratic Citizenship Education, the term refers more specifically to the entire ecosystem modes of communication, vocabularies, belief structures, and so on that frame what is knowable, doable, and be-able.

Competing discourses are always in play.

We go into much more detail on this point in the next two chapters. For now, we want to highlight some of the thinking behind it. In particular, it's important to be aware that the notion of a *hidden curriculum* is not a *hidden agenda*; it isn't pointing to an insidious plot in education that is being managed by some covert, sinister power. On the contrary, while not entirely accidental (since prevailing classroom practices and curriculum content continue to be reflective of early industrialism and the need for minimally literate workers), the hidden curriculum is more a matter of the limitations of human consciousness than anything else. As developed in Chapter 2.2, humans can only be consciously aware of a thin, thin slice of their experience, and so the hidden curriculum mostly comprises aspects of schooling that have been allowed to fall out of awareness. They weren't suppressed; they were simply forgotten.

We have already offered several examples of this forgetting, such as the implicit ways that knowing and learning are understood. Indeed, this book is driven by a Democratic Citizenship Education sensibility – namely that there is an obligation to be critical of one's inherited assumptions and, through that awareness, seek more encompassing, more powerful alternatives. To illustrate, using the example of learning, as noted in Moment 1, within the Standardized Education mindset, learners are typically described in terms of *deficiency* that must be corrected, completed, filled, or traversed. Within the Authentic Education movement, it is recast in terms of *sufficiency*, whereby learners are challenged to elaborate their adequate-but-evolving webs of understanding. Within a frame of Democratic Citizenship Education, the learner is seen in a different way still, as neither deficient nor sufficient, but as *partial* – that is, in the twofold sense of the word as *incomplete* and *biased*.

With regard to the first of these two meanings, the individual knowings are recognized to be fragmentary – but that doesn't mean they're deficient (in the sense that is implicit in Standardized Education). Rather, this sense of partiality points to the way the knowledge is distributed among humans, with each person participating in a planetary web of knowing. That each person's knowing is partial is seen as a strength, not a deficiency. It is partiality that places every human in dynamic and dependent relationship with every other human. We need one another, and so education is about both opportunity and obligation.

As for the second of the meanings, partial as *biased*, Democratic Citizenship Education embodies the realization that every action in the world is prejudiced – that is, oriented by pre-judgments. In this sense, it is impossible to have a clear, unbiased view of the world. Everyone is prejudiced, and most prejudices are absolutely necessary. They are the expectations, the beliefs, and the assumptions that are rooted in each person's unique-but-culturally-embedded histories. They enable thought as they are imposed on the world automatically without conscious mediation, opening up possibilities for creative action by freeing up working memory. At the same time, prejudices can completely shut down possibilities.

We are trying to be cautious in our explanations of these two meanings of partiality. To re-emphasize, *partiality* is a reference neither to the assumption of learner deficiency with Standardized Education nor to the construct of learner sufficiency within Authentic Education. It is neither. Rather, our use of the notion of partiality is to foreground that schooling is an ethical enterprise. The critical issue for educators is *not* that humans are partial, but that humans so often fail to notice their partialities. Such ignorance can open the door for dangerous attitudes – believing that enough is known, being blind to enacted ideologies, not putting forward the effort to make sense of other worldviews, and so on.

This point cannot be understated. Until the emergence Democratic Citizenship Education, the topic of ethics was either completely ignored (within Standardized Education) or minimized (within Authentic Education, where it was considered only insofar as it related to the rights of the individual). As might be expected, it is a core thematic within Democratic Citizenship Education – and an important topic within this theme is the critical part played by the individual in the whole.

The word *prejudice* is usually used and heard in negative terms. Here, it is intended as a matter-of-fact quality, not a criticism. Derived originally from the Latin for "pre-judgment," prejudice is used to highlight that every perception, every interpretation, every action is conditioned by prior, culturally situated experiences. These experiences channel what is noticeable, thinkable, doable.

Without prejudice, one would be unable to act. In this sense, prejudices are both enabling and constraining.

Participation and conscientization

Unfortunately, insights around *partiality* and *ethics* are difficult to translate into curriculum and pedagogy. What/how does one teach in manners that do not simply replace one set of partialities with another or that risks superimposing one group's system of ethics onto that of a different group?

In response to such concerns, proponents of Democratic Citizenship Education have avoided the temptation to prescribe curriculum content or teaching methods, and have instead focused on:

- **participation** – that is, understanding one's part in the social dynamics of learning, including the collective processes through which knowledge is produced; and
- **conscientization** – that is, the cultural dimensions of learning, focusing in particular on the privilegings and partialities that are knitted into established patterns of acting.

These two emphases are deeply complementary, perhaps even overlapping. However, they tend to be treated separately in the educational literature. As will be explicated in Chapter 3.2, the topic of participation is most often encountered in discussions of **sociocultural theories of learning**, whereas conscientization is the domain of **critical pedagogy**. One is focused on how minds are cultured, the other on how culture should be minded.

Before digging into these two emphases, it's probably worth noting that they are drawn from branches of study that are different from the usual sources for educators, at least through most of the 1900s. When the three of us were earning our Bachelor of Education degrees and in the 1970s and early 1980s, the field of education was explicitly defined as an "applied psychology" (and, more recently, as "applied neuropsychology"). In other words, the major conceptual influences were seen to be domains that inquire into the complexities of the individual psyche – which helps to explain why there is such a strong, individualistic flavor to modern schooling.

In fact, where collective processes were noticed,

Conscientization **was coined by Brazilian educator and activist, Paulo Freire to refer to the process of becoming aware of social and political contradictions, thus enabling and motivating informed action against the oppressive elements in one's life.**

they tended to be criticized and efforts were made to minimize them. Examples include **peer pressure** (a group-based force that suppresses good judgment in one's efforts to belong) and **groupthink** (a sort of mob mentality that "turns off" one's educated awarenesses). From the vantage of the individual, any process that diminishes personal autonomy is likely to be seen as bad.

Proponents of Democratic Citizenship Education acknowledge the perils of mindless following, but criticize this tendency to ground education in discourses of the psyche as ignoring the manner in which *all* personal action has a social dimension. A psychology-driven approach to education might seem to be justified by the fact that humans tend to experience themselves as individuals who are insulated from one another. However, somewhat paradoxically, it turns out that this sense of isolated individuality is utterly dependent on a culture for its realization. In particular, the cultural tool of language plays a powerful role in processes of individuation and self-identification. As such, there has been a broad recognition that education must also draw on areas of research that offer insights into the complexities of social and cultural phenomena, including sociology and anthropology. In this sense, and within the frame of Democratic Citizenship Education, teaching might also be described as a sort of "applied socio-anthropology." The notions of participation and conscientization are certainly reflective of this attitude.

Chapters 3.2 and 3.3 are devoted to explicating these notions in the context of schooling. For now, it is useful to know that the construct of **participatory culture** has been developed to underscore that influences between an individual and a collective always flow in both directions. As **Henry Jenkins** has explained, participatory culture is one that, among other qualities, manifests the following:

- It has relatively low barriers for creative expression and civic engagement.
- It has strong support for creating and sharing creations with others.
- It has some type of mentorship to pass the expertise of the most experienced to novices.

The word *participatory* first entered popular usage in the phrase "participatory democracy," used within student protests of the 1960s. Since then, it has been taken up in many domains, including education where it has lost its activist edge.

Participatory has the same deep roots as *partial*, namely the Latin *pars*, "part" – and the sense of being part of a grander whole is critical to understanding the notion. Being participatory is much more than playing a role; it is also about sharing in, partaking of, contributing to, and sharing responsibility for.

- Members believe their contributions matter.
- Members feel some degree of social connection with one another.

This particular list was published online in 2006, and both the means and the timing are important. It was at the historical moment that the Internet was shifting from a one-way source of information to a multidirectional communication-and-information system. That is, the Internet had come to offer an unprecedented platform for participation – to work collaboratively with others, to generate and share knowledge, to connect with people with similar interests – and this amplification of communicative and collaborative possibilities is having some major impacts on educational practice.

Online collaborations are living demonstrations of how humans can put their minds together to create new possibilities. In contrast to earlier collective efforts, digitally mediated co-laboring has the advantage of leaving detailed traces of the sorts of supports that are most useful, the sorts of contributions that move things along, and the sorts of behaviors that enable healthy communities. This information, in turn, is useful for the development of theories of learning that focus on such collective dimensions as interpersonal dynamics, the roles of technologies, and the processes of apprenticing.

These details are particularly evident to us as we craft this book. The first edition, written in the late 1990s, was anchored to our readings of print-based refereed publications and it was assembled in rooms lined with shelves of books and journals. As we were writing the second edition, nearly ten years later, we once again drew principally on refereed publications – with one major shift. We were able to access most of these online through our university libraries. For this edition, the big transformation is that we are expending much less energy on propping up arguments and defending claims by referring to refereed publications and much more energy on pointing to freely available online sources and resources that, we hope, will enable an interested reader to pursue topics of interest.

One of Democratic Citizenship Education's strongest influences was known as the *Frankfurt School*, a consortium of scholars in the first half of the 1900s. Members of this school aimed to integrate works of such varied thinkers as Immanuel Kant, Karl Marx, Sigmund Freud, Jean-Paul Sartre, and Jürgen Habermas, among many others. This range of influence highlights that critical theory is attentive to a range of discourses, including antipositivism, Marxism, sociology, psychoanalysis, existentialism, and postmodernism.

That is, in terms of visual metaphor, we're not trying to place this document on top of a heap of published literature, but endeavoring to situate it as a node in a vast and evolving network of knowledge. And our hope is that you will see yourself as more than a recipient of information, but also recognize the opportunity and obligation to pursue details that interest and irk you. Search engines, social networking sites, and instant communications have opened up incredible possibilities that weren't there even a decade ago. It is thus that we recognize this book's creative contribution to be mainly a matter of connecting and pointing, not arguing and defending – and this way of looking at knowledge production is having a more and more significant impact on school practices, especially as the sea of readily accessible information grows deeper and the tools to sift through that information become more powerful.

However, within Democratic Citizenship Education, it is not enough to be keeping pace with ever-evolving possibilities. It's also critically important to be mindful of how one's identity is shaped and how one participates in shaping others' identities through participation in knowledge systems. That is, educators have a responsibility to support conscientization – a critical consciousness.

The word **conscientization** was coined by Brazilian educator and activist **Paulo Freire** in the late 1960s, and he used it to refer to a core goal of a critical education. Engaged citizens, he argued, must have the intellectual skills – which include open mindedness, awareness of current circumstances, access to facts, capacities to weigh information and arguments, and abilities to synthesize and test new perspectives – to interrogate their situations. Without being educated in these sorts of skills, Freire argued, one is much more likely to perpetuate the conditions of one's existence. That is, the notion of conscientization is not simply a theory, ideal, or goal, it is a practice-oriented social movement that is designed to help students recognize the implicit structures and dynamics that afford authority, power, and privilege with a view toward empowering individuals to take constructive action.

A frequently used word within discussions of Democratic Citizenship Education is *hegemony*, which refers to structures of leadership and dominance. Its synonyms include *leadership, dominance, supremacy, mastery, control, power, sway,* and *rule* – a list that has a great deal of overlap with synonyms of teaching within the frame of Standardized Education.

In other words, within Democratic Citizenship Education, the main focus is the realization from the mid-1900s that schooling was actually helping to perpetuate inequitable social and economic structures rather than interrupting them. The notion of conscientization was explicitly designed to empower students to improve their circumstances, first by developing a critical understanding of those circumstances, and second by nurturing a sense of agency.

It's tempting to think that this educational movement is focused on constraints and oppressions that are external to the student, but that line of thought and its implicit assumptions of victimization actually miss the main point. The process of conscientization is reflexive; it is as much concerned about the individual's habits of thought and internalized narratives as it is with actual social and cultural structures. That is, humans are often active participants in their own oppressions. As will be illustrated in the next chapter, beliefs can be more constraining than political or economic obstacles.

In order of popular usage, the meanings of *critical* include:
1. Inclined to find fault;
2. Characterized by careful judgment (a critical reading);
3. Crucial or decisive (a critical point; a critical stage; critical condition);
4. Indispensable or essential (critical information).

The sense of "critical" associated with conscientization entails these elements – but in more or less reverse order. Critical thinking involves analyzing, creatively integrating, and evaluating not just circumstances, but the conditions that have given rise to particular circumstances.

The never-ending project

To be clear, then, Democratic Citizenship Education is not mainly about pointing fingers, assigning blame, and dismantling institutions – although it is certainly attentive to forms of **hegemony**, however they are manifest. For that reason, its principal emphases are on recognizing and understanding partialities – on the levels of individuals, social groups, and cultures – and reformatting those recognized partialities in ways the enlarge possibilities. Further, the goal isn't some sort of perfection, but rather the realization that life is lived collectively in an endless choreography. Democratic Citizenship Education entails constant attentiveness, ongoing investment, and a continuous reflexive criticality, all oriented toward ethical action.

One of the implications of this positioning is that the work of conscientization is never finished. This point has become particularly obvious over the past few decades as great strides have been made to address once-deeply inscribed social inequities rooted in racism, classism, and sexism. While there is still much work to do, the gains have positioned nations to notice and address whole new categories of injustice and oppression. It is thus that discourses of, for example, **ableism**, **ageism**, and **heterosexism** have risen to some prominence in recent years. Doubtless the list will continue to grow as strides toward social equality are made.

To be clear, however, the point of such movements is not that all diversity is good or even that all difference should be tolerated. Few would make that claim, as many categories of difference are obviously destructive of social cohesion. The guiding question with regard to specific diversities is something toward, "Do others have issues with this category of difference because of entrenched beliefs and uninterrogated norms, or because it poses a genuine threat to individuals, social collectives, or society?" Concisely, beliefs and norms are not adequate bases to maintain prejudices toward and oppressions over others.

New categories of oppression also arise as society evolves – and this point has been especially obvious with the recent pace of technological development. As information and communication technologies have contributed to many valuable advances (around knowledge production in particular, as discussed in the next two chapters), they have also spawned **cyberbullies** and Internet trolls who use the veil of anonymity to do damage. More subtly, the very different sorts of access that certain groups have to digital technologies have complicated and amplified existing inequities. In a "knowledge economy," an "information age," and a "digital era," those who own the latest tools and who have the broadest access to digital services have huge advantages over those who do not.

The suggestion is not that these new inequities are evil; it is that inequities are inevitable and it takes effort to monitor and modulate them. This is precisely the point of Democratic Citizenship Education and its two-pronged emphases of participation and conscientization.

The original foci of critical discourses in Democratic Citizenship Education were racism, classism, and sexism. As western societies have grown more culturally diverse, and as critical sensibilities have gained momentum, the discourse has expanded to encompass ableism, ageism, and heterosexism, as well as injustices based on belief systems and ethnicities.

An emergent issue is that some of these categories make for uncomfortable bedfellows, as honoring one can entail discriminating based on another.

Suggestions for delving deeper

1. A focus of Democratic Citizenship Education is designing situations in which people might come together in a collective project that surpasses what is possible by working independently. Have you ever experienced this sort of situation in your formal education? What did it look like? Feel like?

2. Schooling can have major impacts on societal sensibilities. For example, the current recycling movement was motivated in large part by in-school emphases that were carried home by students. As well, younger generations tend to be considerably more "colorblind" – that is, oblivious to racial distinctions – supported by the many and varied encounters they have in today's diversely populated schools. What other social and cultural issues might be deliberately engaged in schools? How might this be done?

3. A tenet of Democratic Citizenship Education is that, no matter how noble teachers' intentions might be, there is always a hidden curriculum. What are some aspects of the hidden curriculum in your teacher education program? In your postsecondary education?

3.2 Knowledge and Learning in Democratic Citizenship Education

Within the field of education, the recognition of the need to address issues of collective knowledge coincided roughly with the dawning of a new millennium. Notions of CONNECT-and-COLLABORATE associated with Democratic Citizenship Education (versus the more traditional educational emphases of COMMAND-and-CONTROL) have thus come to be associated with "21st-century knowing" and "21st-century learning."

We've collected some of the more commonly identified contrasts between 20th- and 21st-century emphases:

EVOLUTIONS IN WHAT IT MEANS TO KNOW		
20th-Century Competence	ASPECT	**21st-Century Competence**
pre-selected, fixed facts and skills	FOCUS	deep learning and adaptive performance
context-free mastery	GOAL	situated action
precise evaluation	FEEDBACK	nuanced interpretation
"carrots and sticks" (promises of rewards and threats of punishment)	MOTIVATORS	growth, autonomy, mastery and purpose – developed through meeting challenges
individualistic generalist	KNOWER	engaged specialist
disengaged observers	AUDIENCE	participating agents

These distinctions and labels are, of course, contested and volatile, but they do signal some changes that are worth thinking about. One way into this topic is through popular culture – specifically, the dramatic differences between two era-defining genres: the quiz-based game shows of the late 1900s and performance-based reality TV of the early 2000s.

Among the most watched game shows in the 1980s and 1990s were *Jeopardy* and *Who Wants to Be a Millionaire?* In these, knowing is represented through the imperative to provide quick-draw responses to prompts that span the breadth of current knowledge. Every question has an unambiguous, preset answer. The judge is the host with answers in hand. By contrast, in more recent shows such as *So You Think You Can Dance* and *American Idol*, knowing is represented by inviting contestants to offer innovative and demanding performances, often with unfamiliar material that requires an extension of expertise from a related domain. The judges are both industry experts and the public at large.

Think about how participants get ready for these two types of contest. On the quiz show, entrants are lone wolves who are responsible for their own preparations. On the performance show, the contestants are supported through access to expert knowledge and sustained practice within a community that includes other contestants.

As for modes of evaluation, in the quiz shows, feedback comes with clinical precision. Contestants are right, wrong, or too slow. In the performance shows, feedback arrives in the form of expert critique that highlights strengths, pinpoints weaknesses, and steers participants toward improved future performances. It is the popular cultural genre of reality TV that, we would suggest, exemplifies 21st-century knowing – where knowing is associated with deep specialization and the capacity to generalize to other domains out of the depth of that expertise. In these settings, to know is to PERFORM ADEPTLY, ADAPT FLEXIBLY, and CONTRIBUTE NOVELTY TO THE COMMUNITY.

The qualities demonstrated through the evolution of quiz-based to performance-based shows begin to paint a picture of 21st-century knowing and learning – which are about something different than preparing people to do well on timed achievement tests. Among the qualities of emerging importance, society seems to be paying much more attention to deep specialization and well-honed skills that are most powerfully developed by starting young, practicing intensively, having expert teaching, and regularly pressing one's efforts past the edges of current mastery.

Collectivity was a topic of frequent critique in the 1900s. For example, in psychology, the word *groupthink* was coined to refer to the manner in which individuals' desires for harmony in a group can lead to undesirable outcomes that don't challenge the status quo. Similarly, in sociology, the phrase *herd mentality* (or *mob mentality*) was used to label the way people are often influenced by their peers to adopt behaviors, share beliefs, and follow trends.

Collectivity and knowing

These transitions in thinking about individual knowing correspond to equally dramatic shifts in thinking about collective knowledge. Through most of the 1900s, "collectives," "communities," and "**cooperative learning** groups" were seen as a potential support to individual learning, but fraught with peril. As mentioned in Chapter 3.1, deprecating phrases were coined to warn against the negative impacts of group processes, such as **groupthink** from psychology and **herd** (or **mob**) **mentality** from sociology.

More recently, however, attentions have been refocused on the incredible power of collective process, with the realization that it is possible for a group of people to be more intelligent than the most intelligent person in the group. This effect is the opposite to that of groupthink or herd mentality, which assume lowest-common-denominator outcomes. Phrases that have emerged to refer to this phenomenon include **hive mind** and **crowdsourcing**. Instances abound, and Internet-based examples are by far the most frequently cited. Some remarkable advances have been attributed to this sort of collective process, and some of those successes serve as powerful illustrations of shifts in sensibility and possibility around the nature of collectivity in knowledge production.

A notable example is **Wikipedia**, self-described as "a collaboratively edited, multilingual, free Internet encyclopedia." Begun in 2001, Wikipedia has become one of the most visited and cited of websites. Many of the details in this book, in fact, have been informed by quick visits there.

With regard to questions of knowing and knowledge, Wikipedia is remarkable in many ways. For example, it has helped to redefine the game of knowledge production through its rocky relationship with the academic world. Wikipedia violates some of the basic rules of epistemic claims – for example, allowing authors to be anonymous and uncredentialed, and omitting a process of rigorous validation such as expert reviews. Partly because it breaks these rules, Wikipedia has overtaken other encyclopedia projects – particularly

In the past few decades, collectivity has been profoundly reframed, as evidenced by current interests in *hive mind* (or *group mind*, or *swarm intelligence*, or *interhinking*), used to refer to the potential capacities of a collective. Along similar lines, *crowdsourcing* is a neologism that refers to processes of soliciting contributions from a large group of people (especially from an online community) to address a matter or solve a problem of shared interest.

Microsoft's Encarta, which was vastly better funded and obeyed the rules of the academic game.

Wikipedia and similar crowdsourcing projects exemplify some recent insights into collective intelligence. For instance, whereas it was once assumed that group members must work in harmony to achieve complex goals, it is now evident that the individual independence is at least as important for a group to be smart. Consensus can actually diminish possibility, as it often leads to lowest-common-denominator actions that neither offend nor inspire.

Phrased differently, both redundancy and diversity are now seen as vital elements in a knowledge-producing system. Redundancy refers to the extent of similarity among the members of a collective, and it plays two key roles. Firstly, it makes it possible for agents to work together. Samenesses such as a common language, similar status, shared responsibilities, and common vision are important for social cohesion, interpersonal harmony, and group stability. Secondly, redundancies among participants give the system its robustness because it makes it possible for one person to step in for another. Systems that lack such redundancy are highly prone to breakdowns.

In sociocultural learning theories, the word *situated* is used to direct attentions to the role played by physical, social, and cultural aspects of one's context – artifacts, tools, habits, vocabularies, customs, institutions … the list has no end. Each element contributes to what is learnable, thinkable, and doable.

Diversity among individuals is an equally vital ingredient – and one that has been largely ignored by redundancy-oriented public schools. The diversity in a knowledge-producing system is found in the varied interests and specializations of its members. These categories of expertise constitute a pool of possibilities that enables (and sometimes forces) a collective to be innovative. Unfortunately, it's often impossible to know in advance which diversities might be valuable to a collective, as illustrated by the current job market. Some economies have many thousands of unfilled positions because of unforeseen shortages of certain specializations. For that reason, it can be important to nurture diversity simply for the sake of diversity.

To be clear, the suggestion is not that all categories of diversity are inherently good. Rather, it is that popular understandings of diversity must be challenged. Within Standardized Education, diversity is seen as divergence from normality, and so often treated as a problem to be remediated. Within Authentic Education, diversity is seen as the birthright of the individual, and so nurtured and celebrated but considered in isolation. Within Democratic Citizenship Education, diversity is considered in the context of its impact on one another and its contribution to the grander collective. It is not a celebration of "it's all good" or "anything goes"; rather, it entails a more engaged, critical consideration of what might be valuable for individuals whose identities are shaped by and realized within collectivities.

Such thinking, in turn, has compelled educators to reconstrue normality, not in terms of ideals or typicalities, but as a cultural construct that operates to limit difference and constrain choice. As detailed in Moment 1, within the frame of Standardized Education it was assumed that the universe dictated what is and is not normal. Within a frame of Democratic Citizenship Education, normal is understood as a collective invention (and hence evolving).

Anchoring effect is a phrase used to refer to the tendency of a learner to latch onto the first viable interpretation (belief, theory, etc.) that she or he encounters and to stick with that interpretation, even when more plausible, more encompassing, and more powerful ideas are presented. Sociocultural theories of learning suggest that one's situation may play a central role in this phenomenon.

The point is not that all assumptions about normality should be jettisoned. That's unlikely to happen, as some shared sense of what's normal appears to be necessary for social cohesion (even when, as frequently noted these days, the "new normal" is understood in terms of difference). Rather, the issue is that democratic citizens should be aware of the norms that they assume, the origins of these norms, and their participation in maintaining and/or transforming them.

Such responsibilities signal senses of knowing and learning that stand in stark contrast to commonsense understandings. Recalling a discussion in Chapter 1.2, everyday habits of speech frame KNOWLEDGE AS AN EXTERNAL, OBJECTIVE ENTITY and LEARNING AS A PROCESS OF INTERNALIZING. (The associated visual metaphor is shown again in the margin of the next page). The sensibility represented within Democratic Citizenship Education is critical of the assumptions of disconnectedness and rigid boundaries within these metaphors, leaning instead toward the notion that knowers already inhabit collective knowledge, and vice versa.

That is, in somewhat different terms, collective knowledge unfolds from and is enfolded in individual knowing. The associated visual metaphor is more toward the one shown on this page, in which the individual knower is nested within collective knowledge. Here knowing is understood as a sort of vibrant interface. Viewed from the vantage of the individual, knowing is about PERSONAL COHERENCE (consistent with the theories discussed in Chapter 2.2). Viewed from the vantage of the social group, culture, or other collective, knowing is FITTING ACTION WITHIN A GRANDER WHOLE.

The notion of knowing thus collects together thinking, acting, identifying, and other elements that simultaneously define the individual's being and constitute the collective's possibility. Learning, in this construal, is bi-directional. At the individual level, learning is an ONGOING PROCESS OF REVISING ONE'S THOUGHTS AND ACTIONS TO FIT WITH THE CIRCUMSTANCES. But that learning also affects the structure and cohesion of the group, and so at that level learning is a CO-EVOLUTION OF AGENTS WITHIN A GRANDER COLLECTIVE.

As with the perspectives on knowing and learning presented in Moment 2, these perspective on sociocultural learning are also coherence theories – albeit that they are concerned with very different sites of coherence. They focus more on how social and cultural collectives hang together through the co-creation of ideas and expectations.

Sociocultural and critical theories of knowledge and learning frame the phenomena in very different ways to commonsense perspectives. Some differences are highlighted in the contrasts between these visual metaphors. Theories associated with Democratic Citizenship Education tend to opt for images involving permeable boundaries (reflecting evolving identities) of nestedness (indicating situatedness).

With regard to formal education, this image is suggestive of both a downward/inward influence of society on individuals undergoing schooling and an upward/outward influence of individuals on society. This phenomenon is perhaps most evident in the ways people tend to describe or identify themselves. Citizens of modern, industrialized nations gravitate toward two methods. Sometimes self-descriptions are focused inward (on personal abilities, qualities of personality, etc.); at other times self-descriptions are phrased in terms of social positioning (careers, affiliations, places of birth, etc.). That is, individual identity is a dynamic interface of the intrapersonal (i.e., *within* the person) and the interpersonal (i.e., *between* persons).

Or, more provocatively, within a frame of Democratic Citizenship Education, KNOWING IS BEING and BEING IS KNOWING. Who one is, what one knows, and how that knowing/being is enfolded in and unfolds from one's situation are not separate considerations.

Situated knowing and learning

Which of these objects in the collection shown in the sidebar does *not* belong – the hammer, the saw, the axe, or the wood? And why does it not belong?

There's no correct answer here. The task is about reasoning, not rightness. For instance, you may have selected "hammer" because the word has two syllables (and the other words have only one). Or perhaps "saw" because the other three objects can easily be used for pounding. However (based on prior results), it's most likely that you chose the wood, since the other objects are manufactured tools.

A very different answer tends to be given by citizens of oral cultures. As **Alexander Luria** noted in a classic study, their answers veer more toward, "They're all needed. If you want to saw, you need a saw; if you want to split something, you need an axe," or "If I had to leave something out, I'd choose the axe, because I can pound with the hammer and split with the saw."

There are two very different types of reasoning happening in the two preceding paragraphs. In the first one, the rationales are based on abstract categories ("two-syllable words," "objects for pounding," and "manufactured tools"). In the second, the reasons are anchored to immediate situations and embedded in narratives of action. Luria noted (and others have since verified) that, whereas schooled and literate individuals tend to use abstract categories when they reason, persons from communities without schooling and with low literacy levels tend to rely on practical operations from everyday life.

The point here is not that one group's thinking is more sophisticated than the other's. It is that each culture has a distinct set of tools available for thinking – that is, such devices as abstract categories and formal logic, or practical action and narrative reasoning. These tools contribute to fundamentally different ways of perceiving, organizing, and acting – that is, knowing and being – in the world. In other words, the funda-

Which item doesn't belong?

Your response to this question – or, more precisely, your strategy for responding to this question – likely reveals much about your cultural background. (See the discussion to the right.)

mental nature of human cognition varies from one culture to another. **Richard Nisbett** has made a similar point by contrasting western (in particular, citizens of wealthier, English-speaking nations) and eastern (in particular, citizens of nations in which Buddhist, Taoist, and Confucianist philosophies are prominent). Some of the trends that he noted are summarized below.

CONTRASTS BETWEEN INTERPRETIVE LEANINGS ON THE CULTURAL LEVEL		
Interpretive leanings in the WEST (especially the English-speaking world)	**ASPECT OF CULTURE**	**Interpretive leanings in the EAST** (associated with mindfulness traditions)
agency & independence	ETHOS	harmony & interdependence
a life free of constraints	GOAL IN LIFE	self-control to minimize friction
tendency toward above average	SELF-RATING	tendency toward below average
work harder when meeting success	MOTIVATORS	work harder when meeting failure
interpret events in terms of stabilities	HABITS	interpret events in terms of change
attend more to objects	FOCUS	attend more to contexts
distinguish and classify according to abstract categories	STRATEGIES TO CLASSIFY	distinguish and classify according to roles and relationships
discomfort; insistence on (singular) correctness	ATTITUDE TO PARADOX	comfort/pleasure in contradictions and paradoxes
miscommunication is the fault of the speaker (for not being clear)	MISCOMMUNICATIONS	miscommunication is the hearer's fault (for not considering contextual cues)
knowledge in framed real/ideal (noun) terms	KNOWLEDGE	knowing is framed in active/practical (verb) terms

Nisbett's assertions are based on scientifically rigorous measurements, but they should not be read as hard-and-fast truths. Obviously there are very socially minded and paradox-embracing westerners and highly individualistic and stability-seeking easterners. The claims are made at the collective, not the individual level, and the assertion is that cultures have tendencies toward these collective "personalities" when considered across all their citizens.

In the literature of learning theories, this quality is captured by the notion of **situatedness**. All knowledge is situated in physical, social, and cultural contexts. These elements – and, in particular, the tools of thought and action that they make available – contribute to habits of thinking as they frame what is knowable, doable, and be-able.

Over the last 50 years or so, dozens of theories of learning that are based on this principle have been embraced by educators, including **social constructionism, situated cognition, sociocultural theory, cultural–historical theory, activity theory, actor–network theory, distributed cognition**, and **semiotic pedagogy**. There are, of course, subtle and important distinctions among these and related perspectives, but their major point of agreement is instructive: individual cognition is entwined with social and cultural situation.

There are many authors to these theories, but within education the ideas are most commonly associated with the work of **Lev Vygotsky**, a Russian psychologist and contemporary of Piaget. (Luria, mentioned above, was one of his students.) He broke with commonsense beliefs by asserting that powers of higher thought are dependent on cultural practices and, in particular, mediated by language and other tools of thought. For Vygotsky, learning was mainly a process of BECOMING ENCULTURATED – that is, HABITUATING TO SOCIAL ROLES and INCORPORATING CULTURAL PATTERNS (of perceiving, interpreting, acting, etc.) into one's own being. Another quick exercise can be used to illustrate some aspects of this insight.

What is this person feeling? Angry? Amused? Dismissive? Puzzled?

Your response to this question may reveal something about the community in which you live. (See the discussion to the lower right.)

Look at the picture in the margin. Which of the following words comes closest to describing this person's emotional state: puzzled, amused, angry, or dismissive?

Once again, there is no correct answer. The images for such **neutral face tests** are selected precisely because the subjects' expressions are neutral and ambiguous.

If we'd asked this question in Moment 2, in the context of discussing theories of learning associated with Piaget, it might've been used to illustrate that your reading of his emotional state is a projection rooted in your personal history. Those who embrace situated theories of learning would agree, but they would add that your projection is also very likely a reflection of your context. For example, it turns out that most (but not all) adults in North America who live in areas associated with more Liberal or Democratic political leanings see the person as puzzled or amused, and most (but not all) adults who live in communities that elect Conservatives or Republicans see him as angry or dismissive. To re-emphasize, the tendency to make these projections is more strongly correlated to where one lives than one's political affiliation. (We asked this question of 400 undergraduate students in Calgary a few years ago. The collected response of 32% puzzled/amused, 60% angry/dismissive, and 8% undecided mirrored the local results of a recent election to within a few points.)

Restated, you tend to reflect your social and cultural situation in your habits of perception, even if you do not consciously align yourself with prevailing opinions and leanings.

Many citizens of the western world find this suggestion insulting – which is precisely what the theory predicts. Where independence, individuality, and freedom of thought are cherished, a demonstration of dependence is much more likely to be taken as an affront. Even so, humans can't help but reflect their situation. Another activity will help to explain why this is the case.

In the margins are two lists of 20 items. Starting with the list on the left, assign each word to the appropriate category by checking one of the boxes. Do it as quickly as possible and don't worry about errors.

Now do the same for the chart on the right. You'll probably notice that you have to slow down and/or that you're more prone to making mistakes. Much more scientific versions of these **implicit association tests** are available online – ones that are structured to avoid priming biases, that are precisely timed, and that cover many, many issues. It usually turns out that people, regardless of their espoused convictions, demonstrate biases that are prevalent in their cultures, including racist, classist, sexist, and homophobic attitudes. Of course, this is not the same as saying that everyone is a sexist bigot. The implication is merely that human knowing is situated.

So, what are the salient aspects of being "situated"? We've already signaled that language and literacy are critical elements of one's situatedness. More broadly, language and literacy might be described as aspects

Male or Business		Female or Home
☐	Ralph	☐
☐	Anna	☐
☐	Curtains	☐
☐	Office	☐
☐	David	☐
☐	Stapler	☐
☐	Peter	☐
☐	Fax	☐
☐	Gloria	☐
☐	Debra	☐
☐	Kitchen	☐
☐	Lawyer	☐
☐	Playpen	☐
☐	Lara	☐
☐	Bathroom	☐
☐	CEO	☐
☐	Parents	☐
☐	Darren	☐
☐	Sarah	☐
☐	Michael	☐

These two charts are the basis of an "implicit association test." Assign each word to the appropriate category by checking one of the boxes. *(Do the one on this page first.)*

of a culture's technology.

The preceding sentence might have seemed a little odd, given that the word *technology* tends to be heard as a reference to recent gadgets. Smart phones and radar detectors are obviously technologies. Hammers and highways are less so. And languages and literacies … well … for some, that's stretching the notion to the breaking point.

The term *technology* is derived from the same ancient roots as the word *text*, tracing back to the Proto-Indo-European *teks*, "to weave, fabricate, make," and the more recent Greek *tekhe*, "art, craft, skill." That is, technology is about more than objects and tools; it refers to the ideas, practices, artifacts, and sensibilities that define a culture. In this sense, it is inevitable that technologies will become so familiar and "natural" that, at some point, they become transparent. They are no longer seen as human inventions or as devices that influence and shape their users.

An analogy can be drawn between these invisible technologies and your automatic System 1. As was developed in Chapter 2.2, your rapid, accurate, memory-based, intuitive-feeling System 1 is responsible for most of your activity in the world. Its workings are not available to consciousness, and that's why it's powerful. By taking care of the familiar details of existence, System 1 frees up your working memory – your conscious, reflective, but much-more-limited System 2 – to grapple with details that are new or less familiar. Cultures, too, appear to have layers of knowing that operate on the collective level very much like System 1 and System 2 act on the individual level. Such technologies as language, supermarkets, paint, woven cloth, and so on are usually shrouded in a cloak of familiarity. They're in that category of things you hardly ever notice when they're there, but are keenly aware when they're missing. Considered en masse, such elements of everyday existence might be seen as comprising a collective System 1. Just look around yourself right now. Almost every artifact, along with almost every action associated with that artifact, is part of culture's System 1. (Extending the analogy, the cultural System 2 comprises what is in our collective

Male or Home		Female or Business
☐	Dinner	☐
☐	Donna	☐
☐	Kevin	☐
☐	Manager	☐
☐	Timeclock	☐
☐	Garth	☐
☐	Gord	☐
☐	Becky	☐
☐	Domestic	☐
☐	Salary	☐
☐	Personnel	☐
☐	Ellen	☐
☐	Linda	☐
☐	Vacuum	☐
☐	Copier	☐
☐	Neil	☐
☐	Sofa	☐
☐	Mary	☐
☐	Overtime	☐
☐	Tom	☐

This is the second part of the implicit association test begun on the previous page. See the instructions there, and *do the one on that page first*.

awareness by virtue of its unfamiliarity or newness. The category would include the latest technologies, what's in the news, and the like.)

The word *situated*, then, is used to signal that your knowing and learning are not just about what's going on inside you. They are also *distributed* in your physical, social, and cultural environments. To be clear, the assertion is that your thinking is not fully contained in your skin; it is also offloaded onto and entangled in artifacts, structures, and habits that enable, constrain, and otherwise channel what can be known and done. The worlds that humans structure around themselves are not just the products of their intelligence; they are also sources of intelligent action. Knowing and learning, then, are embodied in the physical world, the social corpus, and the body politic in addition to the biological body.

One of the upshots of these theories is that human thinking and knowing is more distributed than anyone can be aware. To illustrate this point, read aloud the message in the margin image to the right.

The above is used to illustrate the *distributed* character of knowing. (See the discussion to the left.) Humans are comfortable off-loading their knowledge onto the larger world and have invented many technologies to assist the process.

Chances are that you missed that the "the" is repeated. (Congratulations if you caught it.) As described in Chapter 2.2, many psychologists interpret the tendency to miss such details as instances of projection. That is, humans perceive what they expect to perceive, and so often gloss over important details.

Among theorists who embrace distributed and situated dimensions of knowing and learning, a different reason is usually emphasized. The issue, they argue, is not so much that human perception is mostly about projection; it is that limitations on consciousness force the brain to be strategic. One highly effective cognitive tactic is to economize by leaving most of what you need to know about the world out in the world. The brain glosses partly because it assumes it already knows what's there, but mostly because it trusts the information will still be there if closer scrutiny is necessary. Human knowing, that is, is not just highly reliant on situation; it is completely at ease with distributing its knowing across its situation.

An upshot of this point is that technologies that facilitate cognitive offloading onto the world, such as literacy and shared responsibilities, can simultaneously contribute to both individual and collective possibility. This is why, as noted at the start of Chapter 3.1, the habit of seeing a tension between the needs of the collective and the needs of the individual, as is commonly done in both Standardized and Authentic Educational frames, is understood within Democratic Citizenship Education as a troubling simplification.

Being, participating, consciously participating

To reiterate, within the frame of Democratic Citizenship Education, knowing is most commonly characterized in terms of SITUATED DOING/BEING and learning in terms of APPRENTICING/BECOMING. This is why, and as mentioned in Chapter 3.1, metaphors of PARTICIPATING are growing in popularity, where "participatory cultures" are understood in terms of conditions that invite meaningful and impactful contributions from all community members, regardless of age, developmental level, social positioning, or other category of difference.

The word *technology* is used within participatory and critical frames to refer to any ideas, practices, artifacts and sensibilities that define a culture. People are typically aware of only the cutting edge of technology, but the most influential may be among those that are so familiar that they have faded into invisibility.

As noted above, insights into situatedness of being, sociocultural dimensions of knowing, collective aspects of learning, and related matters are tightly tethered to the research of Vygotsky, who is by far the most-cited researcher on matters related to collectivity and learning.

There is some irony in the fact that Vygotsky has come to occupy such a prominent place within Democratic Citizenship Education. His work was conducted entirely within the Soviet Union, and so it turns out that a major conceptual influence is to be found in the works of **Karl Marx**. Marx's voice was the most prominent and influential in communist and socialist movements though the 1900s. He advanced a perspective on social transformation that involved challenging those economic and political models that produced and sustained class distinctions – including, in particular, capitalism, the economic model that is most commonly associated with modern democratic states.

It would take more space than we care to devote to unravel the issues here. However, it's important to underscore that Vygotsky's and Marx's ideas met around the role of the collective in shaping the thinking of the individual. Marx's writings, however, were much more political in nature and explicitly oriented toward societal-level transformations that would bring about greater equality among citizens. In the vocabulary of contemporary educational thought, whereas Vygotsky focused on participation, Marx focused on *conscious* participation.

Consistent with sociocultural theories of knowing, Marx held that one cannot help but participate in the social and political structures of one's world. Even nonaction – such as choosing not to vote or staying silent on perceived injustices – is a participation in the way the world is organized. It is a choice, and Marx argued that the person who is critically conscious of the reasons for such choices is the true citizen. The important quality of citizenship, that is, is not compliance, but deliberate consciousness of one's actions and critical awareness of the reasons for one's actions.

As developed in Chapter 3.1, this attitude is at the heart of the critical theory movement, which is mainly concerned with the distribution of power and principles of social control. For the most part, Marx argued, the means of maintaining power and control are implicit and therefore difficult to identify and affect. They tend to be woven through common belief systems, shared assumptions, and other taken-for-granted aspects of the world. That they are implicit does not mean that they are not insidious, however.

Consider a few extreme examples:

- In some belief communities, it not only makes sense to punish young girls for learning to read, there is actually an imperative to harm or kill.
- In some cultures it is common practice to murder newborns whose features deviate from expected norms.

Most citizens of modern societies would be horrified at these practices and the beliefs that support them. Yet, within the communities and cultures themselves, these practices and beliefs are commonsensical. The shared worlds are coherent. It wouldn't make sense to do otherwise.

Power, in its broadest sense, refers to ability – the ability to act or do, strength, vigor. Among critical theorists it refers to the social capacity to dominate in any domain (e.g., politics, economics, fashion, opinion, etc.) and to preserve that domination.

In fact, the belief and value systems that support such practices are not really so distant from those that supported **racially segregated schools** in the United States, **Indian residential schools** in Canada, and **Bantu education** in South Africa – all of which persisted through much of the 1900s, and the legacies of which continue to cripple major subpopulations of these nations.

Indeed, the best predictor of children's educational success is not their ability or aptitude, but the extent of their parents' education, and that should give pause. It means that the educational system is perpetuating itself. Populations at an advantage retain their advantage, and populations at a disadvantage remain at a disadvantage.

Critical theorists have endeavored to understand the assumptions and practices that contribute to this phenomenon, concluding that there is a range of (mostly implicit) structures that "teach" students about their social position. And, to complicate matters, most often parents and communities are complicit in these structures. For example, in neighborhoods with lower socioeconomic status populations, schools are much more likely to place a greater emphasis on rote and procedural learning – in large part because parents expect it (or, at least, teachers believe that parents expect it).

More insidiously, it appears that dissonances between the *discourses* within schools and the discourses that frame a child's home life can be debilitating to a learner. This point has been powerfully shown in schools around the world where well-meaning educators from different social and economic classes have attempted to improve educational experiences of the perceived-to-be-disadvantaged by introducing structures and practices from more privileged settings (or, nearly as frequently, moving these children to schools in more advantaged neighborhoods).

It turns out that these tactics are rarely successful – and critical theorists argue that is because many children from different backgrounds are unable to decode and reconcile the discourses at work. By way of simple example, the remark, "Shall we start math class now?" is likely to be heard by middle class children

Metaphors of SOCIAL CONTRACTS and CULTURAL CAPITAL are frequently invoked by sociocultural and critical theorists. Rooted in business and commerce, these notions hint at very different conceptual influences between Authentic Education and Democratic Citizenship Education.

as a directive, but may well be heard as a nonsensical question by children from homes where imperatives come in the form of clear instructions. (Similar communicative difficulties can arise with children whose first language is other than English.)

For a child caught in the midst of these competing and unreconciled discourses, the school can become a means to maintain social stratification, in spite of the most generous of intentions. In blunt terms, owing to different discourses, learners from different backgrounds will likely derive different – and perhaps radically different – understandings from the same situation. A student's learning is likely to be more dependent on background discourses than on the teacher's pedagogy, since those background discourses are that learner's default means for deciphering school.

Phrased differently, the official discourses of schooling are defined by the dominating class. Learners who belong to that class (i.e., who have been enculturated into prevailing discourses) are likely to be well served. In this way, society can preserve its stratifications.

There is no suggestion that such consequences are in any way deliberate. Quite the contrary, it would appear that the explicit intentions of most teachers, in line with the most commonly announced purpose of schools, are to enable all learners. What is at issue hovers beneath the surface of conscious intention, which is why the phrase "hidden curriculum" is used to refer to the practices and structures that contribute inadvertently to the maintenance of inequities.

The goal of critical theory is thus to find ways of becoming more conscious of the diverse discourses at play, how they enable and constrain possibilities, and how people might work together to avoid the pitfalls of dissonant discourses. Once again, this work is concerned with matters of distribution of power and principles of social control, where it is understood that mechanisms of power and control operate silently and invisibly for the most part.

It is difficult work, largely because many of these mechanisms are hidden behind structures intended to nurture and support learners. Classism is concealed in courteous manners of expression; sexism hides in

The *maker movement* (or *maker culture*) is a technology-rich extension of Do-It-Yourself trends. It includes digital-based activities in addition to traditional arts and crafts – and so, along with an emphasis on developing practical skills, there is a stress on innovative applications of emergent technologies.

With its focus on learning through doing in social settings, the maker movement blends Moment-1 and Moment-2 insights into knowledge and learning.

The word *frame* has the same root as the word *from*. Both terms point to origins and movements. People are framed by where they are from. As used throughout this book, the word frame is roughly synonymous with the word *discourse*, defined in Chapter 3.1.

elementary schools filled with female teachers and secondary schools dominated by males; heterosexism lurks in the families depicted in primary-level reading materials; racism lurks in gifted programs with disproportionate numbers of Caucasians; ableism is masked efforts to attract additional resources by assigning labels to different learners. And so on.

The point is not that one must be aware of all of these implicit structures. It is that one should be open to the possibility that what is held as dear and good may not have the effects that are hoped. No belief is neutral and no act is innocent. Critical theory asks that all educators bear that in mind.

Educators, that is, are asked within this frame to be counter-normative. However, elaborating the imperative of Authentic Education to be attentive to the fact that there is no normal child, within a frame of Democratic Citizenship Education teachers are asked to be mindful of how they are complicit in constructions of rightness and normality. The teacher here is more than an agent of society; the teacher is a powerful SHAPING AGENT OF CULTURE.

Suggestions for delving deeper

1. Anthropologist John Uzo Ogbu distinguished between *voluntary minorities* (who chose to move to wherever they are) and *involuntary minorities* (who were born there), noting that the former tend to be more successful on virtually every measure of success. Why might that be? How is it that the disadvantages associated with being an immigrant are less disabling than the disadvantages of growing up identifying with a minority group?

2. Throughout this book, we use the word *frame* to refer to different moments in the history of formal schooling. In this chapter, we offered definitions of *situated, technology,* and *discourse* that are tightly related to the implied meaning of frame. How are these notions connected within a frame of Democratic Citizenship Education.

3. Identify a few schooling structures or practices that were designed explicitly as

devices to improve the lives of students. What are some of their possible downsides? Might these issues be avoided or mitigated? How?

3.3 Teaching and Democratic Citizenship Education

Two contrasting ways of thinking about dyads such as self *vs.* other and right *vs.* wrong are as either *dichotomies* or *simultaneities*.

A dichotomy is a radical separation, often represented through the visual metaphor of two discrete, non-overlapping regions.

A simultaneity is a pair of phenomena that always happen together and that shape one another. They are often associated with the visual metaphor of the yin-yang.

Within Democratic Citizenship Education, dyads are almost always understood as simultaneities.

Of this book's 12 chapters, this one was the most challenging to write.

That's not because the theories are difficult or their implications for teaching are vague; it's because many of the tidy distinctions associated with Standardized Education and Authentic Education are shown by Democratic Citizenship Education to be troublesome.

On some levels, this is an amplification of a move by Authentic Educators to challenge such popular dyads as theory *vs.* practice, objective fact *vs.* subjective interpretation, nature *vs.* nurture, and surface learning *vs.* deep learning. Such pairings are not opposites, Authentic Educators argued. Rather, they point to phenomena that exist in dynamic tension – and those tensions can be used productively.

Democratic Citizenship Educators agree, and extend the list of false dichotomies to include self *vs.* other, us *vs.* them, truth *vs.* fiction, right *vs.* wrong, normal *vs.* abnormal, competition *vs.* cooperation, and individual *vs.* collective. Once again, the suggestion is not that these dyads are wrong or useless, but that they are not pairings of opposites. They are simultaneities – that is, phenomena that must happen together and that shape one another.

Teachers must thus be attentive to both elements in each pairing. As will become clear through this chapter, there are no hard and fast rules for doing this, but there are some strong recommendations. One common piece of advice when confronted by a seemingly irresolvable tension is to recognize it as an artifact of a particular mode of thinking. By way of example, the tendency to view schooling in terms of competition (*vs.* cooperation) can be traced to centuries-old philosophies that saw competition as the only dynamic that drove human action. (Cooperation was seen as useful only insofar as it gave a competitive advantage.) More recent studies of the complexity of the human dynamics suggest that cooperation is much more elemental to the species than previously thought. In an attempt to sidestep the competition *vs.* cooperation dyad, then, the notion of **coopetition** has been proposed. Coopetition occurs when agents – individuals and/or collectives – work together with some level of common interest that (it's hoped) will lead to a more valuable or enriching outcome than can be achieved by acting independently. Competition is still a motivator, but that competition is with agents outside the collaboration.

Such rethinking of entrenched and limiting ideas is reflective of a core principle of Democratic Citizenship Education, namely the importance of an open disposition. The teacher must embody a willingness to think differently, to be swayed by the evidence, and to work in the sometimes-uncomfortable spaces of dynamic tensions. At times resolutions can be found by merging sensibilities (as with the coopetition example just mentioned). Often, however, resolutions aren't possible without shifts in perspective. Participants must be prepared to step outside the habits of thinking that gave rise to a tension in the first place.

Democratic Citizenship Educators emphasize that the advice to think differently is a profoundly ethical matter, where ethics is understood not in terms of universal rules of conduct, but as situated and co-constructed accords for interaction. Indeed, Democratic Citizenship Educators have revealed an ethically troubling assumption about schooling that is shared by both Standardized and Authentic Educators: public schooling has been organized around a dominant group's efforts to impose its worldview onto non-dominant groups. Schooling has never been – and perhaps never can be – innocent or benign.

The project of Democratic Citizenship Education, then, is oriented toward its own ethical character. This point is emphasized in different ways across the many

The word *ethics* is derived from the Greek *ethos*, "character, disposition, habit, custom" – which has a very similar definition in modern English. A culture's or community's *ethos* is its character, its spirit. Its *ethics*, then, are its codes of acceptable belief, thought, and behavior. These codes are situated and collectively established, and they can be either implicit or explicit. (Most operate implicitly.)

theories of learning and knowing that inhabit the frame, but it is nonetheless a common theme with the strong, strong focus on *situation* shared by all Democratic Citizenship Educators. Teaching is all about organizing and manipulating the situations that learners inhabit – and, in so doing, enabling and constraining what students are able to be while contributing to the shape of society. It is entirely an ethical project. Teachers are thus invited to be cognizant of their inevitable partialities.

What should schools be doing?

Both Standardized Education and Authentic Education emerged in eras of relative cultural stability – at least in contrast to today's world. In particular, they unfolded when it was possible to predict with some confidence what an adult would need to know.

That's changed, as might be illustrated by a ranking of 200 midlevel-income jobs assembled every year by CareerCast.com and published online by the *Wall Street Journal*. Below are the top and bottom ten from the 2014 ranking, based on criteria of physical demands, work environment, income, stress, and hiring outlook. (The list actually changes quite dramatically from year to year, so it may be worth checking out the latest one.)

A RANKING OF MIDLEVEL-INCOME CAREERS			
Rank	**Top 10 Careers**	**Rank**	**Bottom 10 Careers**
1	Mathematician	191	Corrections Officer
2	Tenured University Professor	192	Firefighter
3	Statistician	193	Garbage Collector
4	Actuary	194	Flight Attendant
5	Audiologist	195	Head Cook
6	Dental Hygienist	196	Broadcaster
7	Software Engineer	197	Taxi Driver
8	Computer Systems Analyst	198	Enlisted Military Personnel
9	Occupational Therapist	199	Newspaper Reporter
10	Speech Pathologist	200	Lumberjack

(For those wondering, careers related to classroom teaching and school administration were clustered around #100.)

There are a few details worth highlighting here. Firstly, even though contemporary schools maintain many factory-inspired elements, not one of the above 20 (and very few of the complete list of 200) careers involves assembly-line work. That is, regarding the relationship between the structures of school and the structures of the workplace, the once-tight fit between the school lives of children and the work lives of adults is now an almost-total disconnect.

Secondly, and part of the reason for that disconnect, most of the top 10 (and, indeed, most of the top 100) careers only arose in the last century – and many in the last few decades – highlighting that schools are now tasked with preparing children for careers that may not exist yet. To amplify matters, based on current trends, it's reasonable to expect that most people will move through many careers in their adult lives.

And finally, comparing the top to the bottom of the list, the literacy and numeracy demands at the more desirable end are clearly more intense, suggesting that some traditional school foci continue to be highly relevant. But so are such qualities as focus, goal setting, self regulation, and deep comprehension. Further, the contrast between the two ends of the list signals that, just as an elementary education was deemed culturally insufficient over a century ago, a high school diploma may no longer be an adequate qualification for today's world. All of the careers at the top of the list require more advanced education. With regard to opening up horizons of possibility, formal education is more relevant than ever – even while schools seem to be falling more and more out of step with cultural needs.

These details foreground some critical issues that are not well addressed within other educational frames. Standardized Education's concerns with fixed, measurable outcomes and uniform pedagogy are grounded in an assumption of a stable and predictable career landscape. That is no longer tenable. By the same token, even though Authentic Education offered powerful new insights into how people learn, its focus on the individual blinded it to the growing irrelevance of the school's aims and content.

In other words, there is a clear need to rethink how

< not yet able to attain

< within reach, with support

< able to do unaided

< [SCAFFOLD]

Sociocultural learning theorists foreground that a novice is often able to do more in the presence of an expert than when working unaided. Those capacities that are within reach, with guidance, are commonly described as one's *zone of proximal development* (ZPD) – a phrase coined by Lev Vygotsky.

The SCAFFOLD metaphor refers to the teacher's role, offering support that enables the learner to operate in the ZPD until she or he is able to perform unaided.

the purposes of schooling situate the project within the dynamics of culture – that is, departing from assumed roles of disseminating knowledge and preparing students for the future, to acknowledge the school's participation in defining individual and collective possibilities. Of course, such is precisely the focus of sociocultural theories of learning.

Collectivity as both topic and means of teaching

As developed in Moment 2, one of the implications of Authentic Education's individualistic focus is that, from the perspective of the person, there is no "wrong" interpretation or action. Every idea, every behavior can be explained and justified by appealing to that person's unique history.

Cooperative learning is perhaps the best-established group-based classroom strategy. It includes many methods to encourage interdependence (such as assigning roles or parsing expertise), compelling learners to draw on one another, offer supportive critiques, and monitor one another's activities.

Few cooperative learning models are truly participatory. Very often they serve as group-based settings designed to support individual achievement – as opposed to genuinely productive and potentially innovative sites of joint inquiry.

Democratic Citizenship Educators (and sociocultural learning theorists) recognize this point, but do not allow the discussion of right *vs.* wrong to end there. They grant that idiosyncratic interpretations may be explained by appealing to unique histories, but they also recognize that a person's interpretations must exist with those of many others in an ecosystem of coherent thought and action. What may be completely sensible (i.e., "right") on the level of the individual may be untenable and disabling (i.e., "wrong") on the level of the collective.

No doubt some would see this point as so obvious that it's hard to believe it has to be made. Clearly some things are right and some things are wrong.

But the point is actually much subtler than it might appear. It is that a personal interpretation or a collective belief can be simultaneously right *and* wrong, depending on the level of analysis. This possibility of being right-and-wrong reveals a sharp break with earlier moments in education. Within Standardized Education, such a clash would require a correction to the individual's interpretation; within Authentic Education, it would compel the teacher to make sense of where the learner is coming from with a view toward offering productive challenges; but among Democratic Citizenship Educators, it is more likely to be seen as an occasion to negotiate understandings by collectively interrogating how different assumptions can lead to different conclusions. The goal would not necessarily be to find a way of reconciling conflicting interpretations – although that might figure in. The more encompassing aim is always to enlarge the space of understanding for all.

Not surprisingly, then, most of the advice for teachers within a frame of Democratic Citizenship Education is concerned with collective process – or, more accurately, with the simultaneity of enabling individual learning and fostering collective knowledge building. Perhaps the best-developed models for transforming a class from a *collection of learners* to a *learning collective* are in the areas of writing, the visual arts, social studies, and physical education where structures have been developed to help students through the complex processes of **peer critique** of one another's compositions, arguments, and performances. Within these contexts, the teacher's roles include MODELING appropriate feedback, ORIENTING ATTENTIONS to key qualities, SUPPORTING DEVELOPMENT of necessary interpersonal skills, and MEDIATING inevitable tensions. A driving principle of this sort of emphasis is that, in providing critiques, students develop skills that enable them to see their own writing more critically.

Accompanying the emergence of collective-based approaches to classroom teaching have been community-based structures for on-going teacher development. These include *communities of practice* (*CoPs*), *professional learning communities* (*PLCs*), *networks of practice*, and *lesson study* – all of which are inspired by and organized around sociocultural theories of knowing and learning. They thus incorporate elements of life-long learning and the initiation of new members of the profession.

The value of collective processes also extends to domains that are more commonly associated with objectively verified claims, such as mathematics and science. For example, opportunities to voice understandings, deconstruct implicit images in textbook representations, debate the relative merits of different interpretations, co-develop alternatives, and aggregate interpretations can be powerful means to develop mathematical and scientific insight – aided in large part by the fact that students often have better reads of one another's understandings and misunderstandings than the more expert (and, hence, distanced) teacher.

As for the nature of teaching in these situations, some descriptors that highlight important aspects of the teacher's role include:

- MODELING – the teacher embodies a specialized expertise, helping learners to appreciate nuances of a discipline by the manner of engagement, structures of response, foci of critique, and so on.

- ORIENTING – the teacher organizes learning situations, structures tasks, and uses other devices to prompt attentions toward key aspects of concepts at hand.
- MEDIATING – meaning "being in the middle," the teacher helps students to recognize and work with tensions (e.g., between one another, among diverse interpretations of a concept, between individual and collective).
- CHALLENGING – the teacher is always looking for opportunities to "raise the bar" on discussions and understandings by inserting well-timed, context-appropriate challenges to students.
- EMPOWERING – the teacher helps learners to develop senses of efficacy within a task and control over their own learning.

Across these aspects of teaching, it is important to underscore the role of disciplinary expertise. Within this frame, teachers must be fluent and confident with their specializations in ways that enable them to discriminate between productive and unproductive suggestions and to see connections across diverse topics. Lacking such expertise, there are dangers of either reverting to a thinly veiled mode of direct instruction (through, e.g., selecting and emphasizing only those student contributions that fit with what the teacher already has in mind) or devolving into a directionless, anything-goes pedagogy (e.g., by failing to help learners discriminate between powerful and limiting interpretations).

Assuming that the teacher is able to help learners make appropriate discernments and connections within a discipline, various commentators have assembled useful principles of **knowledge buiding** – that is, collective development, testing, and refinement of conceptual artifacts – and **dialogic learning** – that is, an interaction-based engagement in which participants distribute responsibilities for providing arguments, examining claims of validity. For the most part, these principles tend to echo the qualities of a participatory culture, as identified in Chapter 3.1. Prominent pieces of advice include the following:

Dialogic learning (or *dialogic teaching*) is a classroom emphasis that involves shared responsibilities for investigating, interpreting, and arguing claims to truth. It often focuses on tensions or disagreements, but can be developed around any type of assertion.

- individual agency – Students must know that their contributions matter, both to collective process and to the development of their own insights.
- diversity of ideas – The word *intelligent* derives from Latin *inter-* + *legere*, "to choose between, to discern" – a reminder intelligent action relies on a diversity of interpretions to select from.
- redundancies among participants – To work together productively, members of a collective will have to be "on the same page" on some critical details – in particular, with regard to goals, expectations, and necessary background knowledge.
- evolving ideas – Every insight is regarded as improvable.
- situated ideas – Every claim comes from somewhere, and historical and contextual details can provide insight into its contribution, its relevance, and the social dimensions of knowledge production.
- wise use of authoritative sources – Further to the previous bullet, whereas authoritative sources are typically consulted to silence divergent interpretations, in the Democratic Citizenship Educator's classroom they are used to orient inquiry, frame questions, open new issues, and so on.

Other considerations include structures of interaction, means of recording emergent insights, relevance of foci, use of genuine problems, and attendance to interpersonal dynamics. In brief, then, this approach to teaching is complex and demanding and requires extensive preparation – as much in the form of anticipating emergent possibilities as planning lessons, collecting artifacts, and selecting resources.

Knowledge Building (KB) is a model for collective engagement that is tightly aligned with principles of participatory cultures. Explicitly oriented toward developing the skills needed for citizens of a knowledge-age society, it offers strategies, assessment criteria, technologies to moderate interaction, and tools to track production.

Technologies of situated teaching

Arguably the most important element of preparing for teaching is consideration of the role of relevant technologies.

As developed in Chapter 3.2, a major component of human intelligence arises in the ways situations are structured to offload memories and distribute cognition. For instance, kitchens are typically organized to reduce demands on working memory – by keeping spices together, locating pots near stoves, choosing appliances with uncomplicated controls, and so on. Similar can be said of the ways that offices are set up, car dashboards are arranged, textbooks are formatted, and websites are structured. The task of designers in each of these examples is to create a situation that is intuitive (i.e., makes few demands on the reflective System 2) so that consciousness can be devoted to the task at hand.

The same should be true of the classroom. Productive tools of thought should be immediately available – including, most fundamentally, the technologies of vocabulary and discourse. The importance of having adequate access to relevant vocabulary and defining discourses cannot be overstated. It is particularly evident through two populations that are typically not well served by commonplace approaches to teaching: students whose brains are structured in atypical ways, and children from subpopulations that have endured histories of exclusion, deprivation, and suppression. Meeting the needs of those in the former group usually requires combinations of specialized intervention and intelligent strategies of **diversity education**, which will be discussed in the next section. Addressing the needs of members in the latter group requires deliberate, structured pedagogies.

We mentioned in Chapter 3.2 that an ineffective tactic for improving the educational experiences of disadvantaged groups is to parachute them into situations designed for more advantaged populations – either bringing the children to such settings or taking the settings to them. Examinations of the reasons that such efforts are prone to failure lead to matters of vocabulary and discourse, both of which are foci of **semiotic pedagogy**.

With regard to vocabulary, children from lower socioeconomic status homes, from non-English backgrounds, and/or from traditionally excluded groups often have much more limited lexicons than their peers when they enter school. That means that they often miss subtle nuances and implicit meanings. If not addressed early, this disadvantage can snowball through the school years and be completely debilitat-

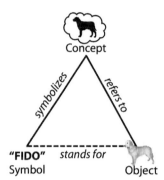

Departing from most sociocultural theories, *semiotics* focuses on *function* rather than *structure*. The discourse deals with the interactions of objects (experienced phenomena), concepts (interpretations, meanings, codes), and signs (language, vocabulary, symbols). *Semiotic pedagogy* aims to enable learners by helping them gain mastery over these elements, on both implicit and explicit levels.

ing by university level, where every discipline has a highly specialized vocabulary.

The point is not that vocabulary should be learned for vocabulary's sake. Rather, it is that vocabulary is one of the most valuable tools of thought. A rich vocabulary is more than a large collection of words. It is a network of associations that extends across time and space, a reservoir of variation, a sea of possibilities. It is a flexible technology that evolves and adapts as needs arise and circumstances change. An elaborated lexicon enables learning by orienting speakers to more fine-grained distinctions and affording access to more concepts. As we flagged at the start of this book, specialized vocabularies aren't intended to exclude; they're necessary for more refined insights in every area of specialization. In practical terms, then, teachers across disciplines must ensure that learners are aware of and fluent with the words being used. Instruction in vocabulary is an aspect of every area of study.

As for discourse, as we introduced in Chapter 3.2, even when vocabularies in place, implicit differences in expectation, interaction patterns, and the ways that ideas are expressed can be debilitating. (For instance, the act of critiquing an authority is unthinkable in some subcultures.) In consequence, resituating the "disadvantaged" into "advantaged" settings can be alienating and incapacitating. In such situations, educators have the choice of redefining what they are up to or, more commonly, giving students access to the prevailing discourse by offering explicit instruction on purposes, expectations, and modes of engaging – in effect, schooling about schooling. Such teaching often involves highly regimented activities (e.g., group chanting of the mantras associated with learning and attendance) in order to make the invisible visible – that is, to ensure that each person is aware of the nature of schooling.

As for other technologies that enable learning, for millennia formal education has been bogged down in debates of which tools should be permitted and which should be omitted. Near 2500 years ago, Plato (in his *Phaedo*) argued against the teaching of writing because it would diminish mental capacities associated with memory and reason.

Networked learning is an umbrella term to refer to strategies to bring people together to support one another's learning.

The movement began in the 1970s, and so has evolved alongside current digital technologies. It is thus associated with a number of technology-focused theories and strategies, such as *Computer-Supported Collaborative Learning*.

It is also associated with *blended learning*, which combines online, and face-to-face pedagogy.

The word *pedagogue* is frequently used as a synonym for teaching within Democratic Citizenship Education – although its original meaning seems to clash with some core principles of the movement.

Pedagogue is derived from the Greek *paidagogos*, a slave responsible for escorting boys to school, from *pedo-* + *agogos*, "child leader." There is some speculation that it was embraced by Democratic Citizenship Educators because of the historical senses of ACCOMPANYING and GUIDING.

He was partially correct. Members of oral cultures, on average, have more agile and trustworthy memories, likely because they must exercise them more. What Plato missed by focusing on the downside of a technology, however, was a more comprehensive consideration its of advantages. Every technology channels possibility; it opens up some capacities while allowing others to atrophy. And so, while literacy diminishes some capacities, it opens up so many other possibilities that it would be absurd to argue against it.

As will be explored in more detail in Moment 4, the same is true (or coming to be true) of other technologies that have faded into transparency through familiarity, including mass print, telephones, televisions, and calculators. However, more cutting-edge technologies remain sites of contestation. On one side, it is noted that smartphones, the Internet, video games, reality-TV, and social networking appear to contribute to the **Flynn Effect** – that is, higher IQs, broader awarenesses, and deeper expertise. On the other hand, actual achievement on standardized schooling tasks can decline when students are permitted to offload details about current affairs, core definitions, complicated procedures, and so on.

Of course, students would probably do much better on these fact-heavy standardized tests if they were allowed to use the technologies in their pockets and backpacks. The crux of the issue, however, is not whether such tools should be permitted. It is around helping learners develop the competencies and wisdom that enable effective use of cutting-edge technologies.

In fact, *every* conceptual tool found in schools was cutting edge at one time or another. Numbers, the alphabet, books, scientific formulae … everything. The implicit assumption seems to be that a technology is appropriate for schooling only when it becomes so ubiquitous and familiar that it disappears from collective consciousness. Democratic Citizenship Educators challenge this habit of thinking, pointing out that it often seems formal education is focused on preserving the best of technologies from the 1600s rather than embracing current possibilities – and this point is amplified daily with the increasing pace of technological development. At the time of this writing, every day nearly 5000 hours of video are uploaded, 2 billion videos are watched on YouTube, and about 1 million new websites are created. Most students in the developed world have near-continuous access to this material, not to mention to one another and to the well-structured resources of Wikipedia, Flickr, Twitter, Wordpress, Facebook, and so on.

Our guess is that the previous paragraph is going to seem woefully limited a decade from now, in much the same way that once-blistering speeds and massive memory capacities of 10-year-old laptops are no longer adequate for even mundane applications. The consequence of failing to come to grips with the issue of technology usage is ballooning, and some hear it as a death knell to the traditional school.

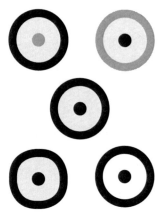

Or, at least, the death knell to Standardized Education, as new possibilities for personalization and specialization arise. The ideas of organizing children into grades based only on age and compelling them to move through factory-shaped experiences are making less and less sense. In contrast, Democratic Citizenship Educators are, by definition, much more attentive to the contexts of education. Those informed by this frame are thus pressing for more enthusiastic embrace of digital technologies – by, for example recognizing online time as class time or permitting Internet access during examinations. They also tend to advocate for thinking differently about the ways that students are clustered together.

Diversity (and) education

Which of the five figures shown in the margin is the most different from the others?

The correct answer to this question is counterintuitive. All but one differs from the "norm" in one way. The upper left has a gray dot; the upper right has a gray border; the lower left is squarish; the lower right has a whiter background. With no unique trait, the middle figure is the most different – even though it's the one that serves as the norm.

This item points to a logical flaw in the notion of "normal" as it has been used to organize formal education. In a species made up of unique beings, a truly normal individual would be truly abnormal. What is normal, then, is difference – as any middle school teacher will confirm. In an 8th-grade classroom, for example, there are likely to be individuals who are well into puberty and dealing with "adult" issues of sexuality and hygiene. There will also be pre-pubescent individuals whose bodily traits and issues are very different. Similar contrasts will be present in the cognitive domain. Some students will be capable of highly abstract and sophisticated thinking. Others will be relying on more concrete, immediate modes of thinking.

In other words, the presence of diversity in classrooms is something that has always been there. The issue is not its existence, but how it is regarded and engaged. Within Standardized Education it is ignored, and extreme differences are sequestered away in **special education** settings. Authentic Education recognized this thinking to be flawed and argued for an **inclusive education** approach based on the inevitable presence of diversities. More recently, there has been a trend to expand the range of differences that merit attention. In particular, earlier concerns with psychological and physical variety have been extended to encompass social, cultural, and economic differences. These contrasts and shifts in sensibility are summarized in the chart at the top of the next page.

It's important to add that the phrases *special education, inclusive education,* and *diversity education* are all in current usage – and, if you were to look up current definitions and descriptions, they would appear to be much more alike than the table suggests. That's not because the table is inaccurate or the details are overstated; it's because each movement has adapted as sensibilities have evolved. The details presented in the chart are reflective of the sensibilities in play when the movements began.

On that count, perhaps the most telling row in the chart is the bottom one, highlighting an evolution in thinking around the place of diversity. The most recent transition, toward recognition of the vital nature of di-

Service learning is an approach to teaching that blends in-class activities with meaningful community service. The intention is to support the development of critical-thinking and self-reflection skills alongside expanded awareness of personal responsibility, civic engagement, and community.

EVOLVING VOCABULARIES OF "DIFFERENCE"			
MOMENT IN EDUCATION:	**Standardized Education**	**Authentic Education**	**Democratic Citizenship Education**
APPROACH:	Special Education	Inclusive Education	Diversity Education
VOCABULARY:	handicaps; special needs; exceptionalities; delays	disabilities; disorders; different ablements	diversities
CATEGORIES:	Mental and physical – defined in terms of measureable departures from statistically based norms.	Cognitive, physical, behavioral, and emotional divergences from typical expectations.	All previously noted categories, plus race, ethnicity, class, gender, sexuality …
STRATEGY:	*Separate* – that is, diagnose and categorize the special need; cluster with others of similar need	*Accommodate* – that is, tailor individual education plans to identified differences, adapting content, pacing, supports, etc. as necessary	*Assimilate* – that is, afford equitable access, in part by structuring collective experiences in ways that all can make meaningful contributions
DRIVING PRINCIPLES:	Difference is a problem – those outside acceptable ranges of "normality" will likely benefit little from standardized approaches and so are best served in other contexts.	Difference is inevitable – education is obligated to serve the individual, no matter the profile. Encountering difference is healthy to the development of every individual.	Difference is vital – diversity is a source of possibility, and so individuals and collectives alike will benefit when it is properly woven into the fabric of schooling.

versity within dynamic sociocultural systems, is rooted in studies of major advances – where, for example, many persons of great prominence, who have served as major catalysts in political, economic, academic, and technical advances, have been "diagnosed" as hyperactive, dyslexic, autistic, economically disadvantaged, or belonging to some other category of difference.

As the current thinking goes, being "differently abled" or "marginalized" can have its advantages. In particular, alternative positionings likely present individuals with alternative vantage points and enable different strengths as they're compelled to find ways to cope with structures that weren't developed with them in mind. In the process, they may come across ways of making sense of the world that give them major advantages. Phrased differently, being defined as "other" or "outside" often helps to reveal the discourses that channel and constrain the thinking of others.

This is one of the major reasons that Democratic Citizenship Education encourages the assimilation of diversities in the classroom. There is much to be learned, not just on how to get along with others, but on how to become aware of habits and assumptions that can be individually and collectively debilitating. The two major strands of Democratic Citizenship Education – that is, the participatory and critical – meet on this issue. But, of course, the critical attitude goes a few steps further.

Critical pedagogy

A theme that is consistent across all the theories that inform Democratic Citizenship Education is that, just as individuals create unique webs of understanding from their personal experiences, communities construct unique systems of belief and interpretation. The key qualities are *sufficiency* and *coherence*. As long as networks of knowing hang together, their elements can and will be taken as truths.

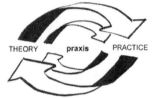

THEORY   praxis   PRACTICE

Praxis is a Greek word meaning "action, doing," and is actually the root of the word *practice*. It refers to the conscious and critical application of theory – and so the word is used to interrupt the false, commonsense dichotomy of theory *vs.* practice.

Critical pedagogy maintains an attitude of suspicion to such collective coherences, insofar as they might unnecessarily or excessively constrain individuals and communities. The movement might be defined as a disposition toward teaching that maintains a skeptical attitude toward the taken-for-granted – which includes, for example, everyday habits, popular assumptions, immediate interpretations, authoritative decrees, clichés, received wisdom, and other elements of prevailing discourses.

The skepticism within critical pedagogy is **praxis**-oriented. In this sense critical pedagogy surpasses critical theory. It moves beyond critique as it searches for more expansive possibilities, the first step of which is to uncover what is usually allowed to be tacit or implicit, such as forgotten histories, concealed power structures, unstated purposes, hidden ideological leanings, and no-longer-defensible beliefs. Descriptions of teaching thus cluster around EMPOWERING, EMANCIPATING, and GIVING VOICE.

Perhaps the most frequently referenced text on the topic is Paulo Freire's *Pedagogy of the Oppressed*. First published in English in 1970, this seminal text is based on Freire's experiences in helping disadvantaged adults learn to read and write.

The book is notable for its detailed account of helping learners to recognize and rethink their own internalized oppressions. At the time of its publication, "oppression" was most commonly seen as something external to and imposed upon the disadvantaged. Freire didn't dispute that, but he helped to show that all members of a society tend to take on those narratives of power and control, creating internal psychological barriers that are as daunting and constraining as any external structure. That is, the oppressor *vs.* oppressed dichotomy is a false one. The work of interrupting entrenched structures has as much to do with critically rewriting one's own narratives as it does with challenging cultural institutions.

As noted in Chapter 3.1, Freire coined the term CONSCIENTIZATION to refer to this process, and he offered pragmatic advice for educators wishing to enact this idea. A starting place, for example, is explicit critique of Standardized Education and its orienting metaphors of KNOWLEDGE AS OBJECT, LEARNING AS ACQUISITION, and TEACHING AS DELIVERY. (Freire collected these notions in what he called a "banking approach" to education.) Freire advocated for more a more situated approach to education and further developed dialogics as an important approach to teaching. In his view, a DIALOGIC PEDAGOGY is one in which all claims and assertions are considered critically within the collective, so their truth-value is a matter of the soundness of the thinking rather than the status of the speaker. (Opposites to dialogics include *opinion* on the personal level and *discourse* on the collective level – since neither is typically subjected to critical interrogation.)

As we explained in Chapters 3.1 and 3.2, critical theory was originally oriented toward Karl Marx's concerns with classism – that is, societal imbalances in access and opportunity that are rooted in social and economic differences. Classism was also the main issue in Freire's work and served as the focus in the translation of critical *theory* into critical *pedagogy* in the 1960s and 1970s. Other concerns and categories of oppression have since been embraced, and the current list of critical attitudes within teaching includes

One of the most insidious influences on cultural sensibilities is popular media, contributing in subtle ways to how citizens see themselves. To illustrate, we recommend doing image searches of "cartoon heroes," "cartoon heroines," and "cartoon villains." The heros are mainly hyper-masculine, tall, handsome, and broad shouldered. The heroines are hyperfeminine, svelt, beautiful, and buxom. And the villains are typically slouched, dark-complexioned, older, and somewhat effeminate.

The most common metaphor within Democratic Citizenship Education is TEACHING AS EMPOWERING.

The notion of "power" at the core of this metaphor is about "the ability to act, to do." A pedagogy of empowerment is thus about affording everything that Standardized Education and Authentic Education aim to provide, with regard to skills and understandings that are useful.

But it goes further to support awarenesses of discourses that enable and constrain possibilities.

feminist pedagogy, post-colonial pedagogy, Indigenous pedagogies, queer pedagogy, anti-racist pedagogy, and **anti-ableist pedagogy.** Common to all emphases are commitments to conscientization, recognizing internalized and external oppressions, and forging strong connections between knowledge and the ability to take constructive action. A few remarks on each:

- feminist pedagogy – seeking to interrupt a broad range of interpretations and structures that are associated with male-dominated domains and patriarchal histories, including attitudes toward knowledge/knowing and inequities in access and opportunity.
- anti-racist pedagogy – seeking to raise awareness of the structures – explicit and implicit, internalized and external – that militate against full participation of members of visible minorities in every aspect of culture.
- post-colonial pedagogy – particularly prominent in countries that were once (or are still) subject to colonial rule, seeking to raise awarenesses of conflicting worldviews, cultural reparation, anti-racisms, hybridization of knowledge domains, and the roles of schooling in cultural suppression.
- Indigenous pedagogies – tending to focus on the recovery and preservation of traditional knowledges of native cultures, typically emphasizing the maintenance of languages, attentiveness to place, sustainability, familial and social structures, strategies of wellness, and traditional lore.
- queer pedagogy – seeking to understand not only how educational matters have been sexed, but how they have been heterosexed – that is, how heterosexism has structured the ways genders are seen and understood.
- anti-ableist pedagogy – an emergent movement, seeking to render visible and interrupt discourses and structures associated with disadvantages of or discrimination toward persons identified as having cognitive, emotional, and/or physical disabilities. The **medical model of disability** is a particular focus of critique.

None of these categories should be seen as isolated. Most critical educators work across more than one.

In addition, critical pedagogues have embraced a range of theoretical movements and conceptual domains, including psychoanalysis, postmodernism, post-structuralism, cultural studies, and ecological thought. Consequently, there is a considerable breadth to current discussions. Across the ranges of emphasis and interpretation, however, education is seen as both a site of struggle and a means to effect change.

As for direct advice to teachers, there are no tidy answers but there are some consistent recommendations. Most important, perhaps, there is an ethical imperative for teachers to be attentive to the ways that classroom dynamics contribute to what can and can't be said, and spaces should be created for diverse opinions. At the same time, teachers should help students be aware of the **echo chamber effect** – that is ways that ideas can be reinforced, amplified, and entrenched through repetition within a closed community. This effect is as much a risk among critical pedagogues as it is among any group. Humans, it seems, want to feel their opinions are "truths" – and one way to do this is to avoid different and competing views. Sometimes that's accidental. Sometimes it's deliberate. It's always limiting.

Really radical responses

For the most part, the concerns and advice of Democratic Citizenship Educators are expressed in ways that fit within the frames of the modern school. While they are typically concerned with interrupting prevailing discourses and transforming core structures, advice is usually given in the form of alternative emphases and strategies.

There are more radical responses. For example, proponents of the **deschooling, unschooling,** and **free schools** movements argue that public schools cannot meet the educational needs of either individuals or society. Two intertwining principles within these movements are, firstly, the conviction that most people learn better when allowed to set their own pace within sufficient but not overbearing structures and, secondly,

By dictating content and prescribing teaching methods, Standardized Education contributed to a de-intellectualization of teaching. As a result, teachers are often seen as society's drudges, whereas they were once regarded as its leaders and luminaries.

In response, an emergent metaphor among critical pedagogues is TEACHER AS TRANSFORMATIVE INTELLECTUAL. Rather than focusing narrowly on producing skilled workers and managers, this manner of teaching aims to provide students with what they will need to be innovators and leaders.

An increasingly popular metaphor, fitted to Democratic Citizenship Education, is TEACHER AS PROVOCATEUR – which makes sense, given some of the (positive and negative) associations between the adjective *critical* and the verb *provoke*.

the realization that society's needs are becoming more and more diversified, in ways that a singular institution can never address.

While growing in momentum, these movements are still small and typically seen as being on the fringe. That said, other influences are starting to appear on the educational landscape that may have impacts that may prove every bit as radical. In particular, advances in technology, the realization of pressing ecological concerns, and the emergence of tran-systemic ways of thinking about knowing and learning are presenting some compelling new alternatives to what education is imagined to be. Collectively, these emergent trends are contributing to what may be an entirely new moment in education.

Suggestions for delving deeper

1. Teacher education is often framed as a conservative enterprise – that is, as though the main purpose of teaching is to preserve and maintain culture. Democratic Citizenship Educators argue that such a project is impossible. Why? How might the obligation to preserve and maintain be reframed as a participatory and/or critical educational project?

2. One of the mechanisms for enculturating new members of a community or professional is **legitimate peripheral participation** – that is, participating in tasks that are simple and low-risk but that still contribute to the work of the community. The idea is that novices should be given opportunities to engage in real work without being overwhelmed, affording opportunities to become more familiar with the vocabulary and discourses of the community. How do the structures of teacher education (in particular, the field experiences) fit with this emphasis?

3. When using an early draft of this book with a group of preservice teachers, one participant suggested that her automatic System 1 and reflective System 2 are analogous to Common Sense (a collective System 1) and Critical Pedagogy (a collective System 2). What might this analogy highlight? What might it obscure?

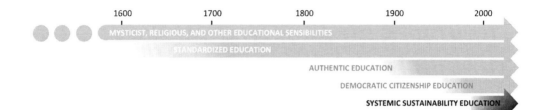

1600　1700　1800　1900　2000

MYSTICIST, RELIGIOUS, AND OTHER EDUCATIONAL SENSIBILITIES

STANDARDIZED EDUCATION

AUTHENTIC EDUCATION

DEMOCRATIC CITIZENSHIP EDUCATION

SYSTEMIC SUSTAINABILITY EDUCATION

MOMENT 4 •
systemic sustainability education

In brief ...
"Systemic Sustainability Education" gathers a range of emerging discourses on complexity, framed by the conviction that discussions of formal schooling have been too narrow – that is, bounded on one end with a focus on the individual and at the other with a focus on society. The biological and the more-than-human have been largely overlooked.

4.1 • The context ...
In addition to shifting cultural landscapes, rapidly evolving technologies, and major advances in brain research, growing environmental concerns have triggered more expansive discussions of formal education. Any one of these happenings should have major implications for schooling. Collectively, they compel dramatic rethinkings of the project.

4.2 • On knowledge and learning ...
Framed by the definition, "complex unities are learning systems," knowledge is understood as a vibrant, LIVING SYSTEM and learning as SYSTEMIC TRANSFORMATIONS or a LIFE PROCESS through which complex unities maintain internal and external coherence.

4.3 • On teaching ...
Embracing elements from all other moments, education is oriented toward the health of persons, social groupings, cultures, species, and biosphere. A key element of teaching is ENLARGING CONSCIOUSNESS – that is, prompting expansive awareness of oneself-in-the-world.

Take a glimpse ...
Suggested YouTube searches: [sustainability education] [ecoliteracy] [ecological education] [transdisciplinary learning] [complexity education]

bioculturalism	andragogy	affordances
complexity science	biomimicry	collectivity
digital age	brain-based learning	conversing
ecohumanism	brain plasticity	crowdsourcing
Gaia hypothesis	comparative dynamics	enabling constraints
global brain	embodied cognition	engaging
global citizenship	hybrid disciplinarity	extend consciousness
Indigenous epistemologies	lifelong learning	game-based learning
interspeciesism	more-than-human world	hive mind
network theory	nested systems	improvising
neurophenomenology	neurodiversity	MOOCs
nonlinear dynamics	power law distributions	neuroeducation
social networking	recursive elaboration	occasioning
systems theory	scale independence	redundancy/diversity
wisdom traditions	self-similarity	third teacher
	transdisciplinarity	universal design
		variable entry

HISTORY & CONTEXT

KNOWLEDGE & LEARNING

DESCRIBING & PRESCRIBING TEACHING

SYSTEMIC SUSTAINABILITY EDUCATION

iconic visual metaphor:
ALWAYS-EVOLVING
DECENTRALIZED NETWORK

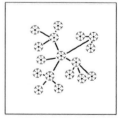

4.1 The Emergence of Systemic Sustainability Education

The nature of schooling will never be settled. Structures evolve, needs change, purposes get redefined. Yet, despite the differences among perspectives on education that have appeared in the modern era, there has been at least one consistent element across the moments of schooling discussed so far: all three focus almost exclusively on the "human."

Of course, that makes sense. Education is a human project.

Or so it has been assumed.

Humanity is facing a growing number of crises that are traceable to deep-set beliefs about its relationship to other species and to the rest of the world. The ages-old conviction that humans are somehow special and separate is not just proving to be untenable; this habit of thought may well be a key contributor to emergent personal, social, cultural, and ecological distresses. That is, climate change, species decline, global epidemics, ocean acidification – the list goes on and on – are crises of how the world is perceived and engaged. They arise when humans act as though the planet were an exploitable resource, a disconnected backdrop, or a disorderly home – metaphors that both place humans in a privileged, dominating role and obscure the fact that the species is one among many.

Until very recently, formal education has been strangely quiet on such issues. The discourses that have dominated discussions of schooling since the Industrial Revolution – that is, Standardized Education, Authentic Education, and Democratic Citizenship Education – have had virtually nothing to say on the

At its root, the word *sustainability* refers to the capacity to endure, but it also had an important dimension of nurturing. Most sustainability discourses focus on long-term societal viability, which has physiological, psychological, social, economic, political, cultural, economic, and environmental dimensions.

more-than-human world. For the past century in particular, analyses have tended to be bookended at one extreme by a focus on societal needs (within the Standardized Education movement) and at the other by individual possibilities (within the Authentic Education movement). Even though Democratic Citizenship Education has helped to interrupt this-or-that thinking by repositioning individual and collective as nested phenomena rather than polar opposites, few critical discussions have escaped the space of the explicitly and narrowly human. An implicit human *vs.* nature dichotomy has been operating for a long time.

This dichotomy works in many subtle ways. For example, it is not only apparent in the manner in which other species, ecosystems, and the biosphere have been ignored or marginalized in discussions of education, it has also been acted out in an associated mental *vs.* physical dichotomy in which *things of the mind* have been positioned as vastly more important than *things of the body*. Indeed, even when topics of physical exercise and bodily health come up in discussions of schooling, they tend to be treated in terms of their service to the mind. A fit, nourished, emotionally stable child learns better, it is often noted. And while that's true, it slips past the realization that a body is not something that a living form *has*; it is something that a living form *is*.

Things are shifting, however. In fact, beliefs and practices have changed dramatically over the past few decades, spurred by developments that have reminded humans that they are embodied beings, and those bodies are part of nature. An upshot of these intertwining realizations is that issues that might at first seem to be utterly unrelated, such as a child's inattentiveness in class and the planet-wide decimation of frog populations, may well be tightly coupled. And, critically, such wide-ranging issues might be tethered to the ways that individual bodies have been treated by and the planetary body has been considered within schools.

A new moment in formal education has arisen in response. It is so recent that no one has managed to propose a name for it that has stuck. We've thus elected to use the phrase Systemic Sustainability Education,

Most generally, the word *system* refers to a whole comprising multiple components working together – whether mechanical (an engine, a computer, etc.) or organic (a body, an ecosystem, etc.). We use it here more in reference to organic forms, consistent with its original meanings. When *system* entered the English language in the early 1600s, it meant "the whole creation, the universe."

and this choice is tied to two important elements of the movement. Firstly, discussions of schooling have come to be increasingly concerned with matters of health and *sustainability* – and considerations include but go well beyond the traditional poles of personal and cultural wellbeing to span the levels of the subpersonal (e.g., neurological, epigenetic) through the supercultural (e.g., ecosystemic, global). Secondly, phenomena at varied levels are increasingly being seen as vibrant, living, and learning *systems* of which humans are part, a significant departure from the inherited belief that the universe is a more-or-less mechanical backdrop for human activity.

Thinking systemically

It's one thing to suggest that formal education might be charged to assist the human species toward healthier, more sustainable habits by expanding the schooling's scope to include a broader range of phenomena. But it's quite another to make this demand in a manner that doesn't overwhelm an institution that is already burdened by so many purposes, such a diversity of theories, and such a breadth of curriculum content.

Phrased differently, it's become clear that there's a need for a way of thinking that brings discourses and demands into conversation, one that helps educators embrace the growing complexity of their roles.

As it turns out, developments over the past century, both inside and outside of education, have set the stage for powerful new ways of thinking rooted in organic rather than mechanistic metaphors. For example, the Authentic Education movement alerted educators to the pervasive use of machine-based metaphors for learning and teaching and, as developed in Moment 2, offered descriptions and advice that drew more on holistic, contingent, and exploratory ways of thinking. The Democratic Citizenship Education movement expanded the conversation, as discussed in Moment 3, by calling attentions to the complex, nested inter-relationships of agent and context, further interrupting the obsessions for order, efficiency, and productivity of the Standardized Education movement.

The word *healthy* calls to mind senses of wellness and wholeness (meanings it has evoked for many centuries. It is derived from Old English *hælp*, "wholeness, a being whole, sound or well").

The term is commonly used to refer to wellness at very different levels of organization (e.g., "heart health" and "planetary health"). We thus use it as a near-synonym to *systemic sustainability.*

These shifts in educational thought coincided with a broad, transdisciplinary move toward what is now known as **complexity thinking** (or "complexity theory" or "complexity science"). By way of preliminary description, *complex* describes those wholes that "are greater than the sums of their parts," to invoke an observation that dates back at least to Aristotle. Complexity researchers, that is, are interested in phenomena that can't be reduced to pieces – like you, for instance. You are more than a compilation of organs, bits of knowledge, and such.

Unfortunately, it is difficult to offer a concise definition of complexity because researchers tend to frame their meanings in terms of whatever they're researching. For example, synonyms for "complex systems" include "nonlinear dynamical systems" (mathematics), "dissipative structures" (chemistry), "autopoietic systems" (biology), "healthy organisms" (medicine), "organized complex systems" (information science), "social systems" (sociology) and simply "systems" (cybernetics). Added to these is a favorite among educators: complex systems are learning systems.

How, then, to proceed?

We don't want to turn this section of the book into a treatise on complexity, yet at the same time we don't want to gloss over a very important shift in thinking that both embraces and elaborates key movements in education over the last century. For that reason, we move on here by offering five different **definitions of complexity**. (We've selected these five for their relevance to formal education. A quick web search will bring up many others.)

We hasten to add that our purpose in approaching the task in this way is not to suggest you should pick the one or two meanings that make the most sense to you. Rather, we are actually attempting to use a principle of complexity to describe complexity – namely that possibilities arise in networked interactions that are not present in any of the elements. That is, our hope is that more nuanced, flexible, and robust understandings of complexity will emerge for you through the effort it takes to blend these different meanings:

Complexity thinking is a transdisciplinary academic movement that is concerned with better understanding those systems that might be described as learning or living.

A sense of the sorts of forms studied, and strategies to represent these forms, might be gleaned from visualcomplexity.com.

- Complexity is comparative dynamics.
- Complexity is the study of emergent transphenom-ena.
- Complexity is distinct from complicated.
- Complexity refers to a category of phenomena with specific qualities.
- Complexity is the study of learning systems.

This list is hardly exhaustive. We've only selected meanings that seem to have particular relevance to education, and so we'd recommend further research on the topic if it is one that interests you.

Meaning 1: comparative dynamics

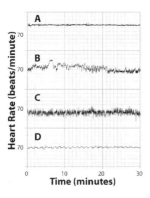

Which, if any, of the traces of heart activity is indicative of a healthy heart? (The answer is discussed to the right.)

The image above is adapted from A.L. Goldberger, L.A.N. Amaral, J.M. Hausdorff, P.C. Ivanov, C.K. Peng, & H.E. Stanley, "Fractal dynamics in physiology," *Proceedings of the National Academy of Sciences*, vol. 99, suppl. 1: 2466–2472. Copyright © 2002 National Academy of Sciences of the United States of America. Used with permission.

Four actual traces of heart activity are presented in the margin to the left. One presents the profile of a healthy heart. Three suggest serious, life-threatening problems. Which is the healthy one? Why did you choose the one you chose?

The first of these traces is indicative of ventricular fibrillation, the third of cardiac arrhythmia, and the fourth of congestive heart failure. The second trace shows a healthy heart rhythm.

Why? The heart is **structurally coupled** to other bodily systems, and collectively those bodily systems are part of grander biological and social systems. That means that the heart has to be adaptive and responsive. It can't have a steady, mechanical rhythm, but must be able to adjust as activities demand more blood flow, thoughts inspire excitement, and so on.

It turns out that *all* greater-than-the-sums-of-their-parts systems manifest this sort of profile. Consider, for example, the familiar images used to show stock market activity, brain function, climate change, traffic volumes, and such.

On the surface, it might seem very strange to compare the dynamics of a heart and those of a stock market or a local climate. Among complexity thinkers, however, such comparisons are commonplace. For this reason, complexity research can be described as a sort of "comparative dynamics," which might be contrasted with the "comparative statistics" approach to research discussed in Moment 1 (and critiqued in

Moments 2 and 3). The following table summarizes some key differences.

COMPARATIVE STATISTICS *vs.* COMPARATIVE DYNAMICS		
Comparative Statistics	FIELD	**Comparative Dynamics**
early-1800s	BEGAN	mid-1900s
Statistics derives from a word that means "hold still," reflecting an approach based on snapshots or still images	MEANING OF TITLE	*Dynamics* derives from a word that means "active" or "energetic," reflecting an approach that follows active, living forms in situ
comparing "like" forms (e.g., one stock market to another, or one heart to another)	FOCUS	comparing different forms (e.g., a stock market to a heart, or an ant to a city, or a mind to an ecosystem)
normal or standard ("mean") distributions, such as the normal curve – that is, it is assumed that objects cluster around a central, mean value	ASSUMED DISTRIBUTION	power law distributions – that is, in which there are very many small events and very few huge ones (and so "arithmetic mean" is virtually meaningless)

The bottom row of this chart is particularly important. For complex phenomena – such as wealth distribution, earthquakes, learning events, wars, Internet hubs, social trends, life forms, questions, articulations, and so on – it makes virtually no sense to talk about "averages" or "norms." For example, it would be silly to calculate the intensity of an average earth tremor. Given that the planet is constantly rumbling, when all the minor shaking is pooled with the few major earthquakes, the result would be a useless, near-0 value. More provocatively, a mathematical average of net worth would be worse than useless, as this sort of datum would mask the fact that the bulk of wealth is in the hands of a tiny elite (i.e., in the "very few 'massive' events" region of the power law distribution).

To be clear, the suggestion here is not that mean distributions are a fiction or that they are inherently flawed. On the contrary, they are useful for describing many phenomena. The point is simply that they may have been over applied and, in the process, they have been used either to distort or to obscure some important qualities of dynamic systems. Studies of comparative dynamics – which include constructivist, sociocultural, and critical theories of learning – seek to restore some of that complexity to conversations as they offer further critiques of educational models based on norms, averages, and means.

Meaning 2: the study of emergent transphenomena

What do the following phenomena have in common: the 2008 stock market crash, the spread of colds and flus every winter, the development of the world wide web, creativity and intelligence, sleep, an ant hill, mathematics, personal identity?

Emergent is a word that was used very little until the middle of the last century, but has surged in popularity since. Among complexity thinkers, it is used in specific reference to the appearance of a whole that exceeds the parts.

While it may seem that the answer is "almost nothing," each of these phenomena might be appropriately described as **emergent**. That is, each is a clearly discernible, coherent phenomenon that cannot be reduced to fundamental parts. Each arises in the entangled interactions of many agents or subsystems and, in the process, exhibits properties and behaviors that are not present in any of those agents or subsystems.

Part of the reason that these phenomena cannot be reduced to the sums of their parts is that they themselves are often parts of grander systems, which in turn influence their properties and behaviors. With regard to humans and human systems, this particular insight is actually central to the Democratic Citizenship Education movement in the realization that identities are framed by contexts – that is, who one is and where one is are inextricably intertwined.

A complex form is thus a *transphenomenon*. That is, understanding a complex, emergent unity usually requires examining at least three levels of organization. One must look at the unity itself, as it manifests qualities that are not present at any other level. If that unity is part of larger systems – such as, in the case of humans, families, social cliques, subcultures, and so on – one will find important clues on the character of the unity by scaling up to look at those systems. Similarly, there will be important information in the subsystems, and so it can also be important to scale down (to extend the example, in the case of individuals, elements of personalities are tethered to brain structure, emotional health, fitness level, etc.). In brief, a transphenomenon is a form or happening that can only be understood by looking across levels of organization.

While the term *transphenomenon* is not in wide use among educators, the sensibility that it flags is becoming more and more prominent. Consider the example of reading ability. A mere generation ago, reading difficulties were seen almost entirely in terms of problems on the level of the individual learner. As it turns out, while it may happen at very different paces, almost all children learn to read – with two notable and obvious categories of exception. First, there are those who have a genuine neurological or vision issue that makes it difficult to decipher text, track storylines, and/or engage in some function that is critical to reading. Second, and more tragically, there are those from minority groups whose members have faced a history of prejudice and oppression. In either case, to attribute or to locate the "issue" with the individual is wholly inadequate. In the first case, one must look to subsystems for roots and to supersystems (e.g., external supports, special tutoring) for responses. In the other, one must look at supersystems for roots and across many levels of organization for suitable responses. Leaving the discussion at the level of the individual is irresponsible, disenfranchising, and unethical.

A *transphenomenon* is a form or event that cannot be well understood by looking only at a single level of organization. Obesity, for example, manifests itself on the individual level, but the fact it is an international epidemic suggests it must be studied at the collective level. At the same time, there are indications of genetic, viral, and other triggers, indicating it must also be studied at the subpersonal level.

As a reminder of this important insight, we use the nested image on the next page as a visual metaphor of emergent, transphenomenal natures of individual learning, the institution of schooling, culture, and the species. Each layer (or body) in this image can be simultaneously seen as a whole, a part of a whole, or a network of wholes.

Like all models, this graphic is far from complete. It actually omits much more than it includes. For example, other levels might have been included (e.g., to acknowledge developments in nanotechnologies, genetics, and augmented perception). As well, other forms, agents, and organizations might have been in-

The Ecosphere, or the Planetary Body (Ecological Theories)

The Species (Biology and Evolutionary Theory)

Society, or the Body Politic (Anthropology, Cultural Studies, and Critical Discourses)

Collectivities: Social Bodies, Bodies of Knowledge, and so on (Constructionisms)

The Person, or Body Biologic (Psychology and Constructivisms)

Bodily Subsystems (Recent studies in Immunology, Neurology, and related domains)

Fitted to the visual metaphor of nested systems discussed on these pages, the notion of *web of life* is an ancient one that has recently re-emerged as a popular and powerful alternative to the idea of the great chain of being (see page 18).

cluded in any given level. Yet further, the tidy layers obscure the overlapping and interlacing complexities of the phenomena listed. In a nutshell, then, the image is intended to be provocative, not exhaustive. It is simply a visual metaphor for the transphenomenal character of every aspect of one's life by gesturing toward a complex web of existence and troubling some lingering beliefs associated the notion of a great chain of being.

Meaning 3: type of phenomenon with specific qualities

If you were to pick up a book on complexity research, chances are the definition it provided of complexity would start with a description of emergence, and the balance of the discussion would revolve around a list of qualities of complex phenomena. For example, complex forms

- self organize (which means very much the same thing as "are emergent," adding that there is no controller or master making things happen);
- self determine (that is, unlike the predictable way a mechanical system reacts to a force or input, the

way that a complex system responds will vary from one unity to the next – and from one moment to the next – as responses depend on the system's structure and history);

- operate far from equilibrium (that is, complex unities are always "off balance," which is why they have jagged activity profiles – they must be responsive to maintain their coherences; to reach equilibrium is to die);
- have decentralized-network structures (that is, they are organized in a very specific way; more in Chapter 4.2 on this vital detail);
- are scale independent (that is, they tend to have the same bumpiness of detail, whether magnified or reduced; for instance, in the nested image on the previous page, the complexity at any layer is comparable to that of any other layer).

The list goes on. Notably, expanded lists often include some figurative elements as well. For example, complex unities are commonly conceived, perceived, and characterized using the metaphor of *body* – as in a body of knowledge, a social corpus, the body politic, or a planetary body. This metaphor, in turn, enables such assertions as "complex unities are embodiments of their histories." As explored in Chapters 4.2 and 4.3, many of these descriptors serve as powerful interruptions to deeply entrenched assumptions about knowing, learning, and teaching.

The word *equilibrium* derives from the Latin *aequus* + *libra*, "equal + balance." It was first used to describe a type of mechanical stability.

The notion was common in discussions of learning for much of the last century, when it was assumed humans seek out balances and stabilities.

However, equilibrium turns out to be a poor metaphor. As studies of complexity reveal, learning and living systems – by definition – must exist in disequilibrium.

Meaning 4: distinct from complicated

Consider the difference between these metaphors:

THE BRAIN IS A COMPUTER.

THE BRAIN IS AN ECOSYSTEM.

Neither of these descriptions is "correct" in the sense of providing a thorough, accurate description of what the brain is and how it functions. However, in these senses, one is certainly more correct than the other.

The differences between the entailments of these metaphors are reflective of the distinction between the meanings of *complicated* and *complex*, as complexity thinkers use the words. Summarized in the table below, complicated systems are governed by physics and are the predictable, determined sums of their parts – vacuum cleaners, colliding particles, clocks, and such. Complex systems, in contrast, can never be reduced to their parts because they are always caught up with other systems in a dance of change. They are spontaneous, have levels of unpredictability, are irreducible, are context dependent, and are vibrantly sufficient.

COMPLICATED *vs.* COMPLEX		
Complicated forms	TYPE	**Complex forms**
	VISUAL METAPHOR	
physics, engineering (machine metaphors; cause–effect language and imagery of Newtonian laws)	SOURCE DOMAINS OF METAPHORS	biology, ecology (ecosystem metaphors; a Darwinian vocabulary of adaptive processes and fitness)
input/output flows (linearity)	DYNAMICS	cycles and feedback loops (recursivity)
deficiency-filling; efficiency-seeking (optimality; goal oriented)	ORIENTATIONS	sufficiency-oriented (adequacy; fitness and development oriented)

Of course, as with any sharp distinction, this one falls apart when it comes to certain phenomena. In particular, some recent technological developments, especially in robotics and artificial intelligence, render the distinction a fuzzy one in some cases. But, on this count, one of the reasons that the boundary is becoming blurred is because the designers of these technologies are deliberately using the images and metaphors presented in right-most column of the chart above.

With regard to education, the distinction between complicated and complex is reflective of the evolution of the field over the last century, as factory-inspired obsessions with efficiency, outcomes, quality management, predictability, uniform methods, and task fragmentation have slowly given way to appreciations of the organic complexity of learning processes.

Meaning 5: the study of learning systems

As we mentioned at the start of this section, the major reason that it is difficult to define complexity is that its proponents tend to offer descriptions that are linked to their own research interests.

We're no different. For us, complex systems are learners – that is, forms that adapt and assert themselves in an endless choreography with and in other learning systems. This insight frames Chapters 4.2 and 4.3, and so we won't say much more about it here, other than to use it as a means to reframe the diversity of disciplines, discourses, and dilemmas that confront educators. We use the graphic below to flag this sensibility.

As with all our other visual metaphors, this one is incomplete, and is intended to be provocative rather than exhaustive. For us, the notion that complex unities are learners offers a means to think about things not only in terms of tensions and discontinuities, but also in terms of a grand, co-implicated conversation. For example, with regard to academic domains, when complex unities are framed as nested learning systems, such diverse disciplines as genetics and geology can be constructively cast as studies of learning – that is, of never-ending, adaptive, and co-implicated processes that operate at particular levels of organization in particular ways. In the same vein, discourses as diverse as constructivism, critical theory, and the **Gaia hypothesis** can be seen as being deeply complementary – each structured around the desire to better understand the emergence of a particular complex, emergent form (i.e., personal understanding, cultural dynamics, and planetary vibrancy). At the same time, each opens up a range of critical issues that schools have been asked to address, some of which are identified in the final column of the graphic.

Included among these issues are all of those we identified in discussions of Authentic Education and Democratic Citizenship Education, highlighting that an intention of complexity thinking is to embrace the insights of other discourses while situating them in wider-ranging conversations.

	INTERIOR	EXTERIOR
INDIVIDUAL	**I** [e.g., identity, consciousness, emotions, will]	**It** [e.g., nutrition, neural activity, stimulus–response]
COLLECTIVE	**We** [e.g., cultures, norms, values, communication]	**Its** [e.g., systems, environment, political orders]

Transdisciplinarity **describes a research sensibility in which multiple systems across many scales are studied at the same time.**

One transdisciplinary theory that has risen to prominence over recent decades is Ken Wilber's *Integral Model* **– which, in contrast to the image on the facing page, organizes phenomena according to the dimensions of interior–exterior and individual–collective.**

The subpersonal through the superpersonal

One of the places that complexivist sensibilities are showing up is in the emergence of **hybrid disciplines** – that is, new domains that traverse disciplinary boundaries that can date back centuries and millennia. Examples identified in the graphic of the facing page include epigenetics, neurophenomenology, and contemplative neuroscience. Others not mentioned include ecopsychology, bioethics, ethnobiology, bioeconomics, and ecosophy – and these represent only a small slice of new fields that have been prompted by the realization that one must look across levels of organization to understand complex phenomena.

Education is, if anything, the epitome of this transdisciplinary sensibility. One need only glance across the titles in a recent annual index of *Educational Researcher*, *Harvard Educational Review*, or *Phi Delta Kappan* to find support for this assertion. These leading journals will have articles on brain function, physical health, personal understanding, social cohesion, cultural trends, and environmental concerns. Breaking with the mid-1900s' construct that "education is applied psychology," within Systemic Sustainability Education the domain is perhaps more appropriately described as an "applied neuro-psycho-socio-anthropo-eco-logy."

This transdisciplinary mindset is precisely what is needed to make sense of some recent findings on learning and systemic sustainability. For example:

- One's level of fitness and the wellbeing of one's immune system have been shown to be tightly coupled, and they have also been shown to be closely tied to attention span, conscious awareness, ability to remember, emotional stability, and social intelligence. (The experimental proof for these associations is recent, but the experiential evidence is ancient. Think about how you respond to challenging mental tasks or difficult emotional circumstances when you have the flu or when you're exhausted.)
- In the early 2000s, spending on psychotropic drugs (e.g., antipsychotics, antidepressants, attention deficit medications) surpassed spending on antibiotics and asthma medications for children.
- Difficulties in behavior, attention, and weight management among children drop precipitously when they engage in regular, vigorous activity.
- Difficulties in behavior, attention, and weight management among children drop precipitously when they have "green time" – that is, when they have regular and sustained access to outdoor green spaces, engage in care of plants and animals, and are otherwise involved in the more-than-human world.
- Alongside climate change, the accelerating paces of species decline, and the threats of worldwide pandemics, the incidences of asthma, autism, allergies, morbid obesity, and hyperactivity among children have all increased markedly over the past decade.

A generation ago, these sorts of issues would have scarcely registered in a discussion of the place of education – partly because they were much less pronounced, but mostly because people didn't have the conceptual tools to see the connections. Biological, medical, and environmental matters were simply not seen (or seeable) as germane to the project of schooling.

On the policy level, the situation is changing.

HUMAN SCIENCES

Psychology, Phenomenology, Developmentalism, Counseling, Exceptionality Studies, Psychoanalysis, Consciousness Studies, Psychiatry

Each of the major moments in modern education has been aligned with a major branch of science.

Standardized Education's main influences were the *physical sciences*, which focus on the study of inanimate natural objects.

Authentic Education was framed by the *human sciences*, which encompass those disciplines concerned with interpretation of experiences,

SOCIAL SCIENCES

Linguistics, Political Science, Anthropology, Economics, Sociology, Cultural Studies, Law, Sociology

activities, constructs, and artifacts associated with human beings.

Democratic Citizenship Education drew mainly on the *social sciences*, sharing a focus on the co-specifying, co-evolving dynamics of individuals and collectives.

Systemic Sustainability Education is closely fitted to the sensibility of the *complexity sciences*, which investigate how relationships among agents give rise to the collective possibilities.

Although varying dramatically from one setting to the next, requirements for health and physical education are trending upward, curricula and classroom resources are beginning to reflect ecological concerns, and more nuanced collaborations are emerging among schools, social agencies, and medical systems. Even so, there's a long way to go. The bulk of these sorts of initiatives are appearing as reactions, lodged in a medical model of illness–treatment (or deficit–remediation, in educational terms).

Of course, when situations have been permitted to devolve into crises, a reactive response is necessary. That said, there are promising signs that a more proactive mindset – one of Systemic Sustainability – is emerging. In this regard, three (among many) notable foci in contemporary discussions of the role of education are wellness at the subpersonal and personal levels, ethics on the levels of the social and cultural, and stewardship with regard to supercultural matters.

In terms of treatments of these three foci, proponents of this moment have tended to complement and elaborate the emphases developed within Democratic Citizenship Education on participation and conscientization. The participatory attitude is extended beyond the realm of immediate human interest to encompass obligations to respect and protect the physicality of existence (e.g., through proper exercise and nutrition, moral behaviors toward others, and wise use of resources). Along similar lines, the conscientization emphasis is extended to encompass an ecological mindfulness that is attentive to the broader consequences of one's beliefs and actions.

On the micro level, these elaborations of participation and conscientization are showing up as greater emphases on exercise and recreation, emotional health, diet and nutrition, time in nature, contribution and service, learning through experience, comfort with change, and relationship and inclusivity – increasingly seen as fundamental aspects of learning, not supports to learning. On the macro level, markers include what might be called **global citizenship** – which extends the notion of democratic citizenship to include an ethical sensitivity to issues and phenomena that exceed the human, coupled to a heightened awareness that one's actions make a difference.

On this count, a complexity-minded sensibility has emerged as crucial. One of the principles of complexity that we didn't mention is that it is impossible to know the consequences of one's actions. This idea is most popularly known as the **butterfly effect**, which amounts to a recognition that there is no such thing as an inconsequential moment or an irrelevant act. It is an insight that amplifies the importance of a participatory, conscientized mindset within a frame of Systemic Sustainability Education.

The bottom line

So, what might Systemic Sustainability Education be all about?

Answers are only just emerging. But one detail is clear: it is not about replicating or perpetuating sensibilities rooted in assumptions of endless growth and human uniqueness. Rather, there is an evident need for creating something new through moments integrating the biological, cognitive, social, cultural, and ecological dimensions of life. It is an education that is realized in the possibilities that might arise when diversities are brought into conversation. It is an education that is not about CONTROLLING or MANAGING, but ENGAGING.

The phrase *butterfly effect* was coined in the late-1900s to refer to the way that tiny events can trigger massive ones over time. The actual phrase was taken from an analogy to the possibility of a hurricane being triggered by the flapping of a butterfly's wings.

It's a fitting image to end this chapter – with its message that "inputs" and "outputs" can be wildly disproportionate for complex phenomena. One implication is that the popular assumption, "teaching causes learning," is laughably inappropriate.

Most important, perhaps, it is an education that is neither beholden to *what was* nor obsessed with *what is*, but that is oriented to the expansive possibilities of *what might be*.

With regard to the specific implications for individual learners, the upshot at this moment in education may be surprising. It arises in the contrast between *complicated* and *complex* perspectives. When a system is interpreted in complicated, mechanical terms (as within a Standardized Education frame), there is a need to ensure that individual parts are free of foibles and quirks – hence an emphasis on generic preparation, management of outcomes, and control of behavior. Nearly the opposite is true for complex, emergent systems. Possibility arises in the diversities and specializations of a system's agents.

In other words, and in a seeming paradox, an education for the greater good – one that anticipates issues rather than simply chasing after desperately needed responses – must be structured to nurture the unique interests of the individual in ways that enable those specialized interests to operate in conversation with others' expertise.

In Chapters 4.2 and 4.3 we look across the emerging culture of expertise in education, attending in particular to the necessity of diverse and deep specialists within an increasingly complex world.

Suggestions for delving deeper

1. When the original edition of *Engaging Minds* was published in 1999, the first image to show up on an Internet search of "nested systems" was the one presented in this chapter (on page 179). That's changed. Use a search engine to find images that are being developed in other domains – psychology, economics, ecology, theology, spirituality, and so on. What do they have in common? How are they different?

2. Much to his mother's embarrassment, 2.5-year-old Michael has started to identify any man with a beard as "daddy" – a habit that illustrates that "errors" are transphenomena. On the level of Michael's thinking, everything is coherent and sensible. On the level of social action, that's not the case. In other words, whether or not something is an error depends on which system you're looking at or through. How is that insight useful for resolving tensions among different moments in formal education?

3. What are some of the contrasting entailments of the metaphors BRAIN AS COMPUTER and BRAIN AS ECOSYSTEM? What are some correlates for discussions of education at other levels of organization (e.g., SCHOOL AS FACTORY *vs.* SCHOOL AS ECOSYSTEM)?

4.2 Knowledge and Learning in Systemic Sustainability Education

A *fractal* is a geometrical form that has the same level of detail whether reduced or magnified. There are many familiar examples of this quality of *scale independence*, including cauliflower florets and fern fronds.

Fractal images serve as powerful visual metaphors for the similar dynamics of biological, cognitive, social, and other complex systems. (For a better sense of their structure, we recommend an image search.)

Think about why you're reading this book, here and now. How did you arrive at this place?

You could probably answer this question with a linear narrative that stretches from the moment of your birth to this instant. But that rendering would be misleading. The path here has been anything but direct. It was more a dance of choices and accidents than a march of progress.

One of the recurrent themes of post-Standardized Educational sensibilities is that there is something deeply troublesome about the habit of describing life in terms of progress along a straight trajectory. Personal histories are better characterized as evolving spaces of possibility, more fitted to trees of ever-branching possibilities than unidirectional arrows.

The same is true of knowing and learning. Rather than the lines, arrows, and enclosed regions of planar geometry, their complex characters are better depicted in terms of **recursion, iteration, feedback loops,** and nested forms.

Such notions were intimated in Moments 2 and 3, where we offered critiques and preliminary alternatives to the planar geometry so prevalent in the Standardized Educational mindset. Knowledge might be understood in terms of nested networks, for example, and learning in terms of nonlinear trajectories. However, it has only been recently that well-articulated alternatives to planar geometry have been offered. We find one of those particularly useful: **fractal geometry**.

You might not have a formal knowledge of fractals, but you're certainly familiar with their forms. We actually referred to one of the defining qualities of fractals in the last chapter: **scale independence**. A fractal image has the same level of complexity – the same bumpiness of detail – whether it's viewed through a telescope or a microscope. This quality may feel counterintuitive, since it contradicts an assumption that has (mis)guided western science for centuries. Many believe that the universe has simplest parts. It might not.

Fractal geometry is relatively new, but humans have long been aware of objects that demonstrate some level of scale independence. In fact, almost every child has noticed that a small twig can strongly resemble an entire tree. The same is true of a broccoli floret, a parsley sprig, or a fern frond. This particular type of scale independence is formally known as **self-similarity**. A figure is self-similar if a well-chosen piece resembles the whole. As the fern illustration on page 189 highlights, this property is associated with a sort of nestedness.

Part of the reason for this constant bumpiness of detail of fractals has to do with the way they're produced. Each is generated through recursion. Recursive processes are based on rules that are repeated, but in a special way that systematically transforms the form they are used to create. The starting place of each stage is the output of the previous stage. An example is illustrated in the margin, based on a simple rule applied recursively.

This example illustrates how surprising detail can quickly emerge from simple rules. It also hints at the pervasive presence of fractals in the natural world – and throughout your body for that matter. Lungs, circulatory systems, neurons, and brains are much better described as fractals than in terms of the shapes of planar geometry. Fractals are not only useful for analyzing structures of living forms; they also appear in traces of their dynamics. Look again at the healthy trace of heart activity on page 175. It is the only one of the four traces that's fractal; its micropatterns strongly resemble its macropatterns.

Throughout this chapter we draw on fractals as a source of visual metaphors for knowing and learning. To further frame the discussion, we pause to "drill

Recursive elaboration is a process of development that proceeds not by accumulation, but by transformation. At each stage, a rule is applied to the outcome of the previous stage, often giving rise to surprising detail in very short order.

The process of recursive elaboration is a useful metaphor for the learning dynamics of complex unities. Each stage of their develop-

deeper" on one phenomenon – hyperactivity – in order to highlight the utility of fractal imagery and to illustrate the importance of thinking in transphenomenal terms.

The transphenomenality of hyperactivity

Within the developed world there is a tendency to interpret complex phenomena in terms of simple causes. **Hyperactivity** is one example.

Many regard hyperactivity (and a cluster of associated diagnoses, including **Attention Deficit Disorder**, Attention Deficit Hyperactivity Disorder, and Hyperkinetic Disorder) as an epidemic of sorts. Typically emerging in early childhood, its "symptoms" include inability to focus, excessive physical activity, inconsiderateness, and impulsiveness at levels that can impair academic performance and social engagement.

It's estimated that 5 to 10% of children suffer from this affliction. These numbers are notable in the fact that the same ratios are typically used in estimates of other categories of "exceptional" difference, including giftedness and depression. (This isn't entirely coincidental; most categories of exceptionality are defined in terms of deviations from a standardized norm.)

Treatments for hyperactivity vary massively. The most newsworthy are chemically based, with the psychostimulant methylphenidate (trade named Ritalin) being prescribed most frequently and at ever-increasing rates. Current estimates are that up to 12% of school-aged children in North America are using it or a related substance. When combined with antidepressants, the total fraction of children taking psychiatric drugs likely exceeds 15%. As striking as they are, these statistics don't actually give the complete picture. Other treatments are used, including dietary regimes (e.g., limiting sugar, protein, and certain fats), **behavior modification** programs (i.e., rigid structures of reward and punishment), neuro-feedback, psychoanalysis, peer-group support, and adult accompaniment. Success is varied in every case.

It can be tempting to think there is broad agreement on what hyperactivity is and what causes it. In fact,

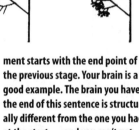

ment starts with the end point of the previous stage. Your brain is a good example. The brain you have at the end of this sentence is structurally different from the one you had at the start ... and you can't get back to the previous one. The next task you take on will be with your recursively elaborated brain, which will once again trigger alterations to its structure.

its symptoms and triggers are vague – and for good reason. It is likely that hyperactivity is most often a symptom itself, triggered by something else. Drug therapies and other strategies may only be masking undiagnosed problems.

That doesn't mean the hyperactivity isn't a "real" phenomenon. It is showing up in many classrooms and there is clear neurological evidence that some children's brains are behaving differently. That said, however, it is notable that use of behavior-affecting drugs and other interventions drop precipitously every summer. When school lets out.

During the school year, however, difficult and disruptive behavior is a growing problem. The trend has prompted extensive research that encompasses biopsychological triggers ...

- low-grade poisoning (e.g., lead, mercury, carbon dioxide);
- malnutrition and nutrient deficiencies (due more to the modern diet and inconsistent eating habits than to lack of food);
- high glycemic-index foods (which contribute to spikes in blood sugar levels);
- chemical dependencies (e.g., alcohol, nicotine, solvents, recreational drugs);
- pollutants (e.g., pesticides, molds, fresheners, repellants, polishes, perfumes);
- conditions that might restrict oxygen or other vital resources in the brain (e.g., lack of exercise, obesity, tumors, trauma injuries, diabetes, allergies, seizures).

... as well as sociocultural-environmental influences ...

- difficulties at home;
- difficulties with or among peers;
- difficulties with classroom tasks (e.g., diverting attention from poor performance);
- permissive parenting that contributes to arrogance, feelings of entitlement, and lack of social empathy;
- excessive information or stimulation, especially in the form of background noise;
- excessive (or inadequate) choice;
- unpredictable changes in context or expectation.

Indicators of HYPERACTIVITY

- poorly sustained attention in most situations;
- low task-persistence when no immediate consequences;
- impulsive, can't delay gratification;
- difficulty regulating or inhibiting behavior in social contexts;
- more active and more restless than most children;
- difficulty adhering to rules.

Just to underscore the incredible complexity associated with that cluster of behaviors and attitudes collected under the umbrella of *hyperactivity*, several educational

These lists should give pause, not in the least because many of the phenomena mentioned have been increasing at rates that roughly parallel the growing incidences of hyperactivity. They also correlate to increased reportings of allergies, asthma, childhood obesity, autism, and learning disabilities – all of which are associated with similar lists of triggers.

A mode of thinking that makes it possible to consider diverse influences all at the same time would seem to be needed. Complexity thinking offers one possible frame, and we find the scale-independent fractal imagery associated with complexity to be useful for organizing lists of considerations and triggers. In the chart below, we've adapted a graphic from Chapter 4.1 (of some nested complex systems) by including a few triggers of hyperactivity:

Indicators of GIFTEDNESS

- poor attention, boredom, daydreaming in specific situations;
- low tolerance or persistence with tasks that seem irrelevant;
- judgment lags behind intellectual development;
- tendency toward power struggles with authorities;
- high activity, may need less sleep than most children;
- questions rules and traditions.

Complex Unity	Possible Trigger
Biosphere	Chemical pollutants
Species	Neurodiversity
Society	Excessive choice
Social collectives	Home difficulties
Person	Test anxiety
Bodily subsystems	Nutrient Deficiencies

researchers have pointed out some perhaps-worrisome relationships between attributes of hyperactivity and attributes of giftedness.

This manner of representation, we believe, presents a compelling case for a "fractal consciousness" – that is, for a mode of awareness that can encompass the subpersonal through the supercultural. As emphasized in the previous chapter, earlier moments in education have been bookended by the needs of the individual on one end and those of society on the other. That span is clearly inadequate.

Rethinking the bookends of discourses

Every evening on the news, there is brief mention of changes in stock market values. No matter the nature of the changes, the announcer always offers a line or two of commentary that, supposedly, explains the day's fluctuations. The same tendency is present in many discussions of children's behavior: "Her parents were too permissive"; "He consumes too much sugar"; "They have lower levels of dopamine in their brains." There seems to be a pervasive desire to reduce complex events to simple causes and effects.

This predisposition to look for simple explanations, we believe, is reflective of two interpretive habits. One is a tendency to over-emphasize boundaries, and the other is tendency to under-appreciate the internal structure of a complex form.

To illustrate the first of these habits, consider the shading of each of the blocks in the image to the right. Most people are surprised to learn that each of the five rectangles is uniformly shaded, even though it looks like each is lighter where it borders a darker block and darker where it touches a lighter one. (That will be more obvious if you cover a border with a pen – which will also reveal that neighboring blocks aren't as different as they seem.)

The graphic of nested complex systems on page 179 employs the same illusion. We did that as a visual reminder that the boundaries perceived between levels aren't as cut-and-dried as uncritical perception might suggest. As a lesson in how people interpret what they see, this illusion illustrates that perception doesn't make absolute judgments; it compares. That is, perception is oriented to difference – to the book out of place, the child who's taller, the misspelled word, the unfamiliar accent. Humans are difference-seeking distinction-makers. And those differences are not just sought out; they're usually amplified when noticed.

This predisposition to look for and over-emphasize differences is really useful for staying alive. Boundaries are the most valuable information in the environment, and so agents that can fish out details about edges and exaggerate them have a huge survival advantage.

Although rooted in biology, the same tendency appears to operate in the conceptual world. Humans have a habit of paying much more attention to minor differences in interpretation than to the similarities – and, unfortunately, distinction making is sometimes carried too far. For instance, humans are virtually

This set of blocks presents an optical illusion, revealing a perceptual habit of amplifying borders. (A more detailed discussion can be found in the text, to the left.)

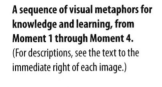

A sequence of visual metaphors for knowledge and learning, from Moment 1 through Moment 4. (For descriptions, see the text to the immediate right of each image.)

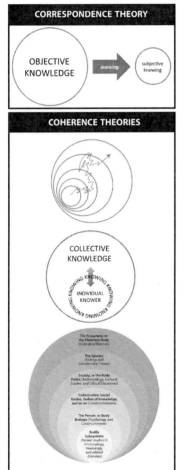

clones of one another. Yet, when people meet, attentions are rarely focused on extensive and profound samenesses. Rather, perceptions are drawn to a few, superficial differences such as height, intonation, skin tone, hairstyle, religion, or perspective on schooling. This proclivity can contribute to major social and cultural prejudices. Keeping it in check requires constant vigilance and a mode of consciousness that is attuned to habits of identification. One must be deliberate about re-perceiving and re-interpreting the boundaries used to organize the world.

This is precisely the thinking behind the visual metaphors we have been using to make sense of conceptions of knowing and learning. To remind, in Moment 1, we offered the image to the left as a representation of the commonsense, boundary-intensive belief that knowledge exists as OBJECTS outside of knowers and learning is a process of INTERNALIZING them.

In Moment 2, we proposed that the visual metaphor of a jagged path across nested developmental levels offers more productive insight into learning, conceived as ADAPTING, CREATING COHERENCE, and EXPANDING POSSIBILITIES.

In Moment 3, we suggested an image that nests individual knowing within collective knowledge, and that rendered their boundaries more permeable was a useful visual metaphor for theories that discuss learning as NEGOTIATING, APPRENTICING, and BECOMING.

In this final part of the book, we take things one step further in the suggestion that knowing-and-learning systems are nested in other similarly complex systems. Of key importance, the boundaries suggested here are recognized to be conveniences. They are over-amplifications that are taken up because they are useful, not because they are absolute. (In the academic world, the emergence of hybrid disciplines, as noted in Chapter 4.1, is a reflection of this re-cognition. These disciplines traverse commonsense borders.)

To be fair, it sometimes seems that the edges of some complex phenomena are absolute. For instance, a person's skin appears to be a pretty definite boundary. Yet closer study reveals skin to be a porous membrane through which air, water, and other substances are constantly exchanged with the environment. Skin doesn't *separate* self from context; it *connects* the individual to the situation. The same is true of the perceived edges of any complex unity – cells, brains, cultures, species, and so on. Edges of complex unities don't separate. They delimit and connect.

This realization has been one of the prompts for a recent branch of research known as **network theory**, a domain more concerned with how elements of a complex system are connected than how they are separated. As it turns out, *all* knowing-and-learning systems – including cells, brains, social groups, bodies of knowledge, and ecosystems – share a similar sort of internal structure. Their elements come together in decentralized networks.

To elaborate, four general categories of networks have been identified: (a) centralized, (b) distributed, (c) decentralized, and (d) fragmented. Much-simplified illustrations are presented to the right, each drawn on top of an identical set of dots.

Each network type has a specific shape, specific advantages, and specific disadvantages. With regard to complex phenomena, all tend to be manifest in one way or another – but the decentralized network is particularly important.

The centralized network, as its name suggests, has a principal hub through which all relationships (e.g., flow of information, channeling of resources) are mediated. This network structure has the advantage of efficient distribution and communication. However, its disadvantages include that it is only as robust and only as flexible as the central hub. That hub determines the system's character. If it fails to adapt to changing circumstances, the entire system will fail.

At the other extreme, a distributed network has tight and extensive local connectivity, but no large-scale systemic connectivity. This netlike structure is very robust. However, distribution and communication is very inefficient – and, by consequence, phenomena with this structure are highly resistant to change.

The third type, a decentralized network, is fractal-like. It has no specific centers but, in a very pragmatic sense, comprises many centers. It consists of clusters

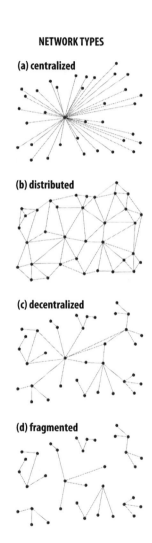

NETWORK TYPES

(a) centralized

(b) distributed

(c) decentralized

(d) fragmented

of interacting parts, and those constituents often turn out to have decentralized structures as well. By way of familiar example, you are part of multiple social systems, which are likely to have decentralized structures. At the same time, your body is a decentralized network of interacting organs. Your brain, in turn, is a decentralized network. And so on. (As noted in the previous chapter, sophisticated, data-based illustrations of these networks are available at visualcomplexity.com.) A reason that these forms are decentralized is that this network structure combines efficient communication with a robust structure, enabling considerable flexibility and high adaptability. In knowing-and-learning terms, the system is reasonably stable (the knowing is robust) while still responsive to emerging circumstances (it learns well).

A fourth category, the fragmented network, lacks a meta-connectivity and so it is often ignored in discussions of system dynamics. While not really a network at all, this type of structure can have at least one powerful advantage: there can be small explosions of diversity within smaller clusters that might, at some point, come together into a grander network. The fragmented network can be an important stage in the evolution of a learning system – as might be illustrated through the creation of hybrid disciplines. When once-separate areas of study are brought together, or when once-disparate views are juxtaposed, powerful new ways of understanding can emerge. The same principle applies at the classroom level. Individual students might have specialized knowledge that, under the right circumstances, could be blended into powerful collective possibility.

That's why, with regard to discussions of knowing and learning, the decentralized network is by far the most important of the four basic structures. It is the fingerprint of a complex unity – which is to say, this network structure is present in all complex knowing-and-learning systems. Many, many phenomena – ranging at least from the sub-cellular to the super-ecosystemic – are decentrally structured. While this recent insight has not yet had a major impact on formal education, it has underpinned restructurings of

Network theory **is a recent branch of transdisciplinary study that's concerned with the relational structure in systems – that is, the ways that parts connect to one another.**

One of the major insights of network theorists is that the fingerprint of a complex (learning) system is a decentralized network structure.

some major institutions and business, including many healthcare systems and a number of multinational companies (such as Apple, Google, and Toyota). The key element in these moments of **biomimicry** – that is, the human-made mimicking the natural – has been the recognition that decentralized structures afford more intelligent and adaptive internal structures than centralized hierarchies.

What are knowledge and learning in this frame?

We've danced around these questions, but have not yet spoken directly to the metaphors of knowledge and learning within a frame of Systemic Sustainability Education. That's because we first needed to present some important vocabulary and images. In particular, notions of complexity, emergence, and decentralized networks are vital for this discussion.

To reiterate, a complex phenomenon/entity is an emergent form. It is a perceptible coherence that

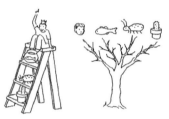

- arises in the interactions of multiple agents/subsystems,
- manifests features and capacities that are not observed in those agents/subsystems,
- maintains itself over some period of time,
- evolves in response to both internal and external dynamics.

Why does this matter in a discussion of knowledge and learning? Because, within this frame, knowledge might be construed as a COMPLEX SYSTEM – a VIBRANT, LIVING FORM that arises in, but is not reducible to, the actions of knowing agents. This suggestion is not a subtle one. The claim is that knowledge is more than a coherence; it is a LIFE FORM, one that "lives in/on/across" the minds of knowers. Correspondingly, learning is seen to be any PROCESS BY WHICH A LIVING SYSTEM MAINTAINS ITSELF. In this sense, evolution is one among many sorts of learning.

To illustrate the point, consider any established body of knowledge. That body somehow maintains itself across generations, moves across populations, and adapts as its circumstances change. It is something more than what people know or what members of a discipline do. It is an entity that grows and matures; it

Evolution is sometimes discussed as a steady upward progression toward perfection. That's a misreading.

Evolution is about *adequacy*, not *optimality*. It is a creative process exploring landscapes of possibility by, in effect, experimenting. The guiding image is not an upward climb toward a pre-given goal, but a drift or branching that leads to a diversity of viable possibilities.

This possibility-oriented (*vs.* goal-driven) interpretation is the one that infuses discussions of complexity.

It is also the basis of a key metaphor: LEARNING IS EVOLUTION. And: EVOLUTION IS LEARNING.

is a being that might flourish or might whither.

A more extreme version of this metaphor is that knowledge is not only a LIFE FORM, it is a PARASITIC LIFE FORM that preys on the minds of knowers. This notion is perhaps most popularly encountered in the suggestion that IDEAS ARE VIRUSES – they are contagious, resilient, unrelenting entities that hijack a host's systems to self-replicate, evolve, and self-perpetuate. This sense gives rise to a perhaps-surprising metaphor of learning, as BEING INFECTED or BEING CONTAMINATED.

Notably, this metaphor is taken literally by some. In particular, within the field of **memetics**, an analogy is drawn between base informational units for knowledge (*memes*) and base informational units of life (*genes*). Memes include habits, skills, songs, stories, theories, mythologies. They are, in brief, anything that might be "copied" from knower to knower – and, in the process of copying, might undergo evolutionary processes of transformation and selection.

We'll return to this topic in Chapter 4.3, in relation to the question of how classrooms might be organized as spaces for vibrant knowledge production. For now, we want to offer some brief glimpses on how the insight is influencing thinking and research across some of the many, many levels of phenomena that are of concern to educators.

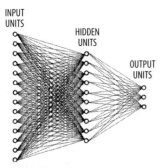

INPUT UNITS
HIDDEN UNITS
OUTPUT UNITS

Connectionism **is a perspective on individual learning and cognition that regards thought and behavior as processes that emerge in intricately interconnected networks of much simpler units. So far it has had relatively little impact on education, but that may be changing soon through its applications in artificial intelligence and brain modeling.**

Cutting-edges of transphenomenal research

From its inception, the field of education has been positioned "in the middle." It sits at the crossroads of many disciplines; it links one generation to the next; it brings together individuals into grander social bodies; it mediates between individual aspirations and cultural expectations.

Complexity-informed rethinkings of edges (as sites of connection) and internal structures (as decentralized networks) have greatly expanded conversations of "what matters" in education. Below we offer brief commentaries on some of the complex, nested phenomena that are now prominent in educational literature. To keep things contained, we have imposed a 100-word limit on each subsection.

Genetic/Epigenetic

Genetics is the study of biologically inherited traits. The field emerged in the late 1800s, when it was assumed that genetic codes were fixed and operated like light switches. Those assumptions frame the hotly contested nature *vs.* nurture debates.

Things aren't that simple. Genes aren't fixed; they can be transformed through experience – and so aspects of lives are passed on genetically. And genes don't operate as simple switches, but as backdrops of possibility that are activated (or not) by circumstances.

Genes were once widely discounted as influential to identity. That's being rethought. They appear to play major roles in personality.

Neurological

Your brain's billions of neurons and trillions of neural connections constitute a dynamic ecosystem. It is a complex, decentralized network, not an assemblage of discrete regions.

Studies of **brain plasticity**, **neural density**, and **life-long learning** show that brains change across the lifespan. Those evolutions are associated with age, deliberate practice, emotional impact, nutrition, fitness, and random experience. New insights into **brain-based learning (neuro-education)** are emerging, along with strategies that support physically and emotionally healthy brains. For instance, repetition strengthens connections and so must be exercised wisely (e.g., venting anger and discussing grief can amplify these emotions by fortifying neural connections).

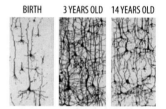

BIRTH   3 YEARS OLD   14 YEARS OLD

Neural density **is a function of both age and learning. Biologically, the density of neurons in the brain is greatest in the toddler years. It diminishes steadily to the teens when there is another surge. It then declines again for the rest of one's life – although the pace and extent of decline can be dramatically affected by good nutrition and taking on personal challenges.**

Physiological

Your physiological system comprises a network of bodily subsystems – brain, heart, skin, guts, and so on. The intricacy of their interconnections is highlighted by the impact of exercise – particularly **green exercise** – which can reduce stress, depression, and anxiety, while improving attention, digestion, and sense of well-being.

These subsystems share many dynamic traits, as exemplified by the extensively studied immune system. Your immune system isn't a machine. Rather, it guesses, errs, remembers, forgets – that is, knows and learns. It can be dumbed down by limiting its experiences or through over-medication. It can be made smarter by meeting appropriate, regular challenges.

Physical

Far from being distinct from or subservient to mental operations, it's clear that the body's movements and poses are integral to thought and emotion. A familiar demonstration is holding your face in a smile, which will improve your mood (and a sustained frown will worsen it). More dramatically, certain poses can alter hormone balances. A confident position can trigger increases in testosterone, in turn raising confidence and decreasing stress.

Conceptually, **gesture studies** have revealed their vital role in comprehension. Think about actions associated with concepts of addition, cold, and acceleration. Those actions are gestural metaphors; they infuse your comprehension.

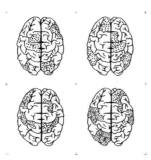

Neurodiversity **refers to a recognition that diverse neurological conditions are a result of normal variations in the human genome. The notion is an explicit challenge to commonsense assumptions that neurological diversity is necessarily abnormal, pathological, substandard, or other deviation from the norm.**

Psychological

Many emergent psychological insights came up in the Authentic Education section. Those have been extended in theories of **embodied cognition**, which assert that the mind is enabled and constrained by the body's form, engagements, and situations.

This is one of the reasons that unstructured, imaginative, exploratory play is now regarded as an essential component of development.

A particularly impactful new topic is **neurodiversity**. People are different, and those differences contribute to a robust, inventive species. Many traits long seen as negative – being hyperactive, hypomanic, autistic, introverted, and so on – are recognized as vital and are disproportionately represented among society's most influential members.

Sociological

The theories presented in the Democratic Citizenship Education section capture many of the important developments here. However, network analyses have highlighted limitations to some of that thinking.

For example, regarding collaboration, group-based projects are appropriate when individuals bring relevant-but-diverse specializations. However, when participants have similar backgrounds, it's usually more productive to ask them to work alone and then pool results. (Exceptions include online collaborations, where privacy and quiet are afforded, and brainstorming, where evaluation is suppressed.)

Peer identifications are also being studied. Contrary to the **nurture assumption**, peers may be more influential than parents and family on habits, tastes, and preferences.

Epistemological

Disciplines such as mathematics and linguistics have discernible layers and "macroscopic" ramifications that cannot be predicted within those layers. That is, they are COMPLEX KNOWING-AND-LEARNING SYSTEMS.

There are several implications for education. First, knowledge domains transcend communities of practitioners (e.g., mathematics is more than "what mathematicians do"). Second, a linear movement through disciplines is antithetical to their decentralized-network structures. Third, traditional separations among disciplines are more porous than commonly imagined, giving rise to hybrid domains and opening awareness to the contributions of non-experts (e.g., teachers and children help to shape disciplines by privileging some ideas and interpretations while ignoring others).

Cultural

With greater interminglings of societies and rapid technological development, cultural evolution can now be observed in "real time."

Among the major current evolutions is the emergence of a culture of specialization, almost completely replacing a culture of generic competencies. Increasingly, careers and pastimes require deep expertise.

That shift is reflected in a rethinking of "inventing." Formerly conceived in terms of creations that spring

Most psychological and sociological research is WEIRD – that is, based on the study of citizens of western, educated, industrialized, rich, and democratic societies. While addressing the experiences of a large portion of the population, WEIRD research barely scratches the surface of insights distributed across diverse cultures.

from individual brains, today's world-impacting devices involve the shared work of many, diverse minds and collaborations among corporations, universities, and governments. It's more a culture of innovation than invention; major developments are principally (recursive) elaborations of previous artifacts.

Anthropological

Until recently, almost all psycho-socio-cultural research has been WEIRD – based on western, educated, industrialized, rich, and democratic societies. Though spanning many countries, it represents a narrow slice of cultural diversity.

For instance, child-rearing practices involving nuclear families, individual beds, scheduled nursing, and same-age playgroups are unique to WEIRD societies – as are Piaget's and most other developmental trajectories.

In contrast to the WEIRD institution of schooling, most cultures frame education in terms of wellness and relationality, communicating important teachings through stories rather than impersonal facts. Such stories needn't be taken literally to be taken seriously; much might be learned by appreciating them as counsel.

As noted in Moment 3, *situatedness* is a core concern of Democratic Citizenship Education. *Situations* define what is knowable, doable, be-able. Moment 4 shares the concern, but extends the discussion to include *location*.

Almost everyone would recognize that the *situation* depicted above is a modern classroom. However, very little can be said about its *location* – including details on landscape, climate, and so on that figure so deeply into one's being. Central to Moment 4, location has been virtually ignored in Moments 1, 2, and 3.

Ecological

Another distinctly WEIRD habit is viewing the planet as a backdrop or resource. That assumption is challenged by the Gaia hypothesis, which proposes that organic and inorganic co-evolve in a self-regulating complex system that maintains the far-from-equilibrium conditions necessary for life.

Within this knowing-and-learning system, humans aren't as unique as often assumed. Other species – including whales, elephants, and great apes – are collaborative problem solvers, are highly social, communicate, and may have self-concepts.

These matters, alongside mounting ecological crises, compel a new ethics and a different sense of culture (e.g., **permaculture**) that are about working with rather than ignoring or exploiting the more-than-human world.

Once again, the above tour through some nested knowing-and-learning systems is in no way comprehensive. We could easily have drilled deeper in any category, or included categories that sit between the ones addressed, or pushed the list of phenomena in both micro and macro directions.

But our hope is that the partial considerations offered are sufficient to foreground the many embedded and interlacing systems that are implicated in any moment of knowing and learning. On this matter, perhaps the most critical insight of Systemic Sustainability Educators is that *every system matters*. Each must be healthy and sustainable. Ignoring or abusing one impacts them all.

Considered all together, these systems can be used to highlight some important new insights into knowing and learning. For example, each system has its own sort of situated intelligence that is rooted in its internal diversities (e.g., "junk DNA" isn't junk at all, but genetic possibility that might prove useful in an epidemic or other crisis; diverse types of specialist knowledge may contribute to unforeseeable collective possibilities). In complexity terms, intelligence arises in the interplay of a system's established repertoire and its improvisational capacity.

The self-similar dynamics across the levels of complex systems mentioned in this section are also useful for illustrating an important detail on knowing and learning. These complex processes are more about SELECTING and DISCARDING than the more commonly assumed activities of COLLECTING or RETAINING. Using a motion-based metaphor, every step of learning is OPENING UP A MYRIAD OF PATHS WHILE OBSCURING ALL OTHERS. This detail is especially apparent in the case of technology, and we turn to that topic now.

Two major themes in Systemic Sustainability Education are *resilience* and *grit*, both of which refer to qualities that appear on the psychological level – and both of which are transphenomena. *Resilience* (from the Latin for "spring back") refers to one's ability to deal with adversity and adapt to stress. It is often seen as an innate trait, but it can be learned and developed.

The same is true of *grit*, which might be described as a mix of resilience, expanded awareness, and perseverance.

The special case of technology

As mentioned in previous chapters, the word *technology* is usually used narrowly, to refer to the most recent inventions. Most technologies are so familiar, so embodied that they're not often noticed.

Yet technology encompasses all human inventions,

and that includes not just tools and machines but all the ideas, practices, and sensibilities that define a culture. In this section we trace some recursive elaborations of communicative technologies, from language, through literacy, to mass print, and culminating with the current digital era. Each of these technologies has been associated with a convulsion of creativity. As with the previous section, we constrain our commentaries, this time to 150 words for each of these innovations.

Language

What is the meaning of this symbol?

/

Of course, the only sensible answer is, "It depends." The symbol might be an "I," an "L," a "1," a "/," or any number of other things. That is, the meaning is not in the symbol, but in the webs of association that the symbol triggers when it is used in a particular context. Such is the power of letters, words, icons, and so on: they collect together and trigger an immensity of associations.

As such, symbols are a powerful technology for thinking. With them, we can chunk together ideas and "smuggle" more into consciousness than would otherwise be possible. Without them, consciousness would be something entirely different.

Language, enables minds to draw from the experiences of billions of other lives and to entertain ideas that have been honed over thousands of generations. It makes it possible for minds to come together into grander cognitive systems that surpass the capacities of isolated individuals. With language, even the young can deal with matters that mystified the ancients.

Perhaps the most useful quality of language is the way it allows speakers to experiment with possibilities without committing, potentially saving time, effort, and lives. A being without language can only learn the consequences of an action by doing, but humans can anticipate, strategize, and plan. That is, language frees the knower from the limits of the here-and-now.

Of course, it's not all good. As with any technology, language succeeds by culling possibilities and channeling thought. In the process, language renders some interpretations automatic and others nonsensical. Language shapes reality.

Literacy

Actually, every technology shapes reality by strengthening some capacities and letting others wither. The written word, for example, increased what could be remembered by off-loading details onto the physical world – even while it impacts brain-based memory consolidation and recall.

Perhaps the biggest transformations triggered by literacy were its contributions to new theories of knowledge. To preserve knowledge in oral cultures means rehearsing it, and accessing it means finding someone who knows. In literate cultures, knowledge can be detached from knowers, thus giving direct access to others' insights, even when separated by seas and centuries. It also affords the creation of abstract ideas and objective truths that can be preserved and accumulated.

Literacy also seems to have been a major scaffold in the development of formal logic as it enabled the orderly, linear presentation of extensive arguments. (The word *logic* derives from the Greek *logos*, "word.")

Mass Print

The invention of movable type in the mid-1400s permitted the mass production of books, which in turn had three major cultural impacts. Firstly, the general populace became more literate with easier access to affordable texts. As the printed word became more pervasive, reading transformed from a mainly public event (i.e., one was read *to* in churches, universities, and public gatherings) into a mainly private one.

Secondly, writing became standardized. Prior to mass print, there were great variations in fonts, grammar, spacing, spelling, and punctuation. Such details had to be standardized for the mass market.

Thirdly, mass print facilitated a sudden proliferation of specialized knowledge. As artisans and academics published details of their skills and insights, craft-knowledge and scientific insight began to amplify one another, setting the stage for the Scientific and Industrial Revolutions, alongside European imperialism and colonization. At the same time, the need for modern schools arose.

Ubiquitous learning is a phrase that has recently grown in popularity. Its meanings vary, but it is typically used to flag the cultural impacts and educational possibilities presented by greater connectivity and continuous access to information – along with the sorts of lifelong learning that accompany relentless technological developments.

Digitality

Language enabled the linking of minds in joint projects. Literacy and mass print amplified that capacity. The emergence of digital technologies represents another major amplification. Electronic devices have enabled collaborations that are so massive that some propose the emergence of a **global brain** – a complex, self-organized, decentralized network of minds and tools.

In fact, in about 2010 the total number of transistors in the global network of computers exceeded the number of neurons in your brain and the number of files in that network rivaled the number of synapse links. The possibility of machine-based intelligence that rivals human brains may be on the horizon.

We don't need to rehearse the massive advances in connectivity, specialization, and capacity afforded by emerging technologies, nor the impact on personal possibility, social engagement, or cultural evolution. These are experienced every moment.

Further recursive elaborations should be anticipated – and perhaps sooner rather than later. Novelty and innovation are now such integral parts of daily life that it's easy to forget how rare they once were. Developments are occurring so rapidly and accelerating at such a pace that some commentators suggest human intelligence might be trillions and trillions times greater by the end of this century – which serves as a reminder that technologies aren't simply the products of intelligence. They also bestow intelligence.

An awareness of the exponential character of technological change further underscores the need for a mode of awareness that is open to but not overwhelmed by rapid evolution, expansive possibilities, vague futures. Prevailing modes of consciousness and habits of awareness are increasingly inadequate.

Fractal (holographic) consciousness

Perhaps the most important word in the previous sentence is *inadequate*. There is no accusation that earlier thinking is "wrong," merely that theories fitted to earlier circumstances may not address current issues. Thinking must evolve with situations and the issues presented by new situations. As Albert Einstein famously observed, "No problem can be solved from the same level of consciousness that created it."

But what, exactly, does a new "level of consciousness" entail?

Investigations into the matter have been pivotal to whole new areas of educational research, such as brain-based learning and **adult education** (cf. **andragogy**). Central to these new subfields are understandings

Andragogy derives from the Greek *andras + ago*, "to lead the (adult) man." It refers to strategies developed for adult learners, framed by the realization that adults aren't large children. *Andragogy* is distinguished from *pedagogy* according to the sorts of motivations, concerns, habits, responsibilities, and mindsets that orient adults.

ADULT BRAIN
ADULT MIND
ADULT SOCIAL WORLD
ADULT PREOCCUPATIONS

of knowing in terms of FITNESS rather than POSSESSING INFORMATION and learning in terms of TRANSFORMATION rather than ACQUIRING INFORMATION. Knowing, that is, refers to a system's ABILITY TO MAINTAIN ITS INTERNAL CO-HERENCE (AMONG SUBSYSTEMS, IDEAS, ETC.) AND ITS EXTERNAL COHERENCE (WITH / IN ITS EVER-CHANGING WORLD). In other words, *knowing* and *learning* are essentially the same phenomenon in this frame – to the VIBRANT SUFFICIENCY of complex, living systems.

This "definition" of knowing and learning applies across levels of organization and includes physical systems, conceptual systems, social systems, and so on. That is, knowing-and-learning is not merely something that goes on in one's head, nor something that is confined to the realm of the human. It describes the dynamic of ONGOING ADAPTATION of any complex form. This sensibility might be seen as an elaboration of the insight of Democratic Citizenship Educators that KNOWING IS BEING and LEARNING IS BECOMING. Systemic Sustainability Educators would agree, but would also suggest KNOWING IS SYSTEMIC COHERENCE and LEARNING IS SYSTEMIC TRANSFORMATION.

With regard to personal knowing-and-learning, an exemplar of these notions is **Robert Kegan**'s **Con-structive-Developmental Theory**, which presents five qualitatively distinct modes of consciousness – that is, five ways of noticing, interpreting, and addressing events in the world. Kegan's model, illustrated to the right, is based on extensive empirical studies of how people in developed nations (as well as followers of wisdom traditions associated with **mindfulness prac-tices**) perceive of and relate to their situations.

Kegan organized his model around the sorts of phenomena that occupy one's attentions and the sorts of phenomena that frame one's attentions. He used the word *objects* to refer to those aspects of experience under one's control, and the word *subjects* to refer to not-noticed aspects of experience that influence action. Objects are available to System 2 and prompt reflective *responses*; subjects activate only System 1 and trigger automatic *reactions*. These are ever-evolving categories. As one learns and grows, subjects become objects. For example, for most young children, emotion is a

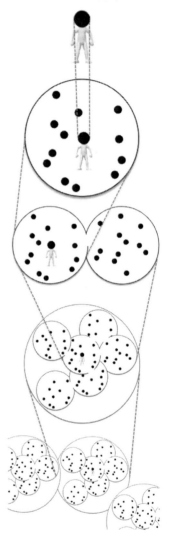

A visual metaphor of Kegan's Constructive Developmental Theory, with 5 levels that parallel stages described on the facing page.

We describe these levels as "fractal" or "holographic" (1) to highlight their nestedness and (2) to flag that, for the experiencer, each has a similar level of complexity.

KEGAN'S CONSTRUCTIVE-DEVELOPMENTAL THEORY*			
Developmental Stage (& typical ages)	Brief description	Objects (can be consciously controlled)	Subjects (cannot be consciously controlled)
1st order: **Impulsive Mind** (~2–6 years)	• idea of "durable objects" un(der)developed • mystified when others have different opinions • need to be repeatedly reminded of rules	attention	impulses and perceptions
2nd order: **Instrumental Mind** (~6 years to adolescence; some adults)	• tendency to view relationships in utilitarian terms (what you can do for me; what I can do for you) • limited ability to take another's perspective or to consider multiple perspectives • seeks out and follows unchanging, universal rules	impulses and perceptions	needs, interests, desires
3rd order: **Socialized Mind** (post-adolescence – and the plateau level for ~60% of adults)	• oriented to maintaining affiliation with one's "tribe" • considers own needs in relation to those of others • capable of goal setting, abstract planning, self-reflection • able to think abstractly and reflect on others' actions	needs, interests, desires	interpersonal relationships, mutuality
4th order: **Self-Authoring Mind** (variable, if achieved – met by ~35% of adults)	• identifies values, principles, and long-term goals • able to hold situation as an object that can be critically interrogated • able to recognize need for affiliations • concerned with competence, responsibility, and meaningful contribution • self-guided, self-evaluative, and recognizes personal responsibility in situations	interpersonal relationships, mutuality	self-authorship, identity, ideology
5th order: **Self-Transforming Mind** (typically over 40 years, if achieved – reached by less that 1% of adults)	• diminished focus on own point of view; able to regard multiple ideologies simultaneously and compare them, being wary of any single one • able to embrace great complexity; tends to move away from "either/or" thinking towards thinking that is more systemic; able to hold the contradictions between competing belief systems • decisions based on translevel (self, organization, society, ecosystem, etc.) considerations	self-authorship, identity, ideology	dialectic between ideologies

* Adapted from R. Kegan, *In over our heads: the mental demands of modern life* (1998, Cambridge, MA: Harvard University Press), pp. 313–314.

subject. They feel joy or anger, but are likely unaware that these feelings can be managed and used. In contrast, these emotions are objects for most adults, who have developed the skills needed to recognize, manipulate, and capitalize on what they are feeling.

For Kegan, such transitions (from subjects into objects) signal the emergence of more complex modes of consciousness. Put differently, a developmental leap is made when one is able to *look at* what was previously *looked through*. In the chart on page 209, we summarize Kegan's five stages and the key *subject ⇨ object* transformations. (More detailed descriptions of these stages can be readily found online, but we recommend Kegan's writings, in part because his ideas are constantly evolving.)

Represented as a visual metaphor in the margin on page 208, these modes or orders might be depicted fractally as expanding spheres of awareness, starting with one's self and potentially extending to a deeply systemic mindfulness. In the visual metaphor, the stages of this model are represented as:

- a single point (1st order, self-centeredness),
- categories (2nd order, awareness that there are other, similar consciousnesses),
- categories of categories (3rd level, awareness of others with very different ways of seeing the world),
- systems (4th level, consciousness of complexity),
- systems of systems (5th order, consciousness of interlacing complexities).

Futures Thinking is an interdisciplinary movement that attempts to anticipate possible futures by analyzing patterns of change and their triggers. Also known as "futures studies," "futurism," or "strategic foresight," the field is oriented toward coping with threats, avoiding disasters, and grasping opportunities through orienting awarenesses beyond immediate circumstances – that is, by enlarging consciousness.

Once again, elaborated descriptions are provided in the chart on page 209.

It's important to emphasize that Kegan didn't suggest that higher levels are "better." That's not always the case, as fitness is the most important quality. One's mode of consciousness must fit with one's situation. As well, there's a difference between attaining a mode of consciousness and inhabiting that mode. Once a level is achieved, it and all the prior levels become available, as demanded by situations.

As with other developmental theories (see Chapter 2.2), this one suggests that the achievement of broader levels of consciousness is triggered by necessity. As

Spirituality **is rarely addressed in "serious" educational research – perhaps because western versions often entail disdain of the bodily, scorn of the worldly, and disregard for evidence that challenges belief.**

Complexity-based discussions offer another route into the topic. With vast research into wholes that surpass their parts, it affords another way to talk about transcendent unities and grander wholes.

For many, this is a new development. For others, it is more a remembering – a recalling that matters of the spirit are, literally, matters of breathing, of constant connection to and exchange with a more-than-human world.

experiences collect and difficulties are confronted, knowers may either ignore emergent complexities or engage in the hard work of reformatting worldviews.

Kegan has asserted that a greater proportion of a population will attain the higher levels of consciousness as a society grows more complex – not because the system supports it, but because the situation demands it. (A caveat of this point is that new, more complex modes of consciousness will emerge as situations become even more complex and greater numbers of people achieve the higher orders.) If correct, it would seem reasonable to assume that societies must pay greater attention to the educational implications of ongoing transformations.

Indeed, it would appear that there has been an increased attentiveness of the educational implications. If you haven't noticed the strong parallels yet, we urge you to revisit the chart and compare the traits of developmental stages (on the left) with the goals of different moments in formal education (on the right):

Instrumental Mind ⇔ Standardized Education
Socialized Mind ⇔ Authentic Education
Self-Authoring Mind ⇔ Democratic Citizenship Education

To re-emphasize, if Kegan and other researchers of consciousness are anywhere near the mark, there is an accelerating need to rethink the purposes and structures of formal education to address a growing need for minds that are capable of higher orders of awareness – of:

Self-Transforming Mind ⇔ Systemic Sustainability Education

It's a matter of cultural and ecological need.

Pulling it together

For several centuries, the prevailing mindset in the western world has been focused on separation and reduction – on finding the simplest parts, specifying the fundamental laws, and so on. For the most part, schooling has reflected this sensibility. The institution has been instrumental in disseminating and perpetuating a worldview that separates selves from others and holds humans apart from the natural world.

Systemic Sustainability Educators contend that formal education is at a crossroads and must either evolve or go extinct. Many, in fact, worry that the institution isn't sufficiently flexible to adapt. Others are more cautious, arguing that immediate small changes might enable appropriate large-scale adaptations as recursively elaborative processes play out. In the final chapter, we outline some of this advice, much of it informed by other cultural traditions and sensibilities.

Suggestions for delving deeper

1. In the chart on page 193 we presented one of our strategies for thinking about the transphenomenality of different aspects of schooling. Select a prominent theme or concern of formal education and, perhaps using a similar chart as a tool to support your thinking, explore how it might be understood as a transphenomenon.

2. In this chapter we offered some focused comments on several nested complex systems (i.e., genetic/epigenetic, neurological, physiological, physical, psychological, sociological, epistemological, cultural, anthropological, and ecological). For each of these levels of organization, identify some possible educational implications of recent developments – both in terms of how formal schooling might have contributed to limited thinking and how schooling might address issues that emerge in part from such thinking.

3. We presented an analysis of the recursive elaboration of communication technologies in this chapter (from spoken language, through written word, and so on). Can you identify similar stages within your own disciplinary specializations?

4.3 Teaching and Systemic Sustainability Education

Below are four different lesson designs, each for a 2nd-grade classroom on the topic of "sums within 20":

A lesson design aligned with Standardized Education

The lesson will open with several review exercises dealing with sums up to 10. The teacher will then pose a few questions where the sums exceed 10. The strategy of counting up along a number line (using the first addend as the starting point and the second as the number of steps) will be introduced. Several examples will be demonstrated. Students will then complete a photocopied set of practice exercises, to be handed in for grading at the end of the lesson. Those who finish early will be permitted to play math games or read quietly.

A lesson design aligned with Authentic Education

The teacher will begin by asking the sum of 4 and 5, requesting that students explain how they know their answer is correct. Additional explanations will be elicited until at least the following strategies are mentioned: grouping objects, counting up, tracing along a number line. Illustrations of these will be recorded on the whiteboard. The teacher will then ask for the sum of 7 and 5 and use the response to remind children of place value (i.e., 12 = 1 ten and 2 units). Finally, using base-10 blocks, examples of sums greater than 10 will be discussed. Students will then work on practice exercises, using blocks if desired.

A lesson design aligned with Democratic Citizenship Education

The teacher will begin the lesson by writing on the whiteboard, "How many ways can you add two numbers together to equal 15?" Children will be invited to work together to generate responses. They will have access to counting blocks, number lines, calculators, and other manipulative tools, and will be required to record all sums that they identify as proper addition statements. A collective discussion of findings will be held when a critical mass of students seems ready to move on. In the meantime, students who finish early will be challenged with other sums within 20.

A lesson design aligned with Systemic Sustainability Education

In advance, the teacher will write some practice exercises of sums within 10 on the board. Students will be asked to respond and to explain their responses. Multiple interpretations will be requested, and students will be required to reiterate and connect to the explanation that immediately preceded theirs. Children will be invited to examine additional sums within 20, of their choosing. Students will be organized in groups of three and invited to use any resources in the room to help them generate responses – with a reminder that they will be expected to explain one another's strategies during discussion time.

In a sense, everything we've talked about so far is reflected in these four brief descriptions – and so it would be easy to get lost in the entangled historical, epistemological, and pragmatic details woven into these designs. For the sake of sanity, we'll limit our analysis to a handful of highlights, in the process offering preliminary thoughts on what teaching might look like within a frame of Systemic Sustainability Education.

As might be expected, the design associated with Standardized Education exemplifies desires for directness, efficiency, and measurable results, reflected in the familiar format of "review, explain, practice, evaluate." The lesson aligned with Authentic Education introduces a concern for conceptual understanding, and thus nests the work in multiple interpretations and opportunities to express insights. The design inspired by Democratic Citizenship Education folds in additional elements of peer-inquiry and some degree of choice, while opening up possibilities for divergent responses.

At first glance, the design associated with Systemic Sustainability Education might look very similar to the Democratic Citizenship Education lesson. But there is an important difference. This lesson is designed around the realization that most children at the 2nd-grade level will likely be operating within Kegan's Instrumental Consciousness. Students are thus being invited to consider others' perspectives – to appreciate how others might be thinking and where they might be coming from. This requirement to take the perspectives of their peers is intended to support concept development and prompt students toward awareness of some of the subjects in their lives (i.e., those elements that frame their attentions, such as their own needs, interests, and desires) and perhaps begin to see them as objects they can influence and use. That is, the lesson is about both curriculum content and enlarging consciousness.

It's important to notice that this expanded emphasis doesn't entail any compromise to curriculum content. It's not uncommon to encounter criticisms of the sorts of more open designs exemplified by the third and fourth lessons, rooted in the worry that students won't have enough practice to develop automaticity. That needn't be the case. In fact, in our experience, the opposite tends to happen. In the presence of a good teacher, students typically engage in *much* more practice than in more rigidly structured formats, because tasks that involve looking for patterns and making generalizations often demand many, many examples.

As for the goal of providing opportunities to enlarge consciousness, the fourth lesson design is deliberately transphenomenal. For example, the description reflects attentiveness to the following levels of complex activity:

- neurological (e.g., reiteration strengthens neural pathways);
- psychological (e.g., access to multiple interpretations affords more flexible understandings);
- social (e.g., shared inquiry supports social skills);

Concerns about *bullying* and *cyberbullying* have reached epic proportions in the past few years, amplified in part by the anonymity of many social media.

Rather than thinking of bullying as of a collection of bad behaviors, one emergent argument is that it is an indicator of a broader, systemic problem. A major response has thus been to emphasize the importance of teaching students how to form and maintain relationships – part of which is the ability to take the perspective of another.

- cultural (e.g., exploration affords greater facility with available artifacts and technologies).

Of course, the students themselves will likely be unaware of this complexity – as should be the case. The teacher is the one responsible for the more expansive awareness.

Teaching as extending consciousness

So what does the word *teaching* entail within a frame of Systemic Sustainability Education?

There's no broad consensus here, but some trends in vocabulary have been emerging over the past few decades as such descriptors as IMPROVISING, OCCASIONING, CARING, CONVERSING, LISTENING, MINDFUL PARTICIPATION, and ENGAGING have become more prominent in the educational literature. Contrasted with the terms associated with teaching in previous educational sensibilities, this vocabulary reflects greater emphases on personal flexibility, attunement to context, and interpersonal relationship.

It also reflects a stronger understanding of the extraordinary human capacity to link consciousnesses – that is, for individuals to coordinate their attentions and to synchronize brain functioning. These capacities make it possible for grander cognitive unities to emerge, through which vastly more ideas can be kept in play, more varied and intricate connections can be made, and so on. And, of course, the likelihood of emergent, collective cognition is greatly enhanced with the presence of a skilled teacher who can serve as an EXTENDED CONSCIOUSNESS OF THE COLLECTIVE.

Consciousness, originally meaning "to know with," is a transphenomenon that is as dependent on collectivity as it is on individuality.

It's also a recursively evolving form. Consciousness is shaped by its own awareness of its awarenesses.

Several critical points are necessary to make sense of this metaphor, starting with the fact that the word *consciousness* is being used in its original sense of a group's shared knowledge rather than the popular current meaning of one's innermost thoughts. Derived from the Latin *com-* + *scire*, "to know with; to be mutually aware," the notion of consciousness entails something much more expansive than personal thoughts, desires, emotions, and intentions. The more ancient understanding is actually being re-asserted through current neurological, psychological, and complexity research. Human consciousness is much more than a self-contained, individualized phenomenon. It requires many layers of complex activity to emerge, and is simultaneously dependent on a brain, a body, a social collective, a context, a language, and so on. Consciousness is a transphenomenon.

Secondly, further developing the notion of collective cognition, the classroom community can and should be understood as a learner – not a *collection of situated learners* but a *situated collective learner*. It has its own coherence and its own evolving identity, and it is part of a similarly coherent and evolving situation. Thirdly, drawing on consciousness research, it has become clear over the past century that personal consciousness is more a commentator than a controller. It doesn't direct, it orients. It contributes to learning not by exerting control, but by highlighting, focusing, and juxtaposing. Consciousness frames what might be noticed or looked for, without dictating what will be perceived or sought out. What one knows and who one is, then, are *not determined by* consciousness, but they are utterly *dependent on* consciousness – in very much the same way that learning is not determined by teaching, but is dependent on it. The metaphor of TEACHER AS AN EXTENDED CONSCIOUSNESS OF THE COLLECTIVE, then, isn't a suggestion that the teacher must somehow be aware of and controlling everything that's going on. It is a description of the teacher's role in ORIENTING ATTENTIONS, offering viable interpretations, and selecting among the options that arise in the collective.

This formulation, of course, only makes sense insofar as there are choices for action and interpretation that might be selected, which brings us to the fourth necessary element of *options*. Across all complex unities, knowing is shaped more by opportunities to select from among diverse elements than it is by instruction. Teachers, then, must ensure that different interpretive possibilities are present in the classroom. In a nutshell, the teaching associated with Systemic Sustainability Education is as much about divergence toward new interpretive possibilities as it is about convergence onto pre-existent truths. It is a participation in a recursively elaborative process of opening up new spaces of pos-

Discussions of lesson preparation have recently been shifting from an emphasis on *planning* (literally, "flattening," see Chapter 1.2) toward an emphasis on *design* (from the Latin *de-* + *signare*, "to mark out"). As we develop in this chapter, this shift in vocabulary reflects an evolution in sensibility, away from prespecifying a path that must be followed toward marking out the boundaries of appropriate activity.

sibility by exploring current spaces – with regard to both curriculum content and modes of consciousness.

The dance of the *designed* and the *emergent*

We suspect that many would hear those last few sentences as academic bafflegab. What, exactly, is being suggested about teaching?

To be honest, we only have the beginnings of responses to this question, and we offer some of those below in the form of principles that might orient teachers' attentions and activities. These principles are informed and influenced by multiple sources, but over the past several years we've noticed them clustered with two core notions: **design** and emergence.

You may have noticed that we used the word *design* rather than *plan* to refer to the brief descriptions of lessons at the start of this chapter. *Design* refers to a more generalized principle, through which structures and activities are intended to be accessible and engaging to the widest possible audience (whereas *plans* are narrower, situation-specific, and usually more detailed). Originally proposed in the field of architecture, the **principle of universal design** has been adapted within the field of education as a collecting place for a range of sub-principles to ensure that learning tasks are adaptable to the inevitable diversities encountered in a group of learners. Some of these include:

The *principle of universal design* was first articulated in the field of architecture to signal a responsibility to make buildings accessible to all and for the widest possible range of activities. It has since been adopted and adapted by many fields, including education, the health professions, and social work.

- providing a range of representations of ideas, with spaces for unanticipated possibilities to emerge;
- allowing for different ways for learners to express what they know and what they're learning;
- offering different ways into, trajectories through, and explorations beyond planned experiences;
- permitting and nurturing the specialized interests of individuals, hopefully in ways that enhance possibilities for the group.

The list could easily be extended, but the above points illustrate the main emphases. Among these elements, the detail that has received by far the most attention over the past few decades is the importance of activities that invite learners to go beyond planned experiences, more popularly described in terms of **open-ended tasks**. More recently, increasing attention has been focused at the other ends of learning activities – that is, on how to design entry points of tasks so that learners, across all their diversities, might be able to adapt activities to fit needs, emergent abilities, and interests. This *variable entry* feature informed the designs of the last three lessons at the start of the chapter. Whereas the first lesson had only one way into the topic, the other three gave learners opportunities to define the task in ways that afforded multiple entry points.

One strategy that we've found to be particularly useful in this regard is the notion of **enabling constraints**. The phrase might at first sound like an oxymoron, but it actually refers to a necessary condition for complex emergence. Complex unities are simultaneously rule-bound (constrained) and capable of flexible, unanticipated possibilities (enabled). That is, enabling constraints define a system's **affordances**.

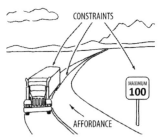

An *enabling constraint* is a design that delimits possible actions, but at the same time opens up powerful affordances. Familiar examples of enabling constraints include the rules of most games and traffic laws.

Some constraints are dictated by context, others by co-actions of agents. The common feature of enabling constraints is that they are not prescriptive. They don't dictate what *must* be done. Rather, they are expansive, indicating what *might* be done, in part by indicating what's not allowed. Familiar examples include the Ten Commandments and the rules of most sports, which dictate what shouldn't be done but don't give much direction on what should happen. Within the space of such enabling constraints there are infinite possibilities for action.

With regard to more immediate examples, our self-imposed limits of 100 words to point to emerging insights across different complex systems (in Chapter 4.2) and to describe four different lesson designs (at the start of this chapter) are illustrative. They were actually inspired by much more limiting rules such as a **Six-Word Memoir, flash fiction**, and **Twitter tweets**, all of which are known for their extreme brevity and their potential for extraordinary profundity.

With regard to what it means to frame a lesson as enabling constraints, consider the lesson intentions associated with the four lesson designs presented at the start of the chapter. The topic specified in the program of studies was simply "sums within 20," which might be translated into action in multiple ways. For example, the four lesson designs might have been oriented, respectively, by these four lesson intentions:

- [Standardized Education] Students will demonstrate adequate mastery of sums within 20 by correctly answering at least 8 of 10 evaluation questions at the end of the lesson.
- [Authentic Education] Each student will be able to explicitly and appropriately discuss at least two interpretations of addition and use these interpretations to explain their responses to sums within 20.
- [Democratic Citizenship Education] Students will work together to list sums of 15 (and other numbers within 20), and this work will serve both as a starting place to examine patterns and a practice space to develop automaticity.
- [Systemic Sustainability Education] Students will present, reiterate, and critique one another's interpretations of addition as they co-produce strategies for and practice sums within 20.

In truth, any of these statements could potentially serve as an enabling constraint – simply because *it's the system that determines whether a constraint is enabling, not the rule itself.* Some rules that appear draconian can be empowering; some that are intended as liberating might shut people down.

That said, the first of the above four intentions is the most likely to be experienced as overly restrictive and permitting the least divergence. This sort of statement is not particularly conducive to triggering robust, flexible understandings. The other three are much more likely to open possibilities – and, in our assessment, the constraints become more enabling as one moves down the list. (Again, different structures will work differently in different situations, so we're not making any strong claims here.)

The guiding principle is that a design should maintain a delicate balance between sufficient structure (to limit a pool of virtually limitless possibilities) and sufficient openness (to allow for flexible and varied

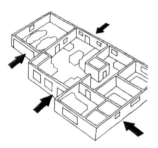

The feature of *variable entry* was developed within Authentic Education. It uses the metaphor of MULTIPLE PORTALS INTO A TASK. That is, learning tasks should be designed in a manner that invites learners to adapt tasks according to their understandings, interests, and expertise – by, for example, adjusting the difficulty, incorporating personal elements, and so on.

responses). These rules are not matters of "everyone does the same thing" (too closed) or "everyone does their own thing" (too open), but "everyone should be able to engage in a manner appropriate to their current situation." On that count, an element that is as vital as an appropriate enabling constraint is a teacher who is attuned to the movements of the collective and able to adapt on the fly – that is, a teacher who is operating as the CONSCIOUSNESS OF THE COLLECTIVE. It's rare that a structure engineered entirely in advance is sufficient to maintain appropriate engagements in the real, complex world of the classroom.

In other words, teaching takes place in the interplay of designed *and* emergent structures. It's never a trivial sequence of planning and implementing, but a complex, recursive process of ANTICIPATING and ENGAGING. In this sense, teaching is far more than a technical competence (as it is framed within Standardized Education), an evidence-based skill set (as positioned within Authentic Education), or a critical, participatory attitude (as described within Democratic Citizenship Education). It involves all of these elements, but is also a mode of working with others that gets much of its inspiration from the complexities of living forms.

Indeed, some of the most powerful insights for teaching are drawn from studies natural designs that arise in the activities of complex systems, some of which have been honed over eons. For example, the third and fourth lesson designs presented at the start of the chapter involve deliberate attempts to organize the classroom as decentralized networks, affording opportunities for deeper expertise and divergent ideas that might then be re-infused into the collective. More broadly, these designs might be described in terms of the intelligent use of network structures, as they modulate between centralized networks (which are useful, e.g., for efficient distribution of information) and decentralized networks (which are more useful for generating alternative interpretations). There are places for each network type in the project of formal education.

Another deliberate feature of these lessons is simultaneous nurturing of redundancy and diversity. As noted in Chapter 3.2, *redundancy* refers to the extent

An *affordance* is a possibility for engagement. The term describes the range of possibilities opened by an enabling constraint. It refers specifically to the way designs invite or enable different usages. A well-known notion in architecture, industrial design, and human–computer interactions, it has recently become more prominent in education.

of similarity among agents in a system – and, as the example of neurons in the brain illustrates, such agents are usually much more alike than different. Redundancy is vital for systemic cohesion and robustness – a point that isn't news to public education. In fact, the modern school could be aptly described as a cultural project to ensure redundancy among citizens. (Notice that, at their hearts, all four lessons at the start of the chapter were aimed at similar, highly redundant content outcomes for all students.) In complexity terms, this emphasis is vital. However, systemic problems arise when redundancy is the *only* focus. It contributes to the stability of a system, but an overly redundant system in which all agents are fully interchangeable is likely to be less intelligent than one in which there is some level of diversity among agents.

Such diversity is present in the specialized functions of different parts of the brain, the range of careers in an economy, and the biodiversity of the planet. In each case, the diversity among agents is a source of possible responses to emergent circumstance. Flexible, intelligent action is not possible without a pool of diverse possibilities. As such, with traditional schooling's overwhelming emphasis on redundancy, the institution may be limiting collective intelligence. Intellectual diversity can be too constrained in contexts defined by individualized tasks, top-down explanations, rote procedures, and inflexible learning outcomes.

Learning Sciences (LS) is a field of study that embraces methods and insights from neurology, psychology, sociology, anthropology, and other domains. LS aims to offer both nuanced understandings of learning and powerful advice on the design of learning environments.

LS is associated with *design-based research* and *design-based learning*, both of which emphasize situated activity, recursively elaborative development, and ongoing critical reflection.

Within a frame of Systemic Sustainability Education, then, a core responsibility of the teacher is to be attuned to variations in interpretation, constantly assessing how these might add to or subtract from conceptual understandings and procedural fluency. This quality is central to the last three lesson designs at the start of the chapter, in which diverse interpretations of addition are deliberately incorporated alongside opportunities for extensive practice.

To re-emphasize a key point, in the space of learning, both conceptual redundancy and conceptual diversity are vital. There is no need to choose between them. Creative, emergent possibility is dependent on both.

Technologies, consciousness, and teaching

For most of human history, and across most societies, redundancy among citizens has been a higher priority than diversity. In the western world, until only a few centuries ago, virtually everyone required highly similar working understandings of such basics as food gathering, navigation, and shelter construction. Individuals still specialized, but even within those specializations responsibilities and competencies tended to be much more alike than different. The proliferation of diverse careers is a very recent phenomenon, and it is occasioned in large part by emergent technologies.

In fact, emergent technologies are forcing major rethinkings of what schooling is all about – in large part making people more aware of the longstanding educational focus on redundancy. At the same time, it has helped to open many, previously unimagined possibilities for diversity and specialization through amplifying abilities to collect, store, analyze, mine, and visualize information. These technologies also enable powerful modeling and simulation techniques, equipping researchers to take on questions that could barely be asked just a few decades ago. With this backdrop, it's making less and less sense to hang on to a model of education that was invented when mass print and steam engines were cutting-edge technologies.

It would be easy to get lost in a survey scanning technological game-changers for teaching, and so we won't even try. Instead we'll point to four exemplars of possibility – gamification, adaptive learning, MOOCs, and augmented reality – that are opening up new forms of pedagogy.

Educational technology, or *EdTech*, is one of the most rapidly evolving areas of educational research and practice. It involves practical study of software, hardware, and Internet applications (such as wikis and blogs), as well as anticipating the educational possibilities of emergent technologies. (For a mapping of the domain, which includes a landscape of anticipated developments, visit http://envisioning.io/education/.)

Gamification and Serious Games

Gamification and **Serious Games** refer to the study and application of game-based strategies and dynamics with a view toward improving learner engagement, motivation, insight, and growth. Main foci include more nuanced understandings of the roles of competition, cooperation, achievement, failure, self-expression, altruism, challenge, and familiarity for promoting learning and development. In practical terms, teachers are exploring such elements as the impacts of meaningful choice, self-defined challenges, self-paced learning, instant feedback, structured brainstorming, and crowdsourcing – in ways and to depths that are simply not possible without electronic aids.

Adaptive learning

Adaptive learning systems are computer- or web-based approaches to teaching that make highly individualized "choices" on tasks, reminders, and other cues based on a student's response patterns. For example, a series of rapid, correct responses will likely trigger more challenging tasks, while a repeated error might activate a sequence of questions intended to address that error. Similarly, indications of sliding interest (e.g., long pauses, unrelated web searches, etc.) might be met with a question or activity tied to a deep personal interest of the learner.

Adaptive learning goes under many, many names, including educational hypermedia, computer-based learning, and intelligent tutoring.

Massive open online courses (MOOCs)

MOOCs are online courses intended for huge numbers of people across a wide range of situations. Structures and approaches vary massively across MOOCs. At one extreme, some have completely centralized teaching, highly standardized curricula, and evaluative grading; at the other, some have decentralized, collaborative approaches, more emergent curricula, and open assessment strategies. Common features include direct (and usually free) access to cutting-edge scholarship and a powerful means to locate persons who might share interests, perspectives, and insights. Learners, across ages and settings, can now have access to the latest insights across domains.

One of the lessons of the 1900s is that educators must be careful about making predictions on the roles and impacts of technology.

For instance, with the development of motion pictures in the 1920s, some commentators confidently forecast that human teachers would soon be unnecessary – as every child could get the same high-quality instruction through film.

Televisions were greeted in much the same way. And the same was true of personal computer – which might be expected, since the major

Augmented reality (AR)

Augmented reality refers to the use of digital technologies to enhance or supplement sensory perception in real time – by, for example, altering sound (e.g., dampening ambient noise or amplifying specific

innovation with most technologies of the 1900s was an improvement in the delivery of information. Motion pictures, radios, and TVs convey details faster and more consistently than earlier technologies – and that meant they meshed well with the prevailing Standardized Education sensibilities.

One of the differences with many of the technologies emerging this century is that they can fundamentally transform how humans perceive, remember, engage, connect, and think – which greatly complexifies the question of how they might be taken up by educators.

voices), maintaining video records (e.g., through wearable cameras), providing feedback on location and movement (e.g., through global positioning devices), accessing information sources, and monitoring others. At present, the most common tools of augmented reality are smartphones and tablet computers, which are evolving rapidly, growing more ubiquitous, and becoming simpler to use. In a profession responsible for extending awarenesses, these developments may herald a fundamental redefinition of what teaching can and should be all about.

With regard to Systemic Sustainability Education, a common feature of these technologies is their potential to support expansive awareness of oneself, others, humanity, and the more-than-human world while they afford enhanced and more engaging access to cutting-edge insights. Doubtless other technological innovations on the horizon will have even greater impacts on modes of consciousness, access to knowledge, and understandings of teaching.

In the face of such developments, some commentators are forecasting an imminent end of the age-indexed, desk-based, time-regimented, and individual-focused school. With the rapidly evolving landscape of technologies, it's ironic that so much of teaching practice is still organized around the linearity of print-based texts, the singular authority of a mandated curriculum, and the ideals of individualism. The irony increases when one considers that the massive successes of video-gaming and information technologies are at least partly due to the ways their creators have deliberately exploited principles of learning related to perception, embodiment, implicit associations, deliberate practice, motivation, collectivity, sociocultural contexts, decentralized networks, and other notions presented in this text. Educational research, it seems, has had considerably more influence in the worlds of gaming, advertising, and politics than in many school settings.

The issue is not that schooling has to change. As we've highlighted throughout the book, it's always been transforming itself. Rather, the point is that its rate of evolution must accelerate to keep pace with that of society. Right now it's falling further and further out of sync.

This is not to say that formal education is becoming irrelevant. On the contrary, to our hearing, most commentators are anticipating an increased need for formal education as a perpetually changing world increases demands for continuous, interconnected learning. It's just that there seems to be an ever-widening gap between "schooling" and "education." With this decoupling, two distinct trends in teaching are emerging. One, aligned with traditional schooling, is clinging to models of linearity and control. The other is exploring notions of expansive growth, systemic awareness, and conscientious engagement.

Given this context, it's interesting to observe that while digital technologies are amplifying the need for more open, flexible, and engaged conceptions of teaching, they're also coming up very short on some key elements to the learning process.

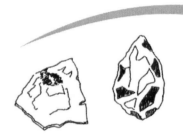

Trusting relationships and bridging experiences

When motion pictures were first invented, many educators saw them as having the potential to streamline instruction and to even out inequities in schooling experience. The hope was that content could be presented uniformly and unambiguously, thus avoiding such "noise" as teacher error and social circumstance. Similar (and even more grandiose) expectations accompanied televisions and, more recently, computers. But these optimistic predictions have never panned out.

One reason for the shortfall seems to be that such technologies operate at low information levels – ones that have been deliberately adjusted to suit what an individual human consciousness is able to accommodate. And so, while these media can give access to immense stores of data, they operate at very low levels of stimulation. Human sense organs, in contrast, function at a capacity that is about a million times greater than conscious perception. In other words, structuring education around "information" technologies may actually result in a starvation of the senses.

Humanity is a teaching species, which means that the discussions of education presented in this book are just a thin slice of the possibilities presented across history and cultures.

That said, it's apparent that conceptions of teaching are tethered to modes of consciousness, which in turn are tied to available technologies. The most ancient tools were likely found rather than made, and so might have been linked to an accidental and unplanned sort of

teaching. When tool-making began, pedagogy likely came to involve more deliberate acts of showing and correcting. As the technology of language developed and supported the technology of myths, teaching likely extended to include telling and interpreting. And the invention of symbol technologies opened up the current range of modes and emphases.

It's fair to anticipate that digital technologies will prompt an equally significant evolution of teaching sensibilities.

This information poverty is one of the reasons that teachers are likely to be needed for the foreseeable future. Learning is much more than an individualized process of ACQUIRING information. It is an ONGOING ENGAGEMENT WITH A COMPLEX WORLD, and that engagement is more powerful when mediated by a knowledgeable, attentive, and trusted person. Indeed, the **teacher–student relationship** has been the subject of much discussion and research over the past several decades, with a near consensus that it is among the most critical aspects of a child's educational experience.

As for the qualities that make for strong teacher–student relationships, actions appear to be much more important than personality traits. The teacher must communicate competence and caring, and that's accomplished more by being responsive, consistent, reliable, composed, and fair than by being warm and friendly. (We hasten to add that it's also good to be warm and friendly; they're just not as important to deep and sustained learning as the confidence-supporting qualities just listed.) Having access to an adult who is perceived as capable and aware will not only support academic growth, it can buffer difficult relationships with peers, problematic situations outside the school, and frustrations with school work.

A sound teacher-student relationship is all the more important because teachers can be the most influential adults in children's lives, often having more sway than even parents on many aspects of personality and moral development. There are two main reasons for this level of impact. One is time: children typically spend much more of their waking lives with teachers than any other adults. Another is context: few other adults are so directly involved with children *inside* their social networks, affecting modes of consciousness by helping to mediate relationships, develop ethical sensibilities, and attune to more aspects of the world.

This detail can be of immense personal and social relevance, given that most children and adolescents are not particularly good at assessing risks, making plans, reading others' emotions, interpreting others' intentions, or recognizing when they're being caught up in feedback loops that might amplify behaviors or emotions in dangerous ways. Across such elements, the teacher has a responsibility to act as an EXTENDED CONSCIOUSNESS OF THE STUDENT, finding ways to bring learners into more nuanced understandings of what's happening and how different choices for action might make things better or worse.

More pointedly, even though it is rare to find much mention of the topic in school acts and curriculum guides, the teacher plays a fundamental role in the development of student consciousness, individually and collectively. What a student notices, how what's noticed is interpreted, and how interpretations shape actions – these are all subject to the teacher's influence. In other words, and returning to the distinguishing feature of the fourth lesson design at the start of this chapter, the teacher has a responsibility to help students develop more expansive awareness of themselves in the world. As introduced in Chapter 4.2, this work involves helping students become more conscious of the subjects of their worlds (i.e., the forms and happenings that they feel *subject to* and beyond their control) and explore possibilities for reconceiving of them as objects (i.e., aspects over which control might be exerted). In the process, one develops consciousness of and senses of agency within ever-grander systems of organization.

That is, within the frame of Systemic Sustainability Education, teaching is about HELPING LEARNERS DEVELOP AGENCY with perceptions, processes, concepts, emotions, relationships, and so on. In this sense, teaching includes but elaborates on the core emphases of prior frames. Returning to the four lesson designs at the start of the chapter, education within this frame includes but elaborates emphases of the prior moments:

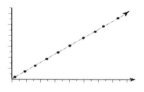

Over the history of modern schooling, different visual metaphors have been applied to *curriculum*. Most commonly, curriculum has been depicted as progress along a linear path (always forward, usually upward) toward a prespecified, fully articulated goal.

In the 1950s, the notions of the "spiral curriculum" rose to prominence. The idea was that, rather than proceeding through topics sequentially, students should be

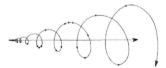

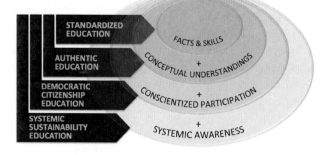

Clearly a different conception of teaching is involved here to the one that was developed half a millennium ago to prepare children to work in factories. And the difference is about more than what the teacher is expected to do. Formal education is about more than perpetuating what is already established. It aims to contribute to the expansion of possibilities at all levels of organization.

Is this really new?

Over the past several years, we have found ourselves involved in educational initiatives with different groups in North America, South America, Africa, Asia, and Australia. These engagements have challenged us in many ways, but most profoundly they have forced us to grapple with the educational baggage that we carry as born-and-bred citizens of a WEIRD society.

In particular, even though we often manage to deceive ourselves into believing that we can see through the structures and intentions of Standardized Education – its object-based models of knowledge, acquisition-based models of learning, and delivery-oriented models of teaching – the truth of the matter is that we are always taken aback when confronted with the very different educational sensibilities embodied in other cultural systems. Most often, in fact, formal education in these other situations seems already to be conceived as transphenomenal and in terms of systemic sustainability – expressed in vocabularies of health, wellness, harmony, wholeness, and similar notions.

That is, some of the most cutting-edge educational ideas in WEIRD societies seem to be commonsensical in many other settings.

As we dig deeper, we typically hear about modes of education that are not articulated in terms of outcomes, objectives, or "end-states." In contrast to the modern, western habit of defining formal education as a preparation for life, in most other cultures education seems to be a constant and integral aspect of every part of existence. Emergent descriptors of teaching, such as **contemplative** and **transformational pedagogy,** are thus entangled with understandings of

introduced to concepts gradually, revisiting topics each year to elaborate understandings. But the path is still defined in terms of convergence onto a prespecified objective.

A complexified conception of curriculum would suggest an image more like a fractal tree, in which each event opens up new possibilities for action, which in turn open still other divergent possibilities. There is no particular direction – except, perhaps, toward the expansion of the space of the possible.

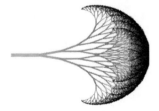

attunement, fitness, wakefulness, mindful participation, and embrace of the not-yet realized. Education in these settings doesn't isolate age groups and parse knowledge, but spans generations and integrates insights while it refuses separations of individual from collective, mind from body, self from other, and human from the more-than-human world. Most strikingly, in every non-WEIRD attitude toward education we've encountered, knowledge and knowing are entangled in an ethics of existence, interlaced with political, social, and ecological realities. "Facts" are thus never encountered as stand-alone truths, but embedded in narratives of action and drenched with considerations of ethical implications.

To be clear, we don't mean to romanticize other cultures and worldviews here. Each has its blind spots and limitations. Our point is merely that the modern, western conceptions of formal education are anomalous historically and culturally. Other perspectives and enactments of education thus offer lenses to observe and interrogate what is taken for granted. For example, we thought we were being innovative when we proposed in the previous edition of *Engaging Minds* that teaching should be explicitly understood as a responsibility to help others develop expanded awareness by acting as an EXTENDED CONSCIOUSNESS. Yet when we present this notion in non-WEIRD settings, the response in every case so far has been more toward "What else would it be?" than "That's different." Systemic Sustainability Education, then, might be better construed as a recovery of lost insights or a resonance with other cultures than a significant development in sensibility.

An upshot is that other cultures already have well-developed understandings of what it means to act as an EXTENDED CONSCIOUSNESS for others and of how to structure experiences to bridge learners' understandings of themselves-in-the-world. We suspect they might also offer insights into what it might mean to frame teaching and learning in terms of DWELLING and INHABITING, rather than TOURING and OBSERVING.

But most important, perhaps, other worldviews offer powerful reminders that teaching is not about

James Carse distinguished between two types of rule-governed engagements: *finite games* and *infinite games*. For finite games, rules are fixed boundaries that constrain play and delimit possibilities. For infinite games, rules are shifting horizons that move with the play.

A finite game has a clear start and end and the goal is to win, but it's not always clear when an infinite game began or when it might be over. The goal of the infinite game isn't to win, but to stay in the game.

Over the last century, discourse on formal education has been shifting from the terms of a finite game to the terms of an infinite game.

The grander environment of educational experience is sometimes called the *Third Teacher* – contributing as profoundly to learning as the first teacher (pedagogue) and second teacher (explicit and hidden curricula).

COMMANDING and CONTROLLING, but about CONNECTING and COLLABORATING. Indeed, the project is most powerful and most enabling when desires to control actions and outcomes are eased and replaced by CONSCIENTIOUS PARTICIPATION IN EXPANDING POSSIBILITIES across all levels of organization.

Teaching, then, is never simply a personal or an interpersonal act. It touches the subpersonal through the planetary. Teaching is a DELIBERATE PARTICIPATION IN WHAT IS. It is about maintaining an awareness that knowing is constantly enacted and learning is always happening.

That means that teaching isn't something that's *done*. Teaching is *lived* as one encounters self and other, individual and collective, past and future, actual and possible. For that reason, within a frame of Systemic Sustainability Education, teachers have an ethical responsibility to look beyond themselves, to be aware of and challenge their subjects and objects of their consciousness.

Suggestions for delving deeper

1. Following the model presented at the start of the chapter, select a topic in your discipline and at the level you intend to teach and craft four 100-word lesson designs that reflect the four moments in education addressed in this book.

2. Develop an enabling constraint around a learning objective from a program of studies. How does it allow for variable entry? What are the affordances of that enabling constraint?

3. In the margin note on page 215, we offered some preliminary thoughts on how the topic of bullying might be understood within a frame of Systemic Sustainability Education. What would you add? How might these emphases contrast with the way bullying might be addressed within the other three moments?

Epilogue

A dozen images that are popularly associated with the profession of teaching are presented in the margins of this Epilogue.

Each serves as a visual metaphor within the field of education. We invite you to think about what various educators might have been thinking when they first selected these images to represent aspects of their work.

A good part of our preparation for writing this book involved scanning the educational literature for discussions of "good teaching." Among other activities, we looked at "How to Teach" manuals that were designed for undergraduate programs, visited countless websites that offer advice to educators, delved into the "effective teaching" literature, attended presentations at academic conferences and professional conventions, and chatted with teacher educators from around the world.

To say the least, there are huge variations on what authors and presenters take for granted. Some people are very much in tune with the evolving characters of education and teaching, but we couldn't help but feel that a great many would feel right at home in a 19th-century conversation on effectiveness and accountability in schooling.

Perhaps even more troubling, a good number of the published resources seemed to be entirely preoccupied with topics that emerged a hundred years ago while oblivious to topics associated with Democratic Citizenship Education and Systemic Sustainability Education. Teaching was most often presented in terms of an uncritical mix of the structures of Standardized Education and the dynamics of Authentic Education. That is, many authors found a way to mix Standardized Education's obsessions with mechanical order and causal control with Authentic Education's conviction that learning is an individualized, organic, non-causal process of unfolding.

In many ways, this situation is not surprising. Humans are associative thinkers and compulsive blenders, able to generate coherences from the raw materials of diverse experiences and unconnected interpretations.

We're not critical of that capacity. On the contrary, it could be argued to be the quality that most enables human ingenuity. However, it strikes us that the educator is obliged to be cautious about this irrepressible tendency – and must be particularly attentive to the ways the habit is exercised around questions of knowing, learning, and teaching.

On this count, an analogy might be drawn to the discipline of medicine. A little over a century ago, it was an uneven, poorly regarded field in which evidence-based treatments were commonly juxtaposed with unquestioned beliefs and inherited practices. The result was a record of hit-and-miss that often wasn't much better (and in some cases worse) than leaving patients untreated. That changed when there was an insistence on interrogating the ground of claims and practices. For example, from antiquity to the late 1800s, the practice of bloodletting was *the most common* medical practice. It was rooted in the metaphors of "humors" and "balances" – that is, in the belief that all bodily fluids (humors) had to be in proper balance to maintain health … and so illness was taken as an indicator of imbalance of humors … and so the sensible treatment for illness was to draw blood in order to restore balance.

Within that frame of interpretation, it all made sense. Even with questionable results.

We would argue that a very similar criticism could be leveled against the culture of INSTRUCTION. It all seems to make sense if one stays inside Standardized Education's web of metaphors and entailments. If knowledge is an OBJECT and learning is about ACQUIRING THAT OBJECT, then it makes sense that teaching should be about DELIVERING THAT OBJECT. However, when you step outside that network of association and examine the evidence, something's amiss.

We thus look forward to a time when TEACHING AS DELIVERING is popularly recognized to be as troublesome as healing by bloodletting. Unfortunately, the complexities of formal education will never lend themselves to the same sort of replication-driven mode of scientific inquiry as medicine. Why, what, and how one teaches can't be unhinged from where, when, and whom one is teaching.

And so we close the book by scanning the horizon in an effort to identify upcoming influences and trends for teaching. We frame those speculations by recapping the four moments of education through a chart that came together as we planned and wrote:

A BRIEF OVERVIEW OF FOUR MOMENTS IN FORMAL EDUCATION				
MOMENT:	Moment 1 **Standardized**	Moment 2 **Authentic**	Moment 3 **Democratic Citizenship**	Moment 4 **Systemic Sustainability**
APPROX START	1600s	early 1900s	1960s	1990s
SCIENTIFIC ATTITUDE	physical sciences	human sciences	social sciences	complexity sciences
INFLUENTIAL DISCOURSES	physics & industry	biology & structuralism	sociology & economics	ecology & systems theory
PREVAILING METAPHORS	MECHANICAL; DIRECTIONAL	ORGANIC; BRANCHING	CONTRACTUAL; COLLABORATIVE	ECOSYSTEMIC; EMERGENT
ICONIC VISUAL METAPHOR				
KNOWLEDGE AND CURRICULUM	OBJECTIFIED FACTS	PERSONAL INTERPRETATIONS	SOCIAL CONSTRUCTIONS	VIBRANT COMPLEX FORMS
	the Canon; skill mastery	meaning; understanding	participation; conscientization	wellness; awareness
LEARNERS	DEFICIENT CONTAINERS	SUFFICIENT ACTORS	PARTIAL AGENTS	COMPLEX UNITIES
AND	correspondence theories	coherence theories		
LEARNING	ACQUIRING; INTERNALIZING; TRAVERSING	CONSTRUING; ADAPTING; EMBODYING	ACCULTURATING; APPRENTICING; CO-CONSTRUCTING	VIABILITY-MAINTAINING; LIFE PROCESSES OF THE KNOWING SYSTEM
TEACHING	INSTRUCTING; DIRECTING	FACILITATING; GUIDING	ENCULTURATING; EMPOWERING	DESIGNING; ENGAGING

We'll suppress the urge to unpack the contents of this table (since that's what the book is all about), but there are several pivotal details that we want to re-emphasize.

First and foremost, it's helpful to notice that formal education has been overwhelmingly dominated by scientific discourses since the 1600s. True, the branch of science that prevails has been shifting (as indicated), but schooling has been squarely framed by discourses of reason and evidence since the Industrial Revolution. Second, as Moment 4 reveals, conceptions of learning and teaching have been evolving (or perhaps *revolving* would be a more fitting term) toward pre-industrialized sensibilities, evidenced in the resurgence of metaphors of PARTICIPATION, WHOLENESS, and LIVING SYSTEMS. Such notions were well represented in pre-modern educational practices, but were eclipsed with the rise of Standardized Education.

The notion that formal education is recovering some ancient insights as it continues its evolutionary dance with the changing world leapt out at us when we gathered together the four of the vocabulary charts that were used to introduce each moment. On pages 238–239, we've assembled them as quadrants of a grander whole – an arrangement that foregrounded that many of the starting places for Standardized Education seem to be culminating sites for Systemic Sustainability Education.

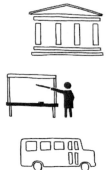

Some might be surprised by this (r)evolution. For us, the more surprising detail is that the project of formal education was somehow blinded to its rich history through its alliance with science and industry. Humans have been teaching for a long, long time. It would make sense that sophisticated insights and strategies would predate the modern school.

Other resurgences in ancient knowledge are being witnessed. For example, as mentioned in Chapter 4.2, matters of **spirituality** are now engaged much more frequently by educators and educational researchers than they were a mere decade ago. Similarly, **storytelling** is gaining considerable interest as both a mode and a focus of formal education. These and other trends remind us of the gnosis *vs.* episteme distinction – and may suggest that schooling is shifting, ever so subtly, to embrace its originating foci on deep knowledge and the arts. Ironically, however, a major impetus is neurological science. Its distinction of **episodic memory** and **semantic memory** provides insight into how narrative-embedded knowledge is more meaningful, more easily learned, and more durable than uncontextualized facts and skills.

The current recoveries of almost-forgotten and once-ignored knowledges of teaching, we think, might be opening spaces for more engaged and nuanced considerations of other discourses and traditions to inform formal education. In addition to pre-modern western conceptions, other emerging influences include non-western ways of knowing, Indigenous epistemologies, and spirituality discourses. For centuries, such sensibilities and approaches have been cast as either naïve of or opposed to science – and therefore of no worth to educators. But more nuanced appreciations of the complexity and evolving character of reality are helping to interrupt assumptions of radical, irreconcilable differences.

Other discernible influences on the educational horizon include the following:

- emergent transdisciplinary fields – which might prompt some rethinking of the sharp disciplinary borders in the current landscape of schooling;
- interspecies studies – which, like intercultural studies in the last century, are already affording new insights into what it means to be a human animal;
- intergenerational studies – which underscore the storied and historied nature of being human;
- technology-mediated realities and engagements – which, as flagged throughout the book, are evolving so quickly that we can say little with great confidence, apart from voicing an expectation of considerable change over the next few years and massive transformations over the next few decades.

No doubt this is just a partial listing. And it doesn't provide much direction. Our hope, though, is that whatever discourses might be engaged and whatever trends might arise, educators will greet them with a blend of openness and caution, taking particular care to interrogate assumptions and entailments ...

... and to be attentive to webs of association ...

AUTHENTIC EDUCATION

DESCRIBING & PRESCRIBING TEACHING

KNOWLEDGE & LEARNING

HISTORY & CONTEXT

active learning		
cooperative learning	accommodation	
deep/surface learning	adaptation	antipositivism
deliberate practice	assimilation	deconstruction
differentiated learning	associative learning	education for all
facilitating	body-based knowing	evolutionary theory
fixed/growth mindsets	coherence theories	existentialism
formative assessment	conscious/unconscious	genetics
inquiry approach	constructivism	Gestalt psychology
manipulatives	developmentalism	human sciences
metacognition	dual-process theory	neurology
PCK	explicit/tacit knowing	phenomenology
Piagetian tasks	genetic epistemology	pragmatism
problem-based learning	multiple intelligences	psychoanalysis
reflective practice	progressivism	rise of middle class
self-regulated learning	schema theory	romanticism
wait time	variation theory	structuralism
activism	activity theory	civil rights movements
apprenticing	actor–network theory	critical theory
conscientization	anticlassism	cultural studies
coopetition	antiracism	feminism
critical pedagogy	antisexism	globalization
critical reflection	critical discourse theory	information age
dialogic learning	distributed cognition	knowledge economy
diversity education	Frankfurt School	Marxism
emancipating	hegemony	participatory democracy
empowering	hidden curriculum	postcolonialism
free schools	participatory culture	postmodernism
networks of practice	power	poststructuralism
peer critique	situated learning	social sciences
praxis	social constructionism	semiotics
PLCs	social contracts	technical revolution
scaffolding	sociocultural learning	
ZPD		

DEMOCRATIC CITIZENSHIP EDUCATION

STANDARDIZED EDUCATION

		best practices
	acquisition model	behavioral modification
Age of Reason	behaviorisms	behavioral objectives
capitalism	cognitivism	Bloom's taxonomy
colonialism	comparative statistics	classroom management
empiricism	correspondence theories	directing
Era of Enlightenment	conduit metaphor	drilling
imperialism	deficiency model	enlightening
Industrial Revolution	epistemology	evaluation
normalism	learning styles	explaining
objectivism	linearity	instructionism
physical sciences	mentalisms	lesson planning
positivism	normal distributions	remediation
rationalism	order	rubrics
Scientific Revolution	planar geometry	special education
standardization	representationism	standardized exams
urbanization	taxonomies	value-added modeling
bioculturalism	andragogy	affordances
complexity science	biomimicry	collectivity
digital age	brain-based learning	conversing
ecohumanism	brain plasticity	crowdsourcing
Gaia hypothesis	comparative dynamics	enabling constraints
global brain	embodied cognition	engaging
global citizenship	hybrid disciplinarity	extend consciousness
Indigenous epistemologies	lifelong learning	game-based learning
interspeciesism	more-than-human world	hive mind
network theory	nested systems	improvising
neurophenomenology	neurodiversity	MOOCs
nonlinear dynamics	power law distributions	neuroeducation
social networking	recursive elaboration	occasioning
systems theory	scale independence	redundancy/diversity
wisdom traditions	self-similarity	third teacher
	transdisciplinarity	universal design
		variable entry

SYSTEMIC SUSTAINABILITY EDUCATION

Ready ... set ...

In the second edition of the *Oxford English Dictionary*, published in 1989, the longest entry was for the verb *set*. Its 430 meanings required 60,000 words (roughly the length of this book!).

The third edition of the OED is currently in progress, and so it's not clear which entry will take the title in this version. That said, the leader at the time of this writing is the verb *run*.

This shift in definitional weight from *set* to *run* since 1989 is reflective of shifts in education and teaching over the same period. In the same way that the language seems to have tilted from setting the course (i.e., planning, preparing, establishing foundations, etc.) to running a course (i.e., actually engaging), the project of education is now less about providing children with an imagined-to-be-fitting toolkit "to set them up" for adult life and more about engaging them meaningfully and pragmatically in the shared world.

What might that mean for teaching? As authors, we have no illusions that we have somehow managed to point to a conception of teaching that answers that question. However, we do feel that the attitude we have presented – of critical embrace of diverse sensibilities and expanded spheres of awareness – will be vital to ensuring that teaching and formal education continue to be fitted to a rapidly evolving world.

SET!   RUN!   TRIUMPH.

Formal education has been overwhelmingly regarded as the first of three stages in one's career trajectory, followed by the "rat race," and culminating in retirement.

That's the dominant sensibility within Standardized Education, and it's shared by many advocates of Authentic Education and Democratic Citizenship Education. Emergent sensibilities, however, suggest that the visual metaphor, above, may be an entirely unfortunate way of understanding the relationship between formal education and the rest of life.

Suggestions for delving deeper

1. Take a look at rubrics, checklists, and questionnaires that are used to assess and evaluate teaching. (Many samples are available for free online. If you're in a university program, chances are there will be forms available for course evaluations as well as student-teacher observations.) Which moments of formal education are represented? Which moments are privileged? Would you change the form(s)? If so, how? If not, why not?

2. BusinessDictionary.com defines *education* as follows: "The wealth of knowledge acquired by an individual after studying particular subject matters or

experiencing life lessons that provide an understanding of something. Education requires instruction of some sort from an individual or composed literature. ..."

This description clearly aligns with Standardized Education – including an OBJECT-based view of knowledge, an ACQUISITION-oriented view on learning, and an INSTRUCTION-focused conception of teaching. Given the source (business), that's not surprising. Locate and/or script definitions of education that are from different perspectives. How do they fit with different educational moments described in this book?

3. A dozen of the most popular icons of schooling are collected in the margins of this Epilogue. Which, if any, resonate with you? Why? When and why were those symbols likely taken up? As visual metaphors, what are their entailments for knowing, learning, and teaching? Can you think of alternatives that are more fitting with what you imagine formal education to be all about?

Influences

As we noted in the Prologue and Chapter 3.1, a major difference between this version of *Engaging Minds* and previous editions is a different strategy for locating the discussion in the literature.

Rather than relying on standard in-text referencing and a typical bibliography, we have elected to acknowledge influences and sources in a manner that reflects how they were experienced during the writing. Apart from the handful of authors, researchers, and educators who are named explicitly in the text, most of our "sources" were not directly consulted during the writing process. Rather, their influence was experienced as the sort of lingering reflection that is prompted by a good teacher.

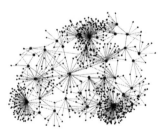

To that end, the names on the next two pages represent a partial listing of people who have had profound impacts on this writing – for the most part, through their impacts on society, schooling, and teaching.

We do recognize the risk in this mode of acknowledgment. Among academics, there is a strong culture of perfomance evaluation in which citations are a vital tool to measure impact, rank quality, and argue for promotion. By not including any direct references to specific publications, we could be seen as refusing to pay scholars in the currency of their profession.

That, of course, is hardly our intention. Rather, we see ourselves more as participants in a grander movement, reflected in so many crowdsourced online resources, toward acknowledging important influences while being attentive to growing criticisms of academia's economy of citation.

AUTHENTIC EDUCATION

INFLUENTIAL EDUCATORS & EDUCATIONISTS

THEORISTS OF KNOWLEDGE & LEARNING

SEMINAL THINKERS

Sylvia Ashton-Warner		
D. Jean Clandinin	Horatio Alger, Jr.	
Elliot Eisner	Jerome Bruner	Simone de Beauvoir
Friedrich Fröbel	Mihaly Csikszentmihalyi	Charles Darwin
Alfie Kohn	John Dewey	Sigmund Freud
Loris Malaguzzi	Carol Dweck	William James
Max van Manen	Erik Erikson	Immanuel Kant
Maria Montessori	Howard Gardner	Jean-Baptiste Lamarck
A.S. Neill	Ernst von Glasersfeld	Charles Lyell
Johann Pestalozzi	Bärbel Inhelder	Gregor Mendel
Ken Robinson	Daniel Kahneman	Maurice Merleau-Ponty
J.J. Rousseau	Lawrence Kohlberg	C.S. Peirce
Lee Shulman	Jean Piaget	Jean-Paul Sartre
Rudolf Steiner	Michael Polanyi	Ferdinand de Saussure
Carol Ann Tomlinson	Carl Rogers	August Schleicher
Dylan Wiliam	Robert Sternberg	Giambattista Vico
James Banks	Theodor Adorno	Hannah Arendt
Michael Apple	Mary Belenky	Mikhail Bakhtin
Carl Bereiter	Clifford Geertz	Pierre Bourdieu
Basil Bernstein	Judith Rich Harris	Jacques Derrida
Deborah Britzman	Ivan Illich	Michel Foucault
Lisa Delpit	Henry Jenkins	Hans-Georg Gadamer
Elizabeth Ellsworth	Susanne Langer	Antonio Gramsci
Paulo Freire	Jean Lave	Martin Heidegger
Michael Fullan	A.R. Luria	Jürgen Habermas
James Paul Gee	John Ogbu	Thomas Kuhn
Henry Giroux	Walter Ong	Imre Lakatos
Madeleine Grumet	Neil Postman	Jean-François Lyotard
bell hooks	Barbara Rogoff	Marshall McLuhan
Nel Noddings	Roger Säljö	Karl Marx
William Pinar	Lev Vygotsky	Margaret Mead
Marlene Scardamalia	Etienne Wenger	Richard Rorty
Roger Simon	James Wertsch	Max Weber
John Willinsky		

DEMOCRATIC CITIZENSHIP EDUCATION

STANDARDIZED EDUCATION

Francis Bacon	Harold Bloom	Mortimer Adler
René Descartes	Robert Gagne	Benjamin Bloom
Euclid	Carl Linnaeus	Franklin Bobbitt
Thomas Hobbes	Horace Mann	Jere Brophy
John Locke	Ivan Pavlov	John Hattie
Pierre-Simon Laplace	B.F. Skinner	Madeline Hunter
Gottfied Wilhelm Leibniz	Frederick Taylor	Doug Lemov
Niccolò Machiavelli	Lee Thorndike	Robert Marzano
John Milton	John B. Watson	Diane Ravitch
Isaac Newton		Robert Slavin
Plato		Ralph Tyler
Pythagoras		
Adam Smith		

A.-L. Barábasi	David Abram	Ted Aoki
Gregory Bateson	Antonio D'Amasio	C.A. Bowers
Rachel Carson	Thomas Berry	Greg Cajete
Noam Chomsky	Fritjof Capra	Peter Blaze Corcoran
Daniel Dennett	James Carse	William Doll, Jr.
Gilles Deleuze	Suzanne Cook-Greuter	Paul Hawken
Jane Jacobs	Terrance Deacon	Lous Heshusius
Alicia Juarrero	Jared Diamond	Tim Ingold
Stuart Kauffman	Merlin Donald	Richard Kahn
James Lovelock	Katherine Hayles	Jay Lemke
Benoît Mandelbrot	Robert Kegan	Rebecca Martusewicz
Lynn Margulis	George Lakoff	Sugata Mitra
Humberto Maturana	Joseph LeDoux	Nel Noddings
Edgar Morin	Ference Marton	David Orr
Martha Nussbaum	Jane McGonigal	Parker Palmer
Francisco Varela	John Muir	Peter Senge
Duncan Watts	Eleanor Rosch	Linda Tuhiwai Smith
Ken Wilber	Edward O. Wilson	

SYSTEMIC SUSTAINABILITY EDUCATION

Index